Studies in International Economics and Institutions

Springer
Berlin
Heidelberg
New York
Barcelona
Budapest
Hong Kong
London
Milan
Paris
Santa Clara
Singapore
Tokyo

Studies in International Economics and Institutions

H.-J. Vosgerau (Ed.), New Institutional Arrangements for the World Economy
IX, 482 pages. 1989

M. Rauscher, OPEC and the Price of Petroleum
XII, 206 pages. 1989

F. Gehrels, H. Herberg, H. Schneider, H.-J. Vosgerau (Eds.), Real Adjustment Processes under Floating Exchange Rates
VI, 302 pages. 1990

T. Tivig, Flexible Wechselkurse aus der Sicht des Finanzmarktansatzes
IX, 226 Seiten. 1991

S. Berninghaus, H. G. Seifert-Vogt, International Migration Under Incomplete Information
VIII, 116 pages. 1991

H. Kräger, K. F. Zimmermann (Eds.), Export Activity and Strategic Trade Policy
VI, 190 pages. 1992

J. Hentschel, Imports and Growth in Highly Indebted Countries
XVI, 210 pages. 1992

H.-J. Vosgerau (Ed.), European Integration in the World Economy
VII, 819 pages. 1992

A. Razin, H.-J. Vosgerau (Eds.), Trade and Tax Policy, Inflation and Exchange Rates
V, 296 pages. 1997

Nicholas C. Baltas · George Demopoulos
Joseph Hassid (Editors)

Economic Interdependence and Cooperation in Europe

With 2 Figures
and 15 Tables

Springer

Professor Nicholas C. Baltas
Professor George Demopoulos
Athens University of Economics and Business
76, Patission Street
10434 Athens
Greece

Professor Joseph Hassid
University of Piraeus
80, Karaoli-Dimitriou Street
18534 Piraeus
Greece

Library of Congress Cataloging-in-Publication Data
Die Deutsche Bibliothek - CIP-Einheitsaufnahme
Economic interdependence and cooperation in Europe / Nicholas C. Baltas ... (ed.). - Berlin; Heidelberg; New York; Barcelona; Budapest; Hong Kong; London; Milan; Paris; Santa Clara; Singapore; Tokyo: Springer, 1998
(Studies in international economics and institutions)
ISBN-13: 978-3-642-72113-7 e-ISBN-13: 978-3-642-72111-3
DOI: 10.1007/978-3-642-72111-3

Softcover reprint of the hardcover 1st edition 1998

Hardcover-Design: Erich Kirchner, Heidelberg

SPIN 10075798 42/2202-5 4 3 2 1 0 - Printed on acid-free paper

Contents

Introduction

Nicholas C. Baltas, George D. Demopoulos and Joseph Hassid

Economic integration is the most noteworthy development in international economic policy at the end of this century. Enthusiasm for the European Union (EU) has been infectious. This has led to lengthy discussions for integration issues which overwhelmingly and understandably focused on its effects on the levels and competition of interregional trade and their consequences for national development. Yet, there are many aspects of the EU and its consequences that still remain obscure and which warrant further careful scrutiny. The major challenges for Europe at the turn of the century are Economic and Monetary Union (EMU) and the integration of the Central and Eastern European Countries (CEECs) within the EU.

Economists and political scientists coming to grips with transition issues in the Central and East European Countries could do worse than adopt, as a working hypothesis of what transition implies, the outcome suggested by classic literature [describing what happens] when market economies are opened to international trade and investment. The predominant expectation is that such a development will lead to gains from trade and from investment opportunities that will arise. The domestic markets that consumers and producers previously faced are now expanded as economic actors are free to operate in a wider marketplace. There will be mutual benefits associated with the realisation of the trading partners' comparative advantages made possible thanks to the liberalisation of exchange between them. In reality, however, things do not work in this idealized fashion. There are inherent economic and political inefficiencies in the transition process itself which are apt to slow down its pace, divert it from its proper course and, in some cases, even endanger its sustainability.

The essays in this book, are an important contribution to these issues. They were originally presented at an International Conference held in Athens, Greece, on 28-29 September 1995, organised by the Hellenic University Association for European Studies (EPEES) and sponsored by the Ionian Bank of Greece.

The volume is divided into five chapters. Part I presents the historical case of a monetary union. Panayotis Korliras provides an interesting case study of the financial history of the Ionian Islands in the 19th century, from which one could draw some useful conclusions for contemporary issues. One of the perennial issues in the analysis of transformation and economic development is the importance of establishing the proper institutions. This is particularly significant for the CEECs, which are facing major problems of domestic reorganisation and restructuring, not only for reasons of economic development but also for social and political stability. The second useful conclusion to be drawn concerns the process of monetary union, an issue of high topical importance and the subject of heated debate in Western Europe.

In Part II, Gelb with Hillman and Ursprung argue that the presence of pervasive rents associated with ambiguities in property rights in economies in transition from socialism are the main impediment to the operation of the idealized free trade scenario. Based on the contestable rent-seeking hypothesis, one can satisfactorily answer a number of crucial questions such as: Why is the transition overall such an extended affair? Why have some countries fared better than others? And, when can the transition be expected finally to come to an end? Their suggested solution to the transition taking too long is for a redefinition of the role of government in transition economies. As the authors put it in concluding their paper: «If the property rights ambiguities that persist permit personalised political markets to determine individual income and wealth, the solution appears to be the establishment of non - contestable claims, albeit in a socially just way with exit of government from the type of political discretion that underlies the creation and assignment of rents. Where contestability is due to government «desertion», the solution is a legal regulatory and institutional structure which makes political discretion less valuable.»

Peterson, on the other hand, commenting on the case of Poland, highlights the distributional effects of various fiscal policy reforms which may potentially lead to more inequality in income distribution. A reformulation of the institutional setting in the countries in transition and accompanying reductions in discretionary interventions via a strategy of depoliticization is also a central proposal of the paper contributed by Petersen. He sees the standard characteristic of the role of a successful politician in such countries changing from interventionism to causal therapy of the imperfect contemporary institutions and instruments.

In Part III, Savic first presents and analyses the trend of the main economic magnitutes exhibited by all CEECs in transition. He then identifies macroeconomic stability as the major precondition for the ultimate success of the transition process. Finally,he traces out the lines along which economic policies in these countries must develop in order to achieve positive rates of growth. He concludes that sustainable growth in the CEECs will only be possible if and when macroeconomic stability and the reform of the private and state sectors are successfully completed.

Pitic focuses on macroeconomic adjustment problems faced by the CEECs' economies as they transform into market - oriented ones. He first analyses the role of fiscal, monetary and exchange rate policy management in providing the desirable economic stability in these countries and then concentrates his interest on the direction that the reform of the banking and financial system should take in order to ensure the ultimate success of the transformation process. Pitic concludes that all successful transformation processes had started with a major stabilisation effort at the macroeconomic level accompanied by major structural efforts to achieve institutional reform and change the behaviour of the economic units at the micro level.

The subject of Mladenov's contribution are the transition problems associated with the reform of the Bulgarian monetary sector. After identifying the major trends in the performance of the private sector, he reviews the developments in the fiscal, monetary, external transactions and foreign debt areas of the Bulgarian economy as it embarked on its transition to a market-oriented regime. He concludes by pointing out that in Bulgaria's case the critical success factors are sound and well co-ordinated monetary and credit policies to underpin the long-overdue structural reform of the state and private sectors.

In Part IV, Holmes focuses on and undertakes a critical analysis of the policy measures which the EU Commission suggests in its White Paper that the CEECs ought to adopt as they prepare their economies for eventual integration into the EU's internal market. He concludes that the CEECs are asked to harmonize their competition legislation much more closely with that of the EU than had been required in the past for the EU's founder members or, indeed, for newly acceding member countries, even after their accession. This assymetry raises the question as to whether the underlying motivation is to promote EU business with the CEECs as much as to help these countries in their transition to market economies. Without disputing the desirability of policy harmonisation, nor the value of the prospect of accession as an external incentive to allow liberal policy makers in the CEECs to push through otherwise unpopular policies, the author suggests that the EU must be at least as willing to face up to its own interest groups as it is eager to advise its trading partners to do so.

Spachis argues that the major priority for the CEECs is to prepare themselves for their integration into the single market. Although the CEECs have already made a serious effort to harmonise their legislation, the task before them is nevertheless a complex one. Regarding the likely impact of the internal market enlargement on the economies of the EU member-states, Spachis draws the following broad conclusions: first, trade flows will increase progressively but substantially and stabilise at levels 4-6 times higher than current levels; second, a shift from traditional industries in the CEECs to more sophisticated manufactures which are relatively labour-intensive will take place; third, most of the increased investment from the EU and other sources is intended to serve the expanding domestic markets of the CEECs rather than involving a relocation of existing EC production to these countries; fourth, growth rates in the CEECs will vary from one country to another and it is possible that the richer ones among them will be enjoying income levels comparable to those of the poorest EU countries within a period of 10 years; fifth, although the availability of cheap labour might confer a comparative advantage on firms located in the CEECs, it is likely that any wage cost advantage enjoyed by the CEECs will be offset by lower levels of labour productivity in these countries; finally, on the basis of the precedent of the later accession to the EU of countries with income levels significantly below those of the original member states, it is not expected that any significant labour movements will occur when individual CEECs eventually accede to the European Union.

Vosgerau discusses the efficiency shortfalls of the transmission mechanisms allegedly allowing free movement of factors of production and equalisation of their prices across the extended trading area. He stresses the role of trade policy deficiencies and more general market imperfections in preventing goods prices in the EU and the CEECs from equalising. The extended Hecksher - Ohlin model, allowing for different transaction costs for trade, migration and capital movements between the two «markets», proves to be a convenient methodological frame of analysis of the relative role of such transaction costs in approaching an efficient solution. This type of analysis may be followed up by an empirical application resulting in a better understanding of the workings of trade liberalisation and free factor movements between the EU and the CEECs.

In Part V, Pitelis discusses the discrepancies between private and public (firms and government) objectives and suggests ways for their reconciliation. He also deals with the specific issue of investment by foreign transnationals in the CEECs and of its potential contribution to the process of those countries' integration into the world economy. CEEC governments' objectives in seeking foreign investment are extensive (among others: deteriorating capital stock, the need to rebuild infrastructure, technology transfers, etc.). The crucial question put by Pitelis concerns the degree of compatibility between such government objectives and the objectives of transnational companies considering direct investment in CEECs. A concomitant question to which an answer is also being sought is whether the pursuing of private objectives will necessarily yield the outcomes which governments desire. The author's position is that such outcomes are conditional on the individual government's ability to develop coherent industrial strategies. This becomes an even more pressing task given the potential weakening of indigenous industry and the national governments' loss of decision - making power.

Mergos deals with the issues regarding the Common Agricultural Policy in the context of the debate on the EU's eastward enlargement. Agriculture is considered as the key sector for the convergence of the CEECs with the EU. An expansion of the EU to the East to include the six CEECs would increase the EU's agricultural land by one third and double agricultural output and employment. The budget cost of extending the CAP to these countries has been the subject of a long and heated debate and was a major factor in the new reform of the CAP. Estimates of the budgetary implications of the CEEC's accession vary widely, depending upon the assumptions underlying alternative scenarios. The author concludes that alignment with the EU's internal market, the capacity of the CEECs to adopt internal market rules and the strengthening of the free market environment in these countries by privatisation and an opening up to competition are the major priorities for agricultural policy in the CEECs.

We wish to express our gratitude to all those who helped us to organise the Conference as well as to prepare this book. The Hellenic University Association for European Studies (EPEES), in the context of whose activities the Conference took place, has provided invaluable organizational help. We express our appreciation and thanks to the members of the Board of the Association for their support in this endeavour. Our sincerest appreciation and thanks are also due to the Ionian Bank of Greece and its then Chairman of the Board Professor P. Korliras for the generous sponsorship of the Conference.

Mrs Despina Diamandi, the Association's Secretary, provided us with efficient secretarial support. Finally, we are greatly indebted to P. Grevenitis who undertook the editing of this book with skill, patience and good spirit.

Part I Historical Background of a Monetary Union

1 The Financial History of the Ionian Islands in the 19th Century: Lessons from the Past?

Panayotis Korliras
Professor of Economics
Athens University of Economics and Business
76, Patission Str.
Athens, GR-104 34

Summary

The financial history of the Ionian Islands in the 19th century is an interesting case study for reasons which, in a sense, prove relevant to contemporary issues such as the constructive role of institutions and monetary unification. The financial history of these islands in the 19th century is characterised by two major developments: first, the establishment of the Ionian Bank in 1839 and, second, the political and monetary union of the islands with the Kingdom of Greece in 1864. The purpose of this essay is to analyse these developments, both in historical perspective and in connection with what economists can say about some current issues.

1.1 Historical background

The Ionian Island are a complex of seven principal islands (from the north to the south: Corfu or Kerkyra, Paxos, Leukada, Cephalonia, Ithaca, Zante or Zakynthos, Cerigo or Kythira), situated along the western coast of Greece in the Ionian Sea, facing southern Italy. These islands, Greek since antiquity, were the only part of the Byzantine Empire that was never subjected to Ottoman rule and remained for centuries under Venetian domination. In fact, Venice considered the Seven Islands to be important intermediate posts for her extensive naval and trade activities in the Levant during her era of glory as a major Mediterranean power. The dissolution of Venice as an independent state by Napoleon brought about considerable changes in the society of the Ionian Islands while it also affected their position in the Mediterranean trade routes. These were after all, times of change, inspired by the French Revolution and, for these islands, affected by the struggle for independence in mainland Greece.The French occupied the islands for a few years, annexing them as departements of France. This arrangement, which went well beyond mere military occupation, fuelled republican aspirations to overturn the quasi-feudal conditions in the islands and formalised the antagonism between the "popolari" and the landed mobility of the "libro d'oro". The collapse of Napoleon's empire was followed by a half-century of British domination, with some form of more-or-less democratic self-government, as the "United States of Ionian Islands", with the city of Corfu as its capital. The Local Parliament (Senate) became the arena of antagonism between the conservatives, who wanted to preserve their privileges, and the "radicals", who were demanding more democracy and, later on, unification with the independent Kingdom of Greece. The British Governors applied an equilibrating policy, trying to impose some stability in a society with deep class divisions, while at the same time putting-off any attempts from the part of islanders to end British rule and unite with Greece. In the end, Great Britain voluntarily ceded the Ionian Islands, which in 1864 became provinces of the Kingdom of Greece.

1.2 Economic and financial conditions in the early 19th century

The economy of the islands depended heavily on the production and export of olive oil and raisins, making the local economy extremely sensitive to international prices and to political events which facilitated or hindered international trade. Monetary circulation consisted of specie, mainly silver Mexican dollars and Austrian thalers, and it is recorded that there was extensive hoarding of silver and gold coins. In 1825, attempts were made to make the pound sterling the official currency of the islands, and by 1830 the sterling was widely accepted and used. There was no organised credit system, a fact that weighed heavily upon the farmers, who depended upon local usurers for working capital. Having to pay off their debts at exorbitant interest rates, in addition to providing for the land-owners' share, was pushing many farmers to distress and bankruptcy. On top of that, the prolonged price deflation and the crisis in international trade that followed the end of the Napoleonic Wars severely affected the islands' economy. Indeed, the Ionian Islands were never again able to recapture their privileged position in the Levantine trade. In 1833, in order to alleviate these difficult conditions, Lord Nugent, the British Governor, tried to organise a credit system, whereby the farmers would be relieved of the necessity to pay interest rates of up to 30% to local money-lenders. A capital of £35.000 was set aside from the Treasury surplus for providing loans to farmers at 6% interest rate. In fact, Lord Nugent's idea went further, as he proposed to London the creation of a local bank, again with Treasury surpluses and the mobilisation of local capital, which would issue local "money" i.e. fiat money backed by the bank's capital and reserves. Lord Nugent's proposal was ill received in London, however, as it coincided with the fierce debate between the proponents of the so-called "Banking School" and those of the "Currency School", a famous debate which resulted in the 1844 Banking Act concerning the role of the Bank of England. The Banking School held the view that the provision of paper money and credit was merely meeting the genuine "needs of trade" and thus should be facilitated in order to allow economic activity to find its proper equilibrium. By contrast, the Currency School, which became the dominant doctrine of the Treasury officials, saw with suspicion any increase in monetary circulation unless it was backed 100% by gold, fearing inflationary pressures. As a result, Lord Nugent's idea of a local issuing bank was rejected for doctrinaire reasons, despite the fact that it would contribute to more normal (and thus, anti-inflationary) credit conditions.

1.3 The establishment of the Ionian Bank

Sir Douglas Howard, the next Governor of the Ionian Islands, was initially unwilling to get involved into what he considered "commercial matters". The threat to social order posed by deteriorating economic conditions, however, forced him to deal with the issue. In 1837, he submitted a second proposal to London. In the meantime, the establishment of a bank became an issue that preocupied the Ionian Senate, which legislated the creation of the Ionian Bank, an institution combining the functions of central and commercial bank. With London's approval, a public offer was organised for 4.000 shares at £25 each, one sixth of which was to be subscribed by the colonial administration. Unfortunately, the public offer was a failure, as local investors were not fully convinced that such a bank was a viable project, despite it having official government backing. Sir Douglas Howard was, however, a very persistent man, who happened to believe that the creation of a local bank was a necessary condition for normalising domestic economic and financial conditions. He seems to have been a forerunner to all those economists who stress the importance of creating the proper institutional framework for economic stability and growth. Giving up on unwilling local investors, the Governor opted instead to turn to the London capital market. The Ionian Senate approved this initiative and through the services of John Wright, a London banker, and Sir Alexander Wood, the representative of the Ionian States in Britain, the project was launched. On 17 January 1839, a public offer was issued in London and the Ionian Bank came into existence as a legal entity. The Ionian Senate granted the new bank the exclusive right to issue paper currency for an initial period of 20 years (a privilege which eventually was to last until 1920!). Thus, a local issuing or central bank was established with mostly British capital. It also became the only commercial bank in the islands, accepting deposits and granting loans both to individuals and to the British administration itself. By the middle of the century, the Ionian Bank had become a well established and respected institution. Historical records show that it was not accidental that its growth coincided with the maintenance of economic stability in the islands and a rise in general prosperity. The Bank had its headquarters in London, being a British limited liability company. In fact, in 1884 it was granted a Royal Charter, the third bank in English history to be given this recognition. In due time, hoarding was indeed reduced and most of the local merchants and investors became its shareholders. The bank's prestige grew so much that in 1860 the Ionian Senate readily renewed its issuing privilege. Interestingly, having established its first branch in Corfu (seat of its head office), Cephalonia and Zante, the Ionian Bank almost immediately (1840) established "agencies" in the cities of Athens and Patras. In the following years, the bulk of its banking business was carried out in Greece, testifying to the changing pattern of the islands' trade relations and of the mainland's growing importance to their economic prosperity. By the end of the century, when the Ionian Islands had already become provinces of the Kingdom of Greece, the head office of the Ionian Bank in Greece moved from Corfu to Athens. The bank's network of branches started to expand all-over Greece, as Greek territory itself expanded with the liberation of the eastern Aegean islands, Macedonia and Thrace after the Balkan Wars. Eventually, the Bank became established wherever Greeks were present and economically active, as happened in Cyprus and Egypt in the 1900's.

In the Ionian Bank we have a typical example of a financial institution which came into existence when it was badly needed to promote stability and growth. The Bank's prudent policies, managed under English banking laws, soon gave it respectability and widespread trust. The Bank's history makes perfectly clear which is the most appropriate feature of a financial institution, namely to direct its activities where trade indicates. The period between the collapse of the Venetian ancien regime and the end of the long Napoleonic Wars was a time of social and economic upheaval in the Seven Islands. Stability returned with the British occupation and colonial administration. Increasingly, the islands developed strong economic relations with mainland Greece. In this historical context, the existence of a key financial institution operating under universally accepted (and trusted) rules not only underpins monetary stability and economic growth but also acts as a catalyst for regional economic integration, which emerges quasi-naturally from increasing cooperation and deepening interdependence.

1.4 Union with Greece

In 1864, Great Britain gave up its sovereign rights and the United States of the Ionian Islands were united with the Kingdom of Greece. This was a culminating event in the history of the Seven Islands, the closing of an immense historical cycle. Undoubteedly, the union was first and foremost a political one, as the modern Greek state strived to encompass all territories where Greeks were either the totality or a dominant majority of the population. On the other hand, Great Britain saw that the Ionian Islands were not quite like her other colonies. The islands, by then distanced from Venetian political and cultural influence, were so near the mainland, and their local society so much integrated with the mainland's culture and economy, that it would be an anomaly for Britain to maintain her dominian over a self-administered statelet. It must be said, however, that the local aristocracy was not so keen on union with Greece, as this meant the abolition of titles of nobility, and, to some extent, a more egalitarian redistribution of incomes. Since political union also meant monetary union, this hostorical episode can be taken as a case study of how such unions might work.

The banknotes issued by the Ionian Bank were "dollars" or "colonatti", kept at parity with the Mexican silver dollar and the Austrian thaler (the so-called Maria-Theresa thaler) while the pound sterling was to all intents and purposes the official currency of the Ionian States. To avoid criticism, especially by those who in the English monetary controversies of the 1830's warned against over-issue of notes not backed by gold reserves, and also in order to win public confidence, the bank's management and policies were extremely prudent. As a result, the Ionian colonatti were a widely accepted currency, their users being confident that they would not depreciate vis-a-vis the then internationally accepted hard currencies, such as the pound sterling and Austrian thaler. In the mainland, the National Bank of Greece had the exclusive right to issue banknotes. The drachma was pegged to the golden French franc (as Greece later joined the Latin Union, essentially a French franc zone). The young kingdom was, however, facing difficulties in creating stable domestic economic conditions and on several occasions the drachma became temporarily a non-convertible currency.

The Ionian Islands' union with Greece involved their political, economic and monetary integration in a sequence of events which provide a historic example of how these processes can work in an orderly fashion. The salient fact was the deepening economic interdependence and integration between the islands and the mainland, as the islands, no longer part of another regional power (such as Venice), were increasingly leaning towards the young kingdom. Their integration, no doubt facilitated by the strong historical ties linking them to the mainland, involved not only free movement of commodities but also mobility of the factors of production, mainly people. The political union of 1864 merely formalized the pre-existing economic integration. The islands formally became greek provinces , with the same rights and obligations as any other province, while the inhabitants of the islands became Greek citizens. The Ionian Senate was abolished and the islanders could vote for their representative to the Parliament in Athens, travel and deal with the rest of the world on Greek passports, pay taxes to the Greek state, and so on. In other words, a complete political union took place. It was a voluntary annexation based on pre-existing cultural ties and economic integration.

There was also a monetary union. The Treaty of Annexation provided that the privileges granted by the British authorities to the Ionian Bank were to remain, with the bank maintaining its issuing rights. In order to make such a monetary union workable, it was agreed between the two "central banks", i.e. the National Bank of Greece and the Ionian Bank, that a constant parity would be maintained, fixed at six drachmas per Ionian colonatto. This fixed parity, essentially a stable exchange rate regime between two areas (or countries) undergoing thorough economic and political union, was considered an essential element in the process of monetary union. The Ionian Bank would continue to issue its colonatti banknotes for an interim period after which it would issue drachma banknotes, along with the National Bank of Greece. This arrangement meant that the country was going to have a dual system of central banks, issuing the same currency and following the same monetary policy. The Ionian Bank was granted a monopoly in the islands for some years. It was also permitted to expand its branch network throughout Greece, provided that the National Bank would not object in cases of overlapping or redundant branches in some areas. Finally, the two banks formed an alliance to resist repeated attempts by the Greek government to impose compulsory circulation of banknotes and to safeguard their institutions and confidence in the soundness of the drachma.

Like the drachma banknotes issued by the National Bank of Greece, the ones issued by the Ionian Bank were legal tender throughout the Kingdom of Greece. The Greek parliament, respecting the provisions of the 1864 Treaty of Annexation and the obligations contained therein, repeatedly extended the privileges of the Ionian Bank, which kept its issuing right until 1920. After that time, the National Bank remained the only issuing bank until a proper central bank, the Bank of Greece, was established in 1928. The National Bank of Greece, a venerable institution founded in 1841 (two years later than the Ionian Bank), continued, as it still does today, to be the dominant player in the Greek banking sector, becoming a leading European bank. The Ionian Bank took advantage of an expanded economic and geographic area of operations and itself developed into one of the country's biggest banks. It also expanded beyond Greece to regions where Greek communities and/or economic interests were established, such as Cyprus and Egypt. It remained a bank with stable and long-serving management (Sir John Stavridis was its chairman from 1920 to 1948), with the majority of its shareholders still in London. After World War II, it merged with the Popular Bank of Greece into the Ionian and Popular Bank of Greece (still operating and one of the major Greek banks) and the majority of its share passed to Greek investors.

1.5 Concluding remarks: What lessons for today?

The study of history is a rewarding endeavour, provided we learn from it and make good use of past examples of wisdom and folly. It is not my intention to claim too much out of the financial history of the Ionian Islands in the 19th century. Nevertheless, I believe that, apart from its purely historical interest, this episode can help us to draw some useful conclusions about issues that are currently hotly debated and must be resolved.

One of the central issues in any analysis of economic and social transformation is the importance of establishing the proper institutions. Notwithstanding the force of the "invisible hand" and the self-regulating properties of the free market system, it is an undeniable truth that economic activity has to be organized within the framework of appropriate institutional arrangements. One could argue, for example, that inexorable historical trends would eventually push the Ionian Islands towards union with Greece and that the establishment of the Ionian Bank was, historically speaking, an insignificant event. Although history cannot be re-made, the useful conclusion to be drawn is that a proper institution, serving the needs of a changing economy in a differentiated international environment has proved to be an indispensable element in normalizing economic and social conditions and paving the way to a smooth adjustment to oncoming profound changes. The use of the attribute "proper" to describe an institution, especially a credit institution whose reputation is based on public trust must be stressed, so as to differentiate it from the haphazard setting-up of unsound "banks", operating under inadequately strict and effective banking regulations. For the CEECs, facing problems of domestic reorganization and restructuring, while at the same time striving to deepen their integration with Western Europe, the conclusion is useful and the message is clear. It is not an exaggeration to say that such "proper" institutions are needed not only for reasons of economic development but also for reasons of social and political stability.

The second useful conclusion to be drawn from the historical case of the Ionian Islands concerns the process of monetary union, an issue of high topical importance and subject of heated debates in Western Europe. The monetary union of the Ionian Islands with Greece was not only preceded by a sufficient degree of economic integration and interdependence but was also followed by thorough political union. This is not an isolated case, as European history offers more significant but similar historical examples. The numerous German states begun their integration in the 1840's with Zollverein, a customs union which was meant to lead to the creation of a "common market" among sovereign states, with the ultimate purpose of preparing the German unification. The political union into a unified German Reich came two decades later and was founded on the solid ground of pre-existing economic integration. Monetary union came a few years later, when the Reichsmark substituted the three or four co-existing currencies and was adopted after the former individual "states" had transferred their fiscal autonomy to a bigger and stronger "federal" fiscal authority. The German example is duplicated by the example of the Italian unification, where political union came in the steps of a far-reaching economic integration while monetary union followed soon after political union.

At the close of the 20th century, the member-states of the European Union are attempting something which does not conform to those historical examples and is historically original. Having achieved a sufficient degree of economic integration and interdependence, they are embarking on monetary union before attempting political union. The member-states, all sovereign countries, appear to be ready to relinquish their monetary autonomy by fixing the parities of their currencies and by conforming to a common monetary policy which best suits the interests of the country with the hardest currency (Germany). From the viewpoint of economic science, this is either an anomaly or a path-breaking innovation. To give up one's monetary autonomy before the establishment of a common, strong fiscal authority could mean that the member-states may be confronted with disequilibrating phenomena which will not be able to be dealt with by means of a "federal" equilibrating fiscal policy. Moreover, the countries most affected by some external or area-specific shocks will not be able to use monetary policy either. This would indeed be anomalous, especially with a monetary union of so many different economies, in which labour mobility is necessarily restricted by geography and, principally, by cultural and linguistic differences (unlike, e.g. the case of the United States of America). On the other hand, fiscal union, i.e. the quasi-equalization of all tax rates and the emergence of a strong "federal" budget, would imply a decisive move towards political union, only to be followed by a Common defence and foreign policy. If such a federal budget existed, the automatic stabilizers of the federal fiscal policy would sufficiently alleviate any regional imbalances and the effects of disequilibrating region-specific shocks, thus making the loss of monetary autonomy a self-evident ingredient in the creation of a federative state. One could even cite the more recent example of the German's unification in the early 1990's, where again monetary unification came after political union, or rather the annexation of the Lander of the former DDR to the Federal Republic. If not an anomaly, then, the currently attempted monetary union can only be regarded as a major innovation. The criteria of nominal convergence established as a precondition for monetary union may in the future generate conditions that will make fiscal, and hence political, union imperative. Indeed, it may be the case that political (i.e. fiscal) union might come to be seen as a necessary condition for the survival of a monetary union tormented by distabilizing regional disparities. Perhaps the citizens of Europe must first savour the fruits of financial discipline and a stable common currency before they are convinced of the desirability to give-up their (remaining) national autonomy. As it is being attempted, however, monetary union is not based on a pre-agreed plan to go for political union. This, if workable, is truly innovative. One can only guess what the implications of such an ordering of developments will be in view of the envisaged enlargement of the European Union to include some CEECs with even more pronounced developmental, institutional and culture-specific problems. In this light , it was indeed fortunate that the Kingdom of Greece and the United States of the Ionian Islands first decided on a thorough political union and then embarked upon a well -prepared monetary integration.

References

For the political and social history of the Ionian Islands, see:

L.S. Stavrianos: The Balkans Since 1453 (Dryden Press, Hinsdale, Ill., 1958), chapter 12, esp. pp. 198-202.

Douglas Dakin: The Unification of Greece, 1770-1923 (Ernest Benn Ltd, London, 1972), chapter 7.

Greg. Dafnis: John Capodistrias: The Birth of the Greek State (Ikaros Publ., Athens, 1975, in Greek), Part One.

On the Ionian Bank and its role as an issuing bank:

The History of the Ionian Bank (in Greek, Athens, 1953)

Basil Mitsis: The Issuing Privilege of the Ionian Bank 1839-1920 (publ. by Ionian Bank, Athens, 1987, in Greek)

On the "banking school" and "currency school" debate, see:

Jacob Viner: Studies in the Theory of International Trade (Harper and Bros, New York, 1937-reprinted in Kelley Classics, 1975), Chapter 5: English Currency Controversies, 1825-1865.

Joseph Schumpeter, History of Economic Analysis (Allen and Unwin, London, and Oxford University Press, 1954), Part III, Chapter 7, and esp. pp. 688-731.

Charles Rist: History of Monetary and Credit History (Original French edition, 1938, English translation reprinted in Kelley Classics, 1966), chapter 5.

On the role of banking in economic development:

Rondo Cameron (editor): Banking and Economic Development (Oxford University Press, 1972), Chapter 1.

For the 19th century cases of monetary unification, see:

Charles Kindleberger: A Financial History of Western Europe (Allan and Unwin, London , 1984), esp. the section German on the unification (pp.117-129) and the Italian unification (pp. 136-146).

Part II Transitional Economics: Theoretical and Institutional Issues

2 Rents as Distractions: Why the Exit from Transition is Prolonged

Alan Gelb, Arye L. Hillman, and Heinrich W. Ursprung*
Bar-Ilan University,
Department of Economics,
52900 Ramat - Gan - Israel

Abstract

The notions of rent and rent-seeking have a substantial contribution to make in offering a theoretical and analytical framework for understanding events and behavior in the transition. The theory of rent-seeking behavior reveals how economic incentives combined with political discretion and unclear property rights attract individuals' attention to unproductive activities directed at contesting available rents. This paper provides a review of rent-seeking theory with a directed focus on the role of rents and rent-seeking incentives in the transition. We indicate how rents and rent-seeking can be endemic to an economy in transition, and how recognition of rent-seeking incentives enhances understanding of the reasons why the transition to market economy is an extended process..

2.1 Introduction

A classic literature describes what happens when market economies are opened to international trade and investment. There are gains from trade and from investment opportunities that arise. The domestic markets that consumers and producers previously faced are expanded to include the wider market that encompasses the newly trading countries. The interdependence between the markets of the liberal-

---

* Respectively, Director, World Development Report 1996, The World Bank; William Gittes Professor of International Economics, Bar-Ilan University; Professor of Economics, University of Konstanz. This research was sponsored by the World Bank. The views and conclusions contained in this report however reflect the individual viewpoints of the authors and indicate the official position of neither the World Bank nor of any of its affiliated bodies. The research of Arye Hillman and Heinrich Ursprung was assisted by the Max Manok Prize for Economic Research.

izing countries is expressed in realizations of comparative advantage and consequent mutual benefit.

This is an idealized picture of what could possibly be. In considering integration of the post-socialist economies into world markets, one finds impediments to this scenario, in the form of domestic incentives associated with rents and rent seeking. The presence of substantial rents turns people's attention inward, and away from productive activity and market exchange, whether domestic or international. The market relationships that are necessary for gains from trade to be realized are compromised, so long as greater benefits remain to be achieved by directing resources and attention to contesting domestic rents.

Markets, of course, require well-defined property rights. Yet, in an economy where rent seeking is prevalent, property rights are ambiguous. It is the ambiguity of property rights which indeed underlies the possibility of contesting rents. Two economies, one where property rights are well-defined and another where property rights are ambiguous have incompatibilities that inhibit market relationships.

Ambiguous property rights and pervasive rents thus inhibit market participation and integration. We shall proceed now to describe how ambiguous property rights and pervasive rents have characterized the economies in transition from socialism. For the purposes of our discussion, we assume little or no background with the literature on rent seeking. We shall incorporate below a brief review of the basic elements of this literature. We begin with the concept of a rent and the nature of rent-seeking.

What is a rent, and what does rent-seeking entail? A rent is a payment, often politically allocated, in excess of that which an individual or factor of production would earn in a competitive market equilibrium. Theories of rent-seeking behavior describe the quest to influence the allocation of such payments, at the expense of productive activity. The more contestable rents present in an economy, ceteris paribus, the more rent-seeking takes place. Since real resources are used in the attempts to affect the allocation of rents, the more rent seeking that takes place in an economy, the fewer resources are available for allocation to productive activities -- and, consequently, the less well-off is the population relative to potential maximal welfare.

In economies in transition from socialism, economic progress has often been slow, and certainly slower that might have been predicted. The slow progress raises three questions which we shall proceed to address: Why is the transition overall such an extended affair? Why have some countries fared better than others? And, when can the transition be expected finally to come to an end? The answers will also inform us regarding when expanded possibilities can be expected to arise for greater market interaction with the western market economies.

The literature points to a list of difficulties that transition economies have encountered (see, for example, Hillman 1994, Gros and Steinherr 1995, Gylfason 1995, EBRD 1995, The World Bank 1996). The transition was hampered by initial antiquated capital stock, poor product quality, a workforce lacking the knowledge and skills required for production of western goods. The institutions of a market economy were lacking, credit markets could not function, tax administrations were inadequate to the task of revenue collection and market-based international trade could not be conducted. Macroeconomic stability was compromised by central banks and fiscal authorities that did not have the requisite policy instruments - nor, seemingly, the political will to implement the correct policies. At the individual level, the attitudes and mentality necessary for a market economy were often lacking. And, most significantly, the economies were replete with rents which distracted people from productive activity.

Rents and rent-seeking are present in all economic systems to different degrees (see the compendia by Buchanan, Tollison and Tullock 1980 and Rowley, Tollison and Tullock 1988, and the review of the literature by Nitzan 1994). Rent-seeking appears, however, to warrant special attention in the transition. Still, the ideas and framework offered by rent-seeking theories for analysing the motives of economic and political agents have not been central to the transition literature. Although they may not use the terminology, the populations in the transition economies are nonetheless aware that phenomena described by rent-seeking behavior are prevalent in their countries to different degrees. The popular press reminds them daily of the resolution, often by violent means, of rent-seeking contests of the transition, and the population observes personal wealth of magnitudes that often appear inconsistent with earned income under the post-socialist economic conditions.

If rent-seeking theories are not part of the behavioral incentives attributed to economic and political agents, significant transition-related phenomena can remain unexplained.[1] Indeed, if rent-seeking behavior is disregarded, many of the phenomena observed during the transition can appear puzzling and be thought to be attributable to mistakes and random events rather than rational calculations. Only recognition of the way rents and rent-seeking influence behavioral incentives will resolve the enigma of the slow pace of transition. The distraction of people's time and effort, and other resources, to contesting rents contributes to explaining why productive effort has been less than it might otherwise have been. We are better able to understand why output failed to recover as fast as it might have from the drastic declines that occurred at the onset of transition. We are also provided with an explanation for the differential performance of the transition economies, in terms of the different prominence of incentives for rent seeking relative to incentives to be productive. Moreover, a criterion presents itself for discerning the light at the end of the tunnel of transition. To the debate on how to determine where a country stands in the transition process (see Marie Lavigne 1996), rent-seeking theories suggest a focus on the persistence of ambiguous property rights and other sources of incentives which continue distract people away from productive activities.

In the transition economies there is a continuity of behavioral norms established during the previous socialist system. When it is individuals who make allocation

---

[1] The broader issue here is: which parts of western economic theory are more useful for understanding the transition and which are less so? See, also, Peter Murrell (1995).

decisions rather than the markets, as in the planning mechanisms of the socialist economic system, the scope for rent-seeking is maximal. Indeed, the socialist system gave to many languages the word "protectzia", indicating personal relationships that facilitate successful rent seeking. When transition began, social property was assigned to private ownership and other policies determined the population's future income and wealth. The decisions were often made within the retained social mores and traditions that reflected the past personalized relations. Such personalized decisions regarding the allocation of wealth and income are at the heart of rent-seeking theories.

2.2 Identifying the rents in the transition

A first step to placing the transition in the context of rent-seeking is to identify the rents characteristic of the transition. These rents may reflect market valuation and have well-defined legal claimants.[2] Then, illegal activity is involved in appropriating the rents from their legal claimants. The rents created and sustained by government policies, on the other hand, in general have ambiguous property rights[3] ,and the contesting of these rents need not be illegal. The rent may have a designated market value or be valued differently by contenders. In either case, the value of the rent may be uncertain. The rent may provide a purely private exclusive benefit, may be shared by a number of beneficiaries, or may provide public good-type benefits to a coalition of winners. And the rent may preexist, or the policy which would bring the rent into existence may be the object of persuasion. The following sources of different rents, in particular, underlie the rent-seeking prizes that are characteristically present in transition economies.

---

[2] For example, Ricardian rent due to differentially efficient factors of production, natural-resource rents that reflect difference between market value and cost of extraction, or rents earned by factors of production that do not have employment opportunities outside their industry.

[3] For example monopoly profits due to regulation, private benefits arising from protectionist international trade policies, government transfers and subsidized credits to favored individuals or sectors, or opportunities to acquire privatized assets at preferential prices, etc.

2.2.1 Preemption of privatization

In many transition economies, privatization of small enterprises and property took place by sale and restitution but progress was more complex and limited when it came to the privatization of the larger state enterprises (World Bank 1996). For these, the privatization programs were often mere slogans rather than actual policies: privatization programs were drawn up but mass privatization was delayed. Privatization remained persistently "around the corner."

There are, in principle, a number of reasons for possible delays in proceeding with privatization. The delays could be procedural, reflecting an inability to achieve consensus regarding how to proceed. Or, gradual privatization over time of a state enterprise could be part of a concerted strategy of imparting credibility to government efficiency objectives (as proposed by Enrico Perotti 1995). There are also, however, credible reasons for the delay of privatization relating to rents and rent-seeking. The ambiguities in property rights that remained sustained the state enterprises as sources of rents that could be transferred to the private sector (for evidence see Hillman, Mitov, and Peters 1995). The transfer of rents from state to private firms takes different forms. Rents are created via the prices at which non-privatized enterprises transact with exclusively designated private-sector agents. The profit shifting to private-sector agents facilitated by these transfer prices is accompanied by tax evasion, since the private sector is less amenable to tax monitoring than state firms with whom the authorities had a traditional auditing relationship (for examples, see Bogetiæ and Hillman 1995). Once privatization takes place, private owners have incentives to ensure that the rent transfers cease.

The rents that accrue from the preemption of privatization are also shared by the workers whose jobs are artificially sustained thanks to persistent soft budgets for state firms (see Manuel Hinds, 1991, 1992). Moreover, procedural arrangements for financial sector restructuring can give rent creation a finality by transforming accumulated state-enterprise losses to taxpayer liabilities (see Hillman and Ursprung 1997).

2.2.2 Rents from the process of privatization

The opportunity to purchase an asset at less than its fair market value provides the privileged buyer with a rent. The rent is here created by restrictions on competitive bidding for the asset, or by asymmetric information. Outside investors tend to be less well-informed about the true worth of a non-privatized state enterprise than incumbent managers; and since the managers (and workers) can be potential beneficiaries of the means chosen for privatization, it may be in the interest of the incumbent managers to withhold or distort information required for valuation for purposes of privatization. By reporting lower than actual profitability, managers and other insiders can hope to reduce valuation and thereby create a rent to be realized by purchasing state property at less-than-market prices.

In cases where the privatization process has been controlled by managers, state property has been sold at artificially low transfer prices to beneficiaries who were family and friends or to politically well-placed individuals and in instances where foreigners purchased state assets, rents have been shared between the foreign buyers and the managers and other agents of the state negotiating the terms of sale. Managers could, for example, secure for themselves long-term management contracts as informal conditions of sale. Such instances (known as "spontaneous" privatization) often took place when the end of the communist regime appeared imminent but before the introduction of democratic government (see for example Hillman 1994).

In principle, rents and rent-seeking associated with privatization could perhaps be restrained by voucher schemes which distribute equal endowments of means of payment for privatized state property, since thereby individuals are provided with the means to bid for state property on equal monetary terms. Yet, the Russian experience confirms that voucher-based privatization is not sufficient to eliminate the creation and contesting of rents: shareholders' rights could be compromised by ill-defined property rights which allow arbitrary dilution of ownership and by denial of owners' rights to information.

2.2.3 Rents derived from political and bureaucratic discretion

Rents are in general allocated by political or bureaucratic discretion. The discretion can, for example, determine who can lease property owned by the state, the city or municipality who is to receive an export quota, who will be able to buy state property at a preferential price, who can import without paying import duties and who can export without an official quota, who can avoid export duties - or who can have a phone line and with how much delay, who can have property rezoned, who can have access to state-owned refineries, etc. The list goes on. Individuals in the private sector seeking to benefit from such decisions are prepared to pay for preferential treatment. The payments received make displacement of the officials exercising the discretion valuable, which introduces incentives for rent-seeking efforts directed at contesting political office and bureaucratic positions. The more valuable the official discretion that is exercised - in determining the means and timing of privatization, allocation of import and export licenses, assignment of leases and rentals of state property, the identity of recipients of subsidized credits, etc. -, the greater the incentives for others to invest time, effort and resources in replacing the incumbents for whom the exercise of discretion is a source of personal income.

2.2.4 Monopoly rents

Enterprises under socialism had designated assignments of production or distribution. Since duplication was regarded as wasteful and as complicating planning, the transition often released monopolies into a market environment (Hillman 1994). Competition, then, took the form of contesting the right of sole supply vacated by the state, rather than competition in the supply of the output itself. For example, rather than competitive offers to supply products to a retail store, the competition could be for sole supplier of products to the store. In this case, the competition assumes a rent-seeking nature, namely to establish the claimant to the rents from the noncompetitive supply arrangements.

2.2.5 The contestability of non-contrived rents

Non-contrived rents not associated with government policies also arise in the transition, as the quite natural consequence of market valuation of individuals' human capital and formerly suppressed entrepreneurial abilities. The change from planning to a market -based economy also revalued returns to different occupations (with gains to professions such as accountants, lawyers, translators, and bankers). As we have observed, such personal non-contrived rents in general have secure private property rights and can be contested only by illegal activity (extortion, "protection", and theft). We return to the illegalities of rent-seeking below.

2.3 The Social costs of rent seeking: Rent dissipation

The above rents attract resources. The rent-seeking contests wherein the resources are used are similar to auctions, with the difference that participants pay their bids whether they win or lose.[4]

It is the contestability that is the source of social loss: the resources used in contesting a rent could have been used to add to national income or create wealth. Gordon Tullock (1967), in introducing the concept of rent-seeking in the modern literature (but not the terminology, for which see Anne Krueger 1974) , observed

[4] A *contest-success rule* determines how winners of the rent are determined (see Jack Hirshleifer 1989). A common rule views the probability of success as increasing with rent-seeking outlays (Gordon Tullock 1980). This type of contest-success rule is "non-discriminating" since the winner is not specifically designated. An alternative "discriminating" rule identifies the winner as making the highest bid (Hillman and Riley 1989).

the similarities among "the social cost of tariffs, monopolies, and theft". Tullock pointed out that, beyond dead weight losses of protectionist tariffs and monopolies, social losses were also incurred. Theft illustrates the general principle. Consider a number of thieves seeking to steal $1,000. Let each thief have an equal chance of success, if he or she invests the same resources in attempting to be the successful thief. The thieves will then make outlays equal to the expected value of their gain (if risk-neutral), allocating accordingly time, effort, and tools of the trade. Before the identity of the successful thief is established, $1,000 of real resources will have been allocated to the contest to be the successful thief. The one successful thief ultimately gains $1,000. For purposes of evaluation of national income, the identity of the successful thief is of no consequence. Nor is the immorality of theft (or seeking tariff protection or monopoly power) the issue. The negative aspect is the social loss reflected in the resources and time used ex-ante in the rent-seeking contest.

2.3.1 Rent dissipation

If the rents of the transition as set out above are indeed "large", can we also infer that the associated social losses due to rent seeking are likewise "large"? That is, are substantial portions of rents dissipated in rent-seeking activities? This is the focal question posed by rent-seeking theories. If rent dissipation is large, we can point to a substantial source of social loss in the transition.

Gordon Tullock and Anne Krueger, two other early writers who were concerned with the social costs of rent seeking, assumed complete rent dissipation: that is, the resources used in contesting the prize were assumed precisely equal to the value of the prize (as assumed in the above thief example). In that case, the value of the social loss can be inferred from the value of the prize, which is advantageous, since often the prize *is* observable whereas the rent-seeking outlays being made behind-the-scenes are not. The assumption of complete dissipation would imply quite enormous social losses in the transition relative to productively earned incomes. Is complete dissipation, however, a reasonable assumption? Since we do not directly observe rent dissipation, we have to rely on the theory linking the value of the prize to the resources that would be allocated to the contest for the prize by rational rent-seeking agents. Sufficient conditions can be identified which ensure complete rent dissipation:

(i) The contest-success rule specifies the probability of success and not the actual winner,[5]
(ii) contenders are risk-neutral,
(iii) the prize is a source of purely private benefit,
(iv) all rent seekers value the prize equally, and

---

[5] The rule is thus "non-discriminating" and contenders are in effect purchasing lottery tickets.

(v) the contest is competitive (anyone can enter, and a sufficiently large number of people do).

Alternatively, complete rent dissipation arises on average (the expected value of outlays is equal to the value of the contested rent) if risk neutral rent seekers value the prize equally and the highest outlay wins).[6] In general, however, there are too many qualifications to expect rent dissipation to be complete. Nor, in practice, based on observations from western economies, does rent dissipation appear to approach the value of the prize (see Gordon Tullock 1988).

Group size is, in particular, an important element in determining rent dissipation. If the prize is a source of collective benefit to members of a group, there is an incentive to engage in collective rent-seeking (see Ursprung 1990, Nitzan 1991). Consider, for example, the benefits, indicated above, of *deferring* privatization. The benefits accrue to all those individuals who gain as long as the state enterprise remains without the discipline of private ownership. The beneficiaries cannot be expected, however, to coordinate their activities, because of transactions costs of organization and free riding. In such cases, theories of collective action often suggest that larger groups are less effective than small "cohesive" groups seeking a common objective. Rent-seeking theory identifies circumstances where, nonetheless, the likelihood of success of a rent-seeking coalition is independent of the size of the group. This outcome requires that rents be of a pure-public-good nature.[7] Small groups are more effective than large groups, if a rent-seeking prize does not have *pure*-public-good characteristics, since then addition of more members to the coalition reduces the per capita benefit for the group, so discouraging individual rent-seeking efforts. With fewer resources thereby contributed to the collective rent-seeking effort, rent dissipation declines. And if smaller groups have advantages over larger groups, there are of course incentives for insiders to place entry barriers against outsiders seeking to join a rent-seeking coalition (see Gradstein 1995).

Rent dissipation is also influenced by asymmetries in resources available for contesting a rent. For example, foreign investors may have more resources for influencing policies than domestic residents who are credit - and capital - constrained. In such cases, the Nash equilibrium requires that poorer contenders make their bids first (Leininger 1993) and rent dissipation is reduced compared to simultaneous bids. Since poorer contenders have a lower likelihood of success, there is again an incentive to exclude, in this case, better-endowed contenders

---

[6] It does not then matter how many rent seekers enter the contest. Rent dissipation is on average complete, for example, if there are only two contenders (Hillman and Riley 1989).

[7] If the prize provides benefits of a pure-public-good nature, and individuals make noncooperative Nash contributions to the collective effort of the coalition, then the additional contribution made by a newly added person in a coalition precisely matches the combined reductions in contributions of all preexisting coalition members. Total rent-seeking contributions are consequently independent of group size, as is the likelihood that the group will be successful.

from the contest altogether, beyond the usual incentive to keep the number of contenders low to avoid competition. This incentive is for example reflected in laws that exclude foreigners from activities related to the transition. A further influence on rent dissipation is resistance by losers. If the winners and losers belong to the same population, and if an individual does not know to which group he or she will belong until after the contest is decided, rent dissipation is increased by resistance (see Hillman and Riley 1989). Individuals are not only outlying resources to win the rent but also at the same time seek to avoid financing the rent by ending up on the losing side. In more usual circumstances, we can identify in advance potential winners and losers, who are not in the same population. That is, rent seekers who are advantageously placed to participate in a contest will gain at the expense of the general population of outsiders. Then, resistance by losers (for example by consumers resisting a quest for monopoly power) makes the rent-seeking contest less attractive for rent seekers. Although such resistance makes use of otherwise productive resources, the total social cost of rent seeking can decline, because of the adverse incentives that are created for rent seekers, who must now not only compete amongst themselves but also face the countervailing opposition of those who will be the losers if their rent-seeking efforts are successful.[8]

2.3.2 Bribes

Finally, we note the difference between rent seeking and bribes. A social cost is associated with bribery only if a contestable rent is created, which requires the bribes to be prizes in contests to determine the identity of the recipients of the bribes. The social losses depend upon the hierarchical transfer of bribes. A low-level official may be obliged to transfer some part of a bribe to his or her immediate superior, who in turn is obliged to transfer some part to his or her superior, and so on up a chain of political or bureaucratic command. The total sum of bribes accruing at each level of the hierarchy becomes the rent which is received by the incumbent in that position and is the prize in the rent-seeking contest for that position (see Hillman and Katz 1987). For example, a part of a bribe paid to an enterprise manager for private use of the state factory's facilities or labor may be transferred to the government officials who are responsible for monitoring the state enterprise (see Hillman, Mitov, and Peters 1995). The social losses are again incurred ex-ante, before bribes are paid, and take the form of the resources, effort and initiative expended to establish the identity of the managers or government officials who receive the transfers.

---

8 Resistance by potential losers reduces rent dissipation if the highest bid wins (a discriminating contest); if the probability of winning increases with rent-seeking outlays (a non-discriminating contest); and if the number of rent seekers is sufficiently large. On countervailing opposition to rent seekers, see for example Fabella (1995).

Information constraints: What can we observe? Because of the types of favors and preferential treatment that are sought, the contests often take place surreptitiously, out of view of the general population. At best, we may observe people congregating to meet decision makers or paying to have doors opened for them. We might observe the wealth of the decision makers, or the political displacement which changes the identities of those individuals dispensing the rents, or we might observe rent-defending behavior by the same individuals. At other times, the contests take place with no more evidence than "footprints in the sand". Someone emerges with privileged private ownership of formerly state assets or with rights to an export quota; or privileged relations are observed between private agents and non-privatized state firms.

2.4 Rent seeking and models of government

Rent-seeking theories are inconsistent with a model of benevolent government. Rather, rent-seeking theories imply a model of government where policies create rents rather than correct distortions and were income redistribution reflects private self-interest and not conceptions of social justice (see Applebaum and Katz 1987). Underlying the departure from socially desirable policies is a principal-agent problem in the voter's relation with the political agents who are his/her representatives. Voters' monitoring of political agents' activities can of course be quite imperfect. The same problem is present in western market economies. It has, however, been uncommon for political agents and government officials in western economies to be direct beneficiaries of the rents which their policies create. Rather, a more subtle exchange usually takes place of political support for economic benefits. In contrast, in economies in transition, the interplay between government and rent seeking has often been more personal, with a less clear-cut distinction between political agents seeking political returns and economic agents seeking economic benefits. Rents in the transition have tended to be more directly shared with those whose policies have created them.

Rather than active policy, the source of rents can be policy inactivity or "government desertion" (a concept introduced by Istvan Abel and John Bonin 1990). The "desertion" is reflected in delayed privatization, absence of bankruptcy laws, deferrals of tax reforms and of regulatory reforms of the banking and financial system. For example, despite the many policy recommendations (see for example Udel and Wachtel 1995, Bonin, Mizsei, Wachtel 1996), banks in many transition economies were often able to incur losses and declare bankruptcy under dubious circumstances regarding the disposition of depositors' funds (Hillman and Ursprung 1997). Laws were also delayed that would provide for accountability to shareholders of the management of privatized enterprises, while legal systems did not permit enforcement of contracts. In these cases, the *absence of the correct policies* created the rents to be contested.

2.5 Appropriability and ambiguity of property rights: Related literature

There is another literature which examines behavior in the presence of ambiguous property rights and also investigates the incentives to establish and defend property rights. Stergios Skaperdas (1992) models a situation where property can be redistributed by coercion and individuals choose whether to engage in productive or coercive redistributive activities (i.e., rent-seeking). He examines the conditions favoring agreement to refrain from contestability and concludes that more powerful agents will tend to favor coercive over productive activities. Karl Wärneryd (1993) models initially non-secure property rights and investigates whether, in the absence of the rule of law, individuals will agree to respect property rights: a principal conclusion is that, with the same cost of using violence, property rights will be more contestable in poorer societies with greater income inequality. Herschel Grossman and Minseong Kim (1995) model individual choice between "appropriative" (i.e. rent-seeking) and productive activities: property can be defended but is also damaged when contested. Jack Hirshleifer (1995) investigates the choice between productive and "conflictual" activity, when there is no external enforcement of property rights, and establishes conditions under which anarchy is sustainable as a form of spontaneous order. This latter literature describes circumstances similar to those which are the subject of rent-seeking theories, but with different terminology. Also, rent-seeking theories focus on investigating the influences that affect rent dissipation and thereby the social cost of contestability of rents.

2.6 Crime and corruption

Many examples of rent seeking are responses to legally instituted policies or attempts to change such policies. Illegality has, however, a significant role in the rent seeking associated with the transition. The murder of businessmen and bankers is, for example, prominent in Russia (the killers are rarely identified and apprehended). After bankers, the prime target of murder is directors of oil companies (Gregory Kisunko, *Transition*, The World Bank, July-August 1996). The murders are ex-post indications of the contesting of rents. Bankers can dispense credits that may not have to be repaid. The oil company directors are intimately linked to the rents that derive from export quotas and lower-than-world domestic prices. The unresolved murders are consistent with a policy position that rent-seeking contests should play themselves out without the state taking sides.

A broader description of the same picture is the following: "Russia .. is under attack from over 5,000 gangs, 3,000 hardened criminals, 300 mob bosses, and 150 illegal organizations with international connections. Some 40,000 Russian businesses and industrial enterprises are controlled by organized crime ... The Russian Mafia is estimated to be worth $10 billion" (Ariel Cohen, Transition, The World Bank, May-June 1995). The rent-seeking contests thus appear to be quite competitive, at least in Russia.

Again from Russia: "Russian officials charge up to $80,000 to register a bank and up to 15 percent of an oil deal's value to issue a license to export. Managers of government-owned industrial enterprises often bill international customers only 10 percent of the price of exported commodities, with the difference between the contract price and the world market price deposited into their offshore bank accounts" (Gregory Kisunko 1995). In these examples of corruption, government officials are using their positions to create and allocate rents. The bribe to register a bank attests to rents from entry into banking, the bribe to issue an export license to rents associated with export quotas. The illegal transfer abroad by managers of proceeds from export sales reveals rents due to ambiguities in claims to the profits of domestic firms.

As for political agents, the Russian Duma which was elected in 1993 felt obliged to legislate criminal immunity for members of parliament. In October 1995, a bill to reduce the scope of immunity was overwhelmingly defeated in parliament (by 450 votes to 41).

Rents are also created by the gullibility of a public not familiar with wealth creation in market economies. In Russia and elsewhere classic pyramid schemes have defrauded a naive and financially unsophisticated population. A perpetrator of one such scheme in Russia succeeded in moving from jail to parliament, in a by-election, by promising to spend $13 million in the constituency which he successfully contested (he was subsequently expelled from parliament for continuing with *legal* commercial activities in violation of parliamentary rules). Announced candidates for the December 1995 parliamentary elections included a woman in jail pending charges of appropriating $266 million from investors. A list of the Russian Ministry of the Interior identified 85 parliamentary candidates with a known criminal past. These observations point to an interface between the political creation and dispensing of rents, as portrayed in rent-seeking theories.

2.7 Private gains and social losses

Rent seeking, whether legal or illegal, is a socially undesirable activity. If, however, rent-seeking opportunities offer a higher expected return than productive activity, it is privately rational to engage in rent seeking. There is a Prisoners' Dilemma. If all individuals choose to forego rent-seeking opportunities, society is spared the social cost of the resources dissipated by rent-seeking. If some individuals choose to engage in rent seeking while others do not, the productive individuals are disadvantaged: they produce the real output which the others contest.

The efficient outcome which maximizes aggregate output requires individuals to cooperate in refraining from rent seeking. Credible commitment mechanisms for resolving the dilemma are however lacking. We can, therefore, consider two societies with the same real resources. In one society, property rights are well-defined and there are no opportunities for influencing the creation and assignment of rents. In the second society, claims to property and income are contestable. In the first society individuals have no option other than to engage in productive activities while the second society offers opportunities to acquire wealth by influencing redistribution. The dominant strategy in the latter economy is to engage in rent seeking. The society without rent-seeking opportunities will be more productive, with higher real income and higher growth than the society where resources are dissipated in contesting and defending ownership claims. For the reasons we have proposed, the comparison reflects the different circumstances and incentives of mature market economies and of the economies in transition.

2.8 Individual differences among the post-socialist economies

There have been substantial differences in rent-seeking incentives among the post-socialist countries. Yet, their economies broadly shared similar initial conditions. For example, in the Czech Republic, the social organization of the transition and the form taken by the mass-privatization program reduced the scope for rent-seeking opportunities. There was agglomeration of stock holdings but it was achieved by the market activities of mutual funds that diversified individual holdings and respected original property rights. At the other extreme are countries where delayed privatization prolonged ambiguous property rights (for example Bulgaria and Romania), or where post-privatization ownership rights were subordinated to managers' interests (for example Russia). Idiosyncratic institutional influences also affected the scope of rent-seeking. For example, in Poland opportunities for rent-seeking were contained by the presence of the Solidarity workers' movement although there were continual delays with privatization and politicized relations persisted between government and state enterprises. In some Central Asian republics, authoritarian rule contained rent-seeking by limiting the number of insiders placed to participate in rent-seeking activities. In many transition economies, rent seeking declined as the private sector developed and began to offer opportunities for private gain from productive activity: by the mid 1990s, emerging private sectors in many of the post-socialist economies had come to account for around half of GDP, although significant parts of the new private sectors operated outside the formal economy (see the World Bank 1996).

2.9 Concluding observations

It has not been our primary intention to make policy recommendations. We can note, however, some implications about the role of government in the transition. Rent-seeking theories suggest that we should be reluctant, for example, to propose, as the solution to the transition taking too long, a more prominent role for the state sector in economic decision- making. Thus, Lance Taylor (1994) suggests that, in confronting the transition, "the market has met its match" and the state should reenter. However, the problem may not be that *the* market has met its match, but rather that the *wrong* markets have attracted resources and private initiative. If the property-rights ambiguities that persist (see Andrzej Rapaczynski 1996 for examples) permit personalized political markets to determine individual income and wealth, the solution appears to be the establishment of non-contestable claims, albeit in a socially just way with exit of government from the type of political discretion that underlies the creation and assignment of rents. Where contestability is due to government "desertion", the solution is a legal regulatory and institutional structure which makes political discretion less valuable.

A decline in rent seeking appears to be a requisite of the beginning of the end of transition.[9] Rent-seeking theories suggest that the end may come endogenously, since the initial winners will wish to declare the contests over. Thus, for example, although privatization had been under way for a number of years, a Russian presidential decree of August 1995 finally granted protection (in principle) to stockholders against arbitrary dilution of ownership and set out requirements for reporting, dissemination of information, and access to shareholders' meetings.

The resolution of rent-seeking contests will have established a wealth distribution in transition economies that approximates the skewed distribution of mature market economies. When the transition is finally declared to be over, an elite will have been established, based not on its positioning within the framework of Party privilege as under the previous system but on personal wealth acquired during the transition. The new elite may differ little from the old one. Thus, a study in Russia in 1995 concluded that 75% of the new political elite and 61% of the new business elite was composed of people who had also been members of the former communist elite.[10] When the contestability of the rents associated with the

---

[9] There are of course other indicators, such as privatization, political competition, liberalization of economic activity, and the development of market-based institutions (see for example Peter Murrell 1996); observe however that the effect of progress in terms of such other indicators is to diminish the scope of the rent-seeking environment.

[10] Research by Olga Kryshtanovska, published in Izvestiya January 10 1996, cited in *Transition, The World Bank*, January-February 1996.

transition has come to end, questions may well be asked about the means whereby private wealth was acquired. If such questions are raised, one would not wish, for the sake of historical fairness, to forget the era of robber-barons elsewhere.

References

Abel, Istvan and John Bonin (1990), "State desertion in the transforming economies: The economic black hole," paper presented at the annual meetings of the ASIA, Washington, D.C.

Applebaum, Eli and Eli Katz (1987), "Seeking rents by setting rents: The political economy of rent seeking," *Economic Journal*, 97, 685-699.

Bogetiæ , •eljko and Arye L. Hillman (1995), "The choice of a tax system," in •. Bogetiæ and A.L. Hillman editors, *Financing Government in Transition, Bulgaria: The Political Economy of Tax Policies, Tax Bases, and Tax Evasion*, The World Bank, Washington, D.C.

Bonin, John, Kalman Mizsei, and Paul Wachtel (1996), *Towards Market Oriented Banking for the Economies in Transition*, Institute for East-West Studies, Prague.

Buchanan, James, Robert Tollison, and Gordon Tullock (1980), editors, *Toward a Theory of the Rent-Seeking Society*, Texas A@M Press, College Station..

Cohen, Ariel (1995), "Growing crime and corruption threaten not only Russia, but the entire world," *Transition*, The World Bank, Washington DC, 6, #5-6, 7-10.

European Bank for Reconstruction and Development (1995), *Transition Report: Investment and Enterprise Development*, London.

Fabella, Raul V. (1995), "The social cost of rent seeking under countervailing opposition to distortionary transfers", *Journal of Public Economics*, 57, 235-247.

Gelb, Alan, Arye L. Hillman,and Heinrich W. Ursprung (1996), "Rents and the transition," *World Development Report Background Paper*, The World Bank, Washington D.C.

Gradstein, Mark (1995), ""Intensity of competition, entry, and entry deterrence in rent seeking contests," *Economics and Politics*, 7, 79-91.

Gros, Daniel and Alfred Steinherr (1995), *Winds of Change -- Economic Transition in Central and Eastern Europe*, Longman, New York.

Grossman, Herschel and Minseong Kim (1995), "Swords or ploughshares: A theory of the security of claims to property," *Journal of Political Economy*, 103, 1275-1288.

Gylfason, Thorvaldur (1995), "Reforms in Eastern Europe," *Journal of World Trade Law*, 29, 107-133.

Hillman, Arye L. and Eli Katz (1987), "Hierarchical structure and the social costs of bribes and transfers," *Journal of Public Economics*, 34, 129-142.

Hillman, Arye L. and John Riley (1989), "Politically contestable rents and transfers, *Economics and Politics*, 1, 17-39.

Hillman, Arye L. (1994), The transition from socialism: An overview from a political-economy perspective, *European Journal of Political Economy*, 10, 191-225.

Hillman, Arye L., Lubomir Mitov and R. Kyle Peters (1995), "The private sector, state enterprises, and informal economic activity," in •. Bogetiæ and A.L. Hillman editors, *Financing Government in Transition, Bulgaria: The Political Economy of Tax Policies, Tax Bases, and Tax Evasion* , The World Bank, Washington, D.C.

Hillman, Arye L. and Heinrich W. Ursprung (1997), "The political economy of financial-sector reform in the transition", in *Financial Reforms during the Transition*, edited by Mario I. Blejer and Marko Škreb, Cambridge University Press.

Hinds, Manuel (1991), "Incentives and ownership in socialist countries in transition," in Arye L. Hillman, editor, *Markets and Politicians: Politicized Economic Choice*, Kluwer Academic Publishers, Boston and Dordrecht, 137-168.

Hinds, Manuel (1992), "Policy effectiveness in reforming socialist economies," in Arye L. Hillman and Branko Milanovic, editors, *The Transition from Socialism in Eastern Europe: Domestic Restructuring and Foreign Trade*, The World Bank, Washington, D.C., 13-39.

Hirshleifer, Jack (1989), "Conflict and rent-seeking success functions: Different models of relative success," *Public Choice*, 63, 101-112.

Hirshleifer, Jack (1995), "Anarchy and its breakdown," *Journal of Political Economy*, 103, 26-52.

Kisunko, Gregory (1995), "Economic crime in the Russian Federation," Discussion Paper, The World Bank, Washington D.C.

Kisunko, Gregory (1996), "Economic crime in Russia," *Transition*, The World Bank, Washington DC, 7, #7-8, 13-16.

Kryshtanovska, Olga (1996), Izvestiya January 10; reported in *Transition*, The World Bank, Washington DC, 7, #1, 16.

Krueger, Anne (1974), "The political economy of the rent-seeking society," *American Economic Review*, 64, 291-303.

Lavigne, Marie (1996), "Russia and Eastern Europe: Is the transition over?", *Journal of Comparative Economics*, 23, 92-102.

Leininger, Wolfgang (1993), "More efficient rent seeking: A Münchausen solution," *Public Choice*, 75, 43-62.

Murrell, Peter (1995), "The transition according to Cambridge, Mass." *Journal of Economic Literature*, 33, 164-178.

Murrell, Peter (1996), "How far has the transition progressed?" *Journal of Economic Perspectives*, 10, 25-44.

Nitzan, Shmuel. I. (1991), "Collective rent dissipation", *Economic Journal*, 101, 1522-1534.

Nitzan, Shmuel I. (1994), "Modelling rent seeking contests," *European Journal of Political Economy*, 10, 41-60.

Rapaczynski, Andrzej (1996), "The roles of the state and the market in establishing property rights," *Journal of Economic Literature*, 10, 87-103.

Perotti, Enrico C. (1995), "Credible privatization", *American Economic Review*, 85, 847-859.

Rowley, Charles, Robert D. Tollison, and Gordon Tullock (1988), *The Political Economy of Rent-Seeking*, Kluwer Academic Publishers, Boston and Dordrecht.

Skaperdas, Stergios (1992), "Cooperation, conflict, and power in the absence of property rights," *American Economic Review*, 82, 720-739.

Taylor, Lance (1994), "The market met its match: Lessons for the future from the transition's initial years," *Journal of Comparative Economics*, 19, 64-87.

Tullock, Gordon (1967), "The welfare costs of tariffs, monopoly, and theft," *Western Economic Journal*, 5, 224-232; reprinted in J. Buchanan, R.D. Tollison, and G. Tullock, editors, *Toward a Theory of the Rent Seeking Society*, Texas A@M Press, College Station.

Tullock, Gordon (1980), "Efficient rent seeking", in J. Buchanan, R.D. Tollison, and G. Tullock, editors, *Toward a Theory of the Rent Seeking Society*, Texas A@M Press, College Station, 97-112.

Tullock, Gordon (1988), *The Economics of Rent-Seeking and Privilege*, Kluwer Academic Publishers, Boston and Dordrecht.

Udell, Gregory F. and Paul Wachtel (1995), Financial System Design for Formerly Planned Economies, Defining the Issues, *Financial Markets: Institutions and Instruments*, volume 4, number 2, New York University Salomon Center (Blackwell, Cambridge MA).,

Ursprung, Heinrich W. (1990), "Public goods, rent dissipation, and candidate competition", *Economics and Politics*, 2, 115-132.

Wärneryd, Karl (1993), "Anarchy, uncertainty, and the emergence of property rights," *Economics and Politics*, 5, 1-14.

World Bank (1996), *From Plan to Market* (World Development Report), Washington DC.

3 Transformation Process Five Years On: Behavioural Adaptation and Institutional Change in Poland

Hans-Georg Petersen
Universität Postsdam
Wirtschafts und Sozialwissenschaftuche Fakultät
August Bebel Str. 89
144 39 POTSDAM

Summary

The successful transformation of the former centrally planned economies is decisive for establishing democracy in the countries of the 'Eastern Bloc' after the breakdown of communism. Poland was the first country to embark on reforms. This paper describes the development of the Polish effort to handle evolving problems. Budgetary situations occurring during conversion and their effects on the economy are examined. In order to overcome budgetary constraints, new government revenue sources have to be found. The main source can only be additional taxes. In the Polish case, the tax system should be remodeled and might be supplemented by a value added tax. Simulations based on the Kramer and Neneman model provide the data needed for analyzing the distributional effects of various proposals for tax reforms. An important result is that income distribution will become more unequal during transformation. Another topic to be considered is limiting excessive transfers to private households and firms. However, reform of the tax and transfer system has to be accompanied by improved privatization. The introduction of a negative income tax appears as a possible remedy for reforming encrusted societies. Since social assets are often at the top of the political agenda, any government activities in this area have to be evaluated on public choice theory criteria.

3.1 Introduction

Whereas actual transformation processes have already yielded several unambiguous lessons, even a cursory look into the ever-increasing literature on transformation and transition clearly demonstrates that there is a general complaint on the lack of a relevant theory.[1] After five years, even without a general theory, economists are able to define some general as well as country-specific features, with the latter seeming to be more important than the former. These wide-spread complaints could be taken as circumstantial evidence that the economic profession is puzzled, that things are improving without its support - neglecting the fact that this is quite a normal situation in our Western democracies. On a less charitable note, one might think that the call for more theorizing is rather motivated by the hope that the demand for economists' jobs and reports will be stabilized or even increased, thus improving the conditions for the whole profession. From a political-economic point of view, one's motives for helping the countries in transition or one's own profession are often mixed and complex.

Nevertheless, some simple and powerful theoretical knowledge does exist. Here, one has only to mention the discussions on methodological individualism and collectivism, on open and closed societies[2] and, last but not least, Hayek's ideas on spontaneous order which offer an appropriate explanation for the radical behavioural adaptations that have taken place in the Central and Eastern European Countries (CEECs), leading to dramatic institutional change. The peaceful or velvet revolutions took place in the CEECs because their citizens put more trust in political freedom and the market system than in state-paternalism and central planning, mainly convinced by the better performance of the market economies in satisfying material needs. Even if exaggerated, people's hopes for a democratic life and a market economy have made the hardships of the big bang bearable, at least in the first phase of the transition process. The disillusionment and sobering up experienced in the next phases have changed behavioural patterns as well as the sequencing of institutional change and reforms, but up to now have not really endangered the overall development.

Given the enormous risks involved in a transformation process of such magnitude, the Polish example seems to be a very promising one. In contrast to almost all other countries of the former Eastern Bloc, a powerful political opposition emerged in Poland already in the 70s and especially in the 80s from the underground to the political surface, leading to influential, democratically-oriented trade unions. Thus, Poland had already had experienced some economic instability[3] which was unknown in, say, the Czech Republic or the German Democratic

1 See, e.g., Portes (1995).

2 For more details, see Petersen (1993).

3 A good, detailed description of these development patterns are given in Sowada (1993)

Republic (GDR). These experiences might have been helpful for the stabilization process on the one hand, but on the other hand might also have acted as an obstacle to rapid privatization. Because of the limited space and time, only the most important facts and trends will be presented here. This is obviously a personal selection, dictated mainly by the experience and insights acquired from involvement in empirical research projects carried out during the last years.

3.2 Monetary Stabilization and Budgetary Reforms

Discussions in Poland and abroad about the stabilization process are highly controversial. On the one hand, the slowdown of the inflation rate from more than 600 % in late 1989 to less than 14 % in the first six months of 1995 is regarded as an enormous achievement. The success seems even more impressive to those with personal experience of the situation in fall 1989. At that time, all indicators pointed in the direction of hyperinflation: In addition to large amounts of surplus money, a tremendous mistrust in all governmental institutions existed. Polish shops reminded one of a clearance sale: there were fewer commodities than salespersons. The impoverishment of large parts of the population resembled the situation in Germany in early 1923. Thankfully, Poland was not hit by hyperinflation. The question to be answered is: why did hyperinflation not arise or, better, how could it be avoided?

A conventional textbook definition of inflation would be as follows: inflation is the permanent increase in the general price level (above a certain minimum level of 1.0 % to 1.5 %). Usually, the consumer price index (CPI) is referred to when talking about inflation. Most economists agree that in the long run no major inflation can take place without money growth,[4] although there are many other causes extensively discussed in all macroeconomic textbooks explaining short- and medium-run inflationary phenomena. With regard to the transformation process, we will analyze price increases that are not inflationary according to the above-mentioned definition of inflation. Yet, they are usually treated as such because of difficulties in separating them from true inflationary increases. Even monetarist authors like Johnson (1969, p. 115) point out that within a market system many price increases take place which do not have an inflationary character.

In functioning market economies these index problems are thought to lead to an upward bias in the official inflation rate of the above assumed at 1 % -1.5 %. This means that only increases in the general price level above this minimum level can

and (1995).

4 "The answer to the question whether inflation is a monetary phenomenon in the long run is yes" (Dornbusch and Fischer 1984, p. 440)

actually be interpreted as inflation. For the former socialist countries in their very first transformation phase, the correct interpretation of the official inflation rate is essential to enforce the appropriate monetary policy. Prices, wages and interest rates did not result from free market transactions but used to be fixed by central planning offices. It is well-known that such price formation has effects comparable to a price and wage freeze in market economies. In case of a price freeze, commodity prices (at least on official markets) cannot increase and, sooner or later, what was formerly open inflation will merely become suppressed inflation (Cassel 1992, p. 268).

In the "short supply economies" (Mangelwirtschaft) of the former "really existing socialism", the price freeze lasted for several decades. Obviously, a tremendous potential of suppressed inflation existed. Complied with a dangerous monetary surplus, this would result in explosive open inflation if prices and wages were determined by market forces. Furthermore, without the social pricing policies of the former socialist countries, relative prices were drastically changed. Basic commodities (such as food, rents, energy etc.) were highly subsidized, whereas superior commodities ("luxuries") were excessively burdened with specific turnover taxes. Thus, for instance, compared to prices in Western market economies, bread was six times cheaper and a TV-set ten times more expensive. Cheap prices for foodstuffs led to widespread waste (bread was even used as animal feed) and shortages, whereas production of superior commodities was insufficient to meet the enormous demand. The combined result was the formation of ever-growing queues. All this taxed the people's patience until the peaceful revolution swept away the socialist nomenclature.

It is not surprising, therefore, that the removal of the wrong price structures and the switch to scarcity-adjusted Western market prices led to a price explosion and had a tremendous shock effect on society. The main part of the increase in the Polish price level of late 1989 and early 1990 was due to this adaptation to a realistic pricing system, especially in the field of basic commodities. Thus, the resulting increase in the price level should be seen as a temporary structural effect rather than as inflation pure and simple.

Taking all these considerations into account, our analysis still supports the view that the rise in the price index of 1989/1990 was mainly caused by the shock of lifting the price controls and not by monetary reasons. Even since 1991, a large part of the price increases have occurred because of the on-going gradual relaxation of administered prices, and this is still true today.[5] This gradualist approach was adopted in order to avoid yet another shock while further adapting to world market prices, especially in the area of housing, energy and transportation. If all these price increases were eliminated from the commodity prices used for price index estimation, the resulting inflation rate would be much lower. In short: Polish inflation is more of an index problem than a real phenomenon. Or, to put it the other way around, the real phenomenon is the price shock, and this cannot be

5 For more empirical details, see Petersen and Sowada (1995, pp. 386-397).

called inflation!

However, the more serious problem originates from the fact that index illusions did influence economic policy. IMF experts - macro-economically more orthodox than most economists - recommended that the Polish central bank pursue a restrictive policy, much more restrictive than the bank was able to manage. This can be demonstrated by developments in the money stock and inflation in 1990. The IMF proposal was to increase the zloty money supply by 41.2 billion zloty,[6] but the actual increase was 103.9 billion. This increase was necessary because of three reasons: (a) the above mentioned price shock, (b) the rapid growth in monetary transaction volume, and (c) the reconstruction of the real cash for transaction purposes by the Polish private households after the price shocks during the first quarter of 1990.

Under central planning, the monetary transaction volume was comparatively small because of the existence of large combinats. A large part of trade was carried out through internal deliveries according to internal clearance prices. And as monetary theory states, the fewer stages of production exist within an economy, the less money is needed. Decartelization of the combinats and ongoing privatization, however, led to a strong increase of interfirm transactions creating further need for additional monetization. Obviously, this factor had been ignored by the IMF experts when fixing the monetary expansion path for 1990.

Our figures even support the monetarist view once the price shock and administered price increases lost importance; in 1992 the inflationary potential is more or less higher than the increase in the price index. Here, one has to mention that some administered price increases were again included in the price index, so that the actual inflation rate was even lower. Whereas in many quarters from 1989 to 1991 the monetary expansion was too low, in 1992 it was too high, which might cause an increase in the inflation rate in 1993. It is quite clear that Poland has to follow a very careful monetary policy. Polish experts, torn between perceived necessity and IMF recommendations, often changed tack from restrictive monetary policy to expansionary Keynesian measures, practicing a kind of stop-and-go policy. Naturally, a much steadier expansion of the money stock is necessary in the future in order to enable private firms and households to develop stable expectations and regain their trust in public institutions, especially in the state and the Central Bank, which was lost during the shock therapy phase.

Another reason for the success of the shock therapy and the avoidance of German-style hyperinflation was the existence of a stable parallel currency in Poland. Since the late 70s, when travel to foreign countries was allowed, many Polish people have been working, at least temporarily, outside Poland, especially in the shadow economies of the Western European countries. This gave rise to a large inflow of foreign currency. If anecdotal evidence is taken into consideration, it is likely that a large part of all private savings was held in US dollars or DM. Step

---

6 This amount was agreed upon in the Letter of Intent, see Instytut Finansow (1991, p. 30)

by step, the US dollar assumed the character of a parallel currency in Poland.[7] Together with the zloty, the US dollar was used for transaction purposes and, especially, as a store of value and a means for speculation. Because of these multiple functions of the US dollar within the Polish economy, it would seem sensible to redefine the Polish money supply (at least) by including bank deposits in US dollars (for details see Sowada 1993). By defining the money supply in such a comprehensive way, the currency substitution between the US dollar and the zloty would be taken into consideration. In 1989, the US dollar deposits rose to about $ 7 000 million, and it is important to mention that realistic estimates suggest that another $ 2 000 million were held in cash by private households.

Compared to 1988, in 1989 the total money supply increased much more than the zloty money supply because of numerous revaluations of the US dollar exchange rate. It is very important to mention that the income velocity in this period rose from 2.93 to 4.18, mainly because of a the zloty-velocity increase to 7.17. Obviously, the zloty was used for transactions whereas the US dollar was used as store of value. In 1990, the growth rate of the zloty money supply was much higher than that of the total money supply, whereas both velocities remained almost unchanged. The reason for this reversal of the 1989 development is that in 1990 people were forced to liquidate US dollar savings in order to buy commodities for their personal survival during the structural recession. In 1990, the currency deposits of private households increased by 9.2 billion zloty ($ 966 million), or 20 %. But the structure of household savings changed; whereas in January 1990 more than 80 % of the savings were held in foreign currency, this percentage dropped to 60 % in December 1990 (see National Bank of Poland 1991, p. 13). From a theoretical point of view, this development seems to verify the wealth effect often discussed in macroeconomic textbooks (see Petersen 1988, p. 203). The macro-economic consumption function

$$C = C\,(Y/P,\; R/P,\; M/P,\; \$ * e/P) \qquad (1)$$

depends on real income Y/P, real assets R/P, real money stock M/P, and real US dollar holdings $\$ * e/P$.[8] An increase in the exchange rate e creates a positive wealth effect for Polish people possessing US dollars. The revaluations of the US dollar in 1989 increased their purchasing power and supported effective demand in 1990 - an excellent example of a wealth effect induced by exchange rate movements.[9]

---

7 Like the famous cigarette currency in Germany before the 1948 currency reform. For details, see Petersen and Sowada (1995, p. 387).

8 The US price level is not considered here as its changes are negligible compared to those in the Polish price level.

9 Later on, in 1990 and 1991, when the exchange rate was fixed at 9.500 zloty (up to April 1991), a reverse wealth effect took place produced by the fixed exchange rate but

In 1991, the situation became more normal. The price shock of late 1989 was over, leading to a sudden drop in the price indices. Many experts, who were of the opinion that only a currency reform could cure inflation, now learned that the same is possible by inducing a price shock, with the only difference that prices will have some more noughts. In addition, the existence of a parallel currency as well as the currency substitution between the US dollar and the zloty had a stabilizing effect on the Polish economy.

Summing up all these developments, there is strong evidence that the extremely tight monetary policy and temporarily too high real interest rates placed an additional heavy burden (beside the structural deterioration) on the Polish economy. This view is supported even if budgetary policy is taken into consideration.[10] In the presence of the chaotic economic situation in 1989, due to the IMF rules, it is rather surprising that already in 1990 the Polish budget registered a small surplus (0.4 % of the GNP). The greater part of this surplus can be traced back to NBP's profit in 1989 and 1990. But even if this profit were subtracted, the budget would still be more or less balanced.

Because many public expenditures were postponed until the end of 1990, the gap between tax revenue and expenditures widened considerably in early 1991. In political discussions in Poland, this situation was considered much more serious than would be justified in view of the actual problem. Again, the reason behind it was the IMF idea of a sound monetary policy: financing the budget deficit by central bank credits was rejected in early 1991. It soon became obvious, however, that without such credits state financing would collapse. Already in March 1991, the actual deficit was much higher than planned. In August, the deficit was fixed at 24 billion zloty, and this number was corrected in December to 31.9 billion zloty, which was 3.9 % of GNP - almost nothing compared to the deficits in the Western countries and with regard to the malaise experienced by the Polish economy.

The NBP was pressed to finance this deficit by the liquidation of a special fund and by short-term bonds on the virgin capital markets.[11] This was an attempt to follow the 'principle of hope' and had nothing to do with reality. Due to general mistrust of government, private individuals as well as firms were neither prepared nor willing to lend their money to the state. Instead, they lent it to commercial banks. Moreover, the newly established capital markets were not strong enough to finance the budgetary gap. Since no financial sources could be found, the tight monetary view had to change in view of these real pressures: 60.8 % of the deficit was financed by the central bank, thus causing another necessary increase of the

---

still ongoing price increases. In May 1991, a currency basket (45 % US dollar, 35 % German mark, 10 % British pound sterling, 5 % French franc, and 5 % Swiss franc) was introduced, supplemented by a crawling peg in October 1991, which caused an increase in the exchange rate from 10.242 zloty to 11.075 zloty in December 1991.

10 For general problems of budgetary policy, see Calvo and Frenkel (1991b, p. 290 -294).

11 For details on the capital markets problems, see Calvo and Frenkel (1991a).

money supply. Again, we have strong evidence that in times of transformation the simple rules that apply to countries with stable institutions do not hold true. On the other hand, it is good to know that facts are stronger than the often misleading ideas of international organizations and experts.

In 1992, the deficit increased to 69.3 billion zloty, a justifiable amount in view of the tremendous structural problems and recessive tendencies. An increasing part of this deficit could be financed by commercial bank credits and state bonds. Thanks to the relative stabilization, public trust in institutions increased. The fact that in 1992 the Polish economy grew by 1.0 % in real terms contributed significantly to this development. As mentioned above, the first signs of a too expansive monetary policy were observed in 1992, especially if the administered price increases were subtracted from the CPI.

Since the successful introduction of a VAT and income tax system (the topic of the next section), tax revenues have improved substantially. Industrial output has been growing without interruption and reached a growth rate of 12.8% in the first half of 1995. The unemployment rate reached a maximum of almost 17% in July 1994 and came down to 14.7% in May 1995. The budgetary deficit increased slightly, while interest payments on the public debt rose sharply (by 69.4% in 1994).[12] This development is caused by real interest rates which still remain high, at least partly due to the uncertainty associated with the ongoing inflationary climate. Stabilization and consolidation of public budgets by simple budgetary cuts is almost impossible because of the fact that public expenditure, including subsidies to the social security system, has already been cut to the bone. Significantly, wages in the public sector are the lowest in the whole economy. Pressures for wage increases and for subsidies to the state-owned enterprises (SOE) are growing. Thus, prospects are gloomy but not hopeless, especially if the interventionism of the current administration were substituted by an economic policy which improves markets.

12 See Sowada (1995a).

3.3 Restructuring the Tax System

One of the key elements of the transition from a centrally planned to a market economy is the fundamental reform of state financing. A market economy requires a differentiated tax and transfer system and new instruments and institutions that are absent in a centrally planned economy. With respect to taxation, transition calls for a reform of income tax and the implementation of a Value Added Tax (VAT). The need for changes in income taxation results from changes in the ownership structure of the economy. In a centrally planned economy, the bulk of tax revenue is provided by state-owned enterprises. Individuals are (in general) not taxed explicitly. In Poland, the state-owned sector started to shrink while the private sector grew rapidly. This called for an overall taxation of society. Another fundamental change in the Polish taxation system is the introduction of VAT. In addition to being a prerequisite for a possible integration into the EC,[13] this change should stimulate the growth of small businesses and contribute to a decrease of the shadow economy.

The Income Tax on Natural Persons was introduced in Poland on January 1, 1992. It replaced five different taxes,[14] of which the most important were the 20 % Flat Rate Wage Tax paid by employers and the so-called Equalization Tax levied on incomes exceeding a certain multiple of the average wage. However, the Income Tax on Natural Persons was still accompanied by the Tax on Supranormative Wage Increases, which was implemented in 1990 in order to fight inflation caused by excessive wage increases (the so-called wage anchor or Popiwek).[15] The income tax system introduced was quite simple. There were three tax zones with marginal tax rates of 20 %, 30 %, and 40 %, respectively. The annual tax allowance amounted to 840.000 Zl.[16] Exemptions were mainly limited to housing expenditure. Income from capital gains, interest and dividend payments, as well as income from agriculture were free of income tax. Spouses were allowed to

---

13 The VAT implies the possibility of tax refunds for exported goods, which is an important feature for international trade.

14 See Bielawny et al. (1991), p. 4.

15 For a detailed description of the income tax, see Bolkowiak (1995). For a description of Popiwek, see Sowada (1995). Popiwek was first introduced in 1986.

16 On January 1, 1994, a new tax tariff was implemented. Up to then the tax-schedule read as follows (x as taxable income):

$t = 0.2x - 864\,000 \text{ Zl}$ for $x > 64\,000\,000 \text{ Zl}$

$t = 0.3\,(x - 64\,800\,000 \text{ Zl}) + 12\,096\,000 \text{ Zl}$ for $64\,000\,000 \text{ Zl} < x < 129\,600\,000 \text{ Zl}$

$t = 0.4\,(x - 129\,600\,000 \text{ Zl}) + 31\,536\,000 \text{ Zl}$ for $129\,600\,000 \text{ Zl} < x$.

Because of the tax allowance this tariff can be called indirect progressive. In oder to deduce progressivity mathematically the first derivative of the average tax rate function has to be greater than zero, i.e. the average tax rate increases with increasing income, see Petersen (1993a), p. 229.

file joint tax returns. Thus, this so-called income tax had many of the features typical of an expenditure tax system.

The introduction of a Value Added Tax, or, in general, changes in the tax rate, scope and structure have distinct impacts on the redistribution of income.[17] The old Polish tax system can be characterized by its very limited tax base combined with high tax rates.[18] This resulted in progressive income taxation but also in disproportionate tax burdens between different types of households, with a high preference given to the households of pensioners. The new system is more comprehensive, as it encompasses far more goods and services and thus reduces all kinds of differences. Consequently, the new tax system is no longer progressive with respect to income since the progressive effect of taxing luxury goods cannot offset the regressive effect of taxing necessities. For the same reason, the differences between households of different social status or size are smaller now. The role of luxury taxation, although reduced, is still significant, both from the redistribution and the budget revenue points of view.

With respect to the budget and economic efficiency, the change is undoubtedly positive. The new, higher taxes are levied on goods with low price and income elasticities, which results in relatively less tax-avoidance and therefore fewer losses in government revenue. The potential loss in revenue is also reduced by the more uniform scope of taxation and tax rate structure. In the long run, this should stimulate a better allocation of resources, as prices should reflect more accurately scarcity and demand. International allocation is improved as tax compensation at the border is facilitated.

Besides the improved efficiency of the new tax system, the social consequences of such a reform should not be neglected. While the old system transferred income from the rich to the poor, the new system is far more neutral. The fundamental question here is whether sales taxation should have some redistributional effects or not. One may argue that it is more efficient to redistribute on the income side than on the expenditure side. The former could take place in the form of progressive income taxation and/or social transfers. On the other hand, when the analysis is carried out in terms of lifetime income and consumption, the effects of value-added taxation are reduced. This means that a VAT system still implies some redistribution of income, even though to a much smaller extent than in the case of a turnover tax system.

For an evaluation of the total effect of taxation on the different socio-economic groups, tax burdens resulting from both direct taxation and indirect taxation should be analyzed. Inequality resulting from income taxation can either be enforced or compensated for by VAT taxation. Due to data limitations, only rough

---

17 Extensive empirical analyses on the revenue as well as redistributive effects of the VAT have been made by Nagel and Neneman (1995), using the tax simulation model of the „Forschungs- und Arbeitsgruppe Umwelt-Steuern-Transfers“ (FAUST), Potsdam.

18 Mostly luxury goods were taxed, combined with subsidies on basic commodities.

conclusions can be drawn. If we combine the results of both studies (VAT and income tax)[19] carried out within this joint research project we can state that, with respect to all socio-economic characteristics, the differences in the relative tax burden (between the old and the new systems) resulting from VAT are much smaller than the ones resulting from direct taxation.[20] This is why the redistribution of income by direct taxation is much stronger than that by indirect taxation. Whereas income taxation is progressive throughout all income classes, the VAT effect is not as uniform: it puts the highest relative tax burden on the lowest income class and is regressive in the highest income classes. The shift from turnover tax to VAT clearly has an overall regressive effect. Although, after the implementation of the VAT, the group of pensioners carries a slightly below average relative tax burden, it is hit hardest by the reform of indirect taxation, as its members consume mainly goods which earlier used to be tax-free. As pensioner households pay relatively more taxes than they receive income, compared to the average Polish household, and this relation has even become more pronounced by the income tax reform, this is the social group that is hit hardest by the tax system reform. Comparing the relative tax burden resulting from VAT and income tax reform for households of different size we can see that both relative burdens have the same bell-shaped distribution over the households. Hence, the reforms do not work against but rather reinforce the distribution of the tax burden among households. Middle-sized households have to bear most of the tax burden.

The simulation of the Polish income tax system enables us to analyze some distributional effects of income taxation for different socio-economic groups. Summarizing the results of our simulation, it can be stated that in the polish case the aim of an overall taxation of society is not at all realized with respect to taxpayers' social status in society because of a too narrow definition of taxable income, especially as agricultural incomes are exempt from tax. Most of the tax burden is levied on employee and pensioner households whereas farmer households barely have to pay any income tax. On the other hand, the income tax system can be seen as progressive, as the average tax rate increases with increasing income. In addition, the relative tax burden of households with many members is lower than that for households of smaller sizes. To some extent, this would justify calling the tax system socially adjusted since bigger households are usually families with many children.

The freezing of the tax brackets in 1993 (previously they were indexed to inflation) led to increased tax burdens for all socio-economic groups. However, the relative position of households of different size and different social status hardly changed. The analysis with respect to different income classes shows that the income tax system becomes more progressive solely as a result of cold progression,

---

19 Simulations on the effects of the income tax were carried out by Kramer and Neneman (1995).

20 See Figures 14, 17, and 21 in Nagel and Neneman (1995) in comparison to Figures 8, 9 and 10, in Kramer and Neneman (1995).

although income distribution is not essentially changed.

As the group of the self-employed becomes increasingly important in transition processes, the absence of this group in the database distorts any distributional analysis. In the new 1993 survey, however, this group is included. Additionally, as the inflation rate continues to decrease in Poland, the data of the new survey should become more reliable for empirical studies. A simulation study grounded on a more comprehensive data base should give interesting results on the effect of tax reform in the Polish transition.

In order to analyze the total effect of the tax reform with respect to the different socio-economic groups, a study of the overall tax burden, combining the distributional effects of the reform in direct as well as indirect taxation, is called for. This will allow us to identify the overall winners and losers of the newly implemented tax systems.

The last remark enables us to draw some dynamic conclusions, as the tax reform takes place in a rapidly changing economic environment where not only taxes but also income is subject to changes. The transition to a market economy inevitably means a less equal distribution of income. Combined with our model, these results would mean that, in the long run, the new form of indirect taxation favours the better-off. The long-run position of pensioners will worsen as they will be taxed more heavily.

With these additional remarks on income, our model can show - to a certain extent - the winners and the losers of the transition to a market economy. As expected, higher-income employees will be the winners. This may, of course, be controversial in terms of social equity, but has to be accepted as an unavoidable and necessary feature of the market economy because inequality of income is one of its strongest incentives.

3.4 Privatization

A functioning market economy is characterized by private ownership of means of production and by effective competition. Demonopolization and privatization of production and trade structures were thus particularly important in the economic programme of the Mazowiecki administration.

Demonopolization was to be achieved by four different methods. First, company federations, large wholesale and retail trade associations as well as federations of co-operatives were dissolved. Second, Polish monopolists were exposed to foreign competitors by the opening up of the Polish economy, i.e., by drastically reducing duties and non-tariff trade barriers. Third, building up of domestic competition was encouraged by special support to newly established middle-sized companies. Finally, monopoly exploitation was to be eliminated by the Anti-

Monopoly Commission and Anti-Monopoly Court.

In 1989, most industrial enterprises and trade companies were owned by the state or by state co-operatives. The aim fixed in the Balćerowicz Plan was to adapt the property structure in Poland to that of the EC-countries within 5 to 7 years through various measures. A classification of privatization strategies into four groups seems to be helpful. The first group of measures comprises "small-scale privatization", aiming at a new constitution of ownership of small enterprises (especially in the construction, trade and transport sectors). This form of privatization was basically completed by the end of 1990. The second area of privatization concerns those changes in the economy's property structure that are due to the establishment of private enterprises. This is an especially positive development, since, as a general rule, it is accompanied by the creation of new jobs and an increase in capital stock. After phasing out nearly all bureaucratic barriers which had hampered the setting up of private enterprises, lack of capital is now the biggest obstacle to the success of this privatization strategy.

Most difficulties were encountered with the third strategy of "large-scale privatization". The term "large-scale privatization" covers the various methods for transferring ownership of large companies. The most important method, which could be called a "commercial method", concerns the transformation of state-owned enterprises into private companies through direct sale or by transforming them into corporations and selling their shares to private individuals. A very similar method is privatization through liquidation, which is realized by selling the company's assets or by leasing those assets to other companies. Transferring ownership to their work-force and management at a low price is also part of this method. A third possibility is mass privatization, which indirectly leads to the transformation of state-owned enterprises into corporations. The strategy is a mixture of the commercial method - a proportion of shares are to be sold - and free distribution of ownership titles. In the different projects, however, ideas differ strongly about the desirable extent of this free transfer of ownership and the social groups that should benefit from this. Although mentioned in the Balcerowicz Plan, this strategy was put in concrete terms only in the privatization guidelines of late 1990 and early 1991 (Monitor Polski 1990, No 43, item 333 and Monitor Polski 1991, No 13, item 86).

The fourth method contains all measures of reprivatization, i.e. the return of or the compensation for property nationalized by the previous regime. This method was not mentioned in the Balcerowicz Plan and remains something of a taboo to this day.[21]

The most important barrier to Polish privatization processes is lack of capi-

---

21 On this issue, perhaps Poland has made the right decision. In Germany, restitution of physical property to previous owners is sharply criticized by a growing number of economists: „And even if property ownership is deemed to be a higher value, surely the imperatives of wealth creation should have dictated compensation in cash rather than in kind" (Portes, 1995, p. 14).

tal.[22] Recognizing this obstacle, Balcerowicz called for an instant amendment of the laws on state-owned enterprises and the self-administration of these enterprises.[23] It was clear that "large-scale privatization" could only be realized in the long run and that interim regulations had to be adopted. Such an interim solution was the "commercialization" of state-owned enterprises, which means their transformation into corporations, with the state as sole shareholder. These companies were then to act on the market just like private enterprises, their managers being given a large amount of entrepreneurial freedom.

However, in comparison to other CEECs (especially the Czech Republic) the success of the "large-scale privatization" is often judged as insufficient (see, e.g. Belka and Krajewski, 1995, p. 23). Thanks to improved conditions in the stock exchange, the first SOEs are being privatized by the selling of their shares. But the limited success can also be traced back to political and psychological obstacles to immediate privatization. In the first phase, there was strong resistance against foreign capital involvement on the part of trade unions and workers who feared that the working conditions would deteriorate under the new foreign management or that a large number of workers would be fired.[24] Additionally, a serious lack of competent managers became obvious, a problem which in Germany was solved by large-scale relocation of highly-educated human capital to the five new Länder.

Since Poland could not rely, à la GDR, on a "big brother", either with regard to manpower or capital, and given that the social security system had almost collapsed (see next section), the SOEs had to fill the gap. Whereas in Germany the effect of the unavoidable rise in unemployment could be mitigated by unemployment insurance and social aid, in Poland the prospect of even higher unemployment has been prevented by subsidizing employment in the SOEs. Doubtlessly, the price of this policy was high and was paid in the form of a slowdown in privatization. In return, social consensus was less shaken, albeit at the cost of a higher degree of impoverishment of the general population. It seems, therefore, that reform of the social security system is an important requirement for the future success of privatization.

---

22 For a detailed analysis of barriers to privatization, see Rapacki and Linz (1992, pp. 20 - 23).

23 See "Das Wirtschaftsprogramm" (1991, p. 18).

24 The expression "clearance sale of Polish property to foreign firms" encapsulates these popular fears.

3.5 The Open Gap: Transfers

From 1989 to 1992, three different trends characterized social expenditure from the state budget:[25] (1) The systematic elimination of price subsidies to consumer goods (the "price shock" mentioned above) which had been in force in Poland for several decades. These were subsidies to foodstuff, communication and transport, housing, fuel and energy, medicine, goods for children and books. (2) A drop in social expenditure, i.e. education, health care, culture, recreation and sports, translating into a reduction of transfers in kind. Both these measures have reduced the real incomes of the low earners. This was at least partially compensated for by the third trend: (3) An increase in subsidies to social insurance and social assistance funds, part of which is "hidden expenditure" related to increasing unemployment and growing poverty. Simultaneously, new social problems have emerged, mainly unemployment,[26] which claims an ever-growing part of budgetary expenditure, leaving drastically reduced funds for other purposes.

Laws on employment and unemployment were among the first legal regulations in the social sector in the transition period. In 1989, Poland established labour funds, introducing unemployment benefits and setting up an administration for job promotion schemes. The laws were subject to frequent amendments resulting in a reduction of individual cash benefits with growing overall unemployment. At the same time, more and more money has been allocated to programmes which actively combat unemployment.

The high rate of unemployment also affected decisions concerning social insurance. Like in other CEE countries, Poland introduced the right to early retirement or pre-pension benefits. However, the budgetary consequences of such regulations were very negative. Similarly costly has been the introduction of indexation for pensions. Since pensioners represent an influential electoral group, they were able to put forward their claims better than other social claimants. Thus, thanks to increased pension payments, the losses caused by the price shock and the introduction of the VAT have been more than compensated for, so that pensioners overwhelmingly do not belong to the losers of the transition period.

Principally, social insurance has become one of the most difficult areas of the overall reform effort. "Despite loud declarations of the necessity and urgency of social reforms, changes are slow and full of conflicting issues" (Golinowska and Ochocki, 1995, p. 272). As in the Western welfare states, the basic direction of change has been the introduction of the insurance principle, especially for pension schemes. This means that the entitlement to receiving a pension and the amount of

---

25 For more details, see Golinowska (1995).

26 Here, one has to mention that more than one third of the Polish labor force is still occupied in the agricultural sector, often on jobs with extremely low productivity. As in the SOEs, a large extent of hidden unemployment might be involved.

it must depend on the length of the contribution period as well as on the size of the premium paid. What is needed is the introduction of a new formula for calculating pension benefits. This would result in different amounts of the individual pension payments and, obviously, the losers of such an operation would protest vehemently. In Poland, despite a good start in autumn of 1991, further action was paralyzed by social protest and the reluctance of politicians to pursue unpopular options.

Another important field in the transition process is health care. Here, too, attempts have been made to replace the blanket state provision system by a system partly based on the insurance principle. An important change with respect to the financing of health care would be the limiting of full cost coverage by health insurance funds to only basic health care services. This was in fact a provision of a draft act prepared in 1993. Implementing this act, however, would mean abandoning the principle of free provision of medical services which is enshrined in the Polish Constitution. In any case, current practice of health care services provision in Poland includes many fees paid by patients, and not all of them are illegal. Budgetary constraints have resulted in various charges being gradually imposed on patients, first for catering and laundry services in hospitals, and later for transport and costly medical equipment. After the reduction of state subsidies to the pharmaceutical industry, charges for medication have also risen considerably.

Political obstacles to the reform process are enormous. Consequently, critical voices are being raised about the path of reform which obviously leads in the direction of the Western welfare states. For at least the last two decades, these countries are also in serious trouble, especially because of the exploding costs connected with an ever increasing redistribution of income, overwhelmingly from one pocket into the other of the same individual. Skepticism about the efficiency of compulsory state provision and insurance schemes has increased because such schemes are often accompanied by a socialization of individual responsibilities, thus increasing the influence of public bureaucracies. A diminishing market sector was substituted by public activities, giving political operators more opportunities to act in favour of newly defined group interests with the aim of maximizing their vote base. As a result, moral hazard, rent-seeking, and free-rider behaviour became dominant, not to mention widespread complaints about tax avoidance and evasion as well as social security fraud.[27]

A promising alternative would be a strategy to satisfy basic needs through a social aid system with additional protection being supplied by a private insurance system which reflects the individual preferences much better than any compulsory system could ever do. Such an alternative would be much easier to implement because most of the current public provision has already come down to a minimum level. In addition, the existing income tax system could be used as an integrating anchor between the tax and social transfer system. The introduction of a negative income tax (NIT) as a measure to satisfy the basic needs for the real poor

---

27 For more details, see Petersen (1995).

could be a better solution for overcoming current problems in social security provision - ironically not only in the CEECs but also in Western democracies, in which the egalitarians of all political parties have caused the current malaise of the welfare states.

3.6 Social Reform: Acceptance and Feasibility

Because of the collapse in social security, subsidies to the SOEs have been used to mitigate the consequences of explosive unemployment connected with the transition period. To a much larger extent than in the former GDR, Polish industrial policy is dominated by social concerns. Whereas in Germany the desirability of an industrial policy is under serious criticism, in Poland, due to the lack of a functioning social aid system (and because of its enormous costs), industrial policy is seen as an inevitable instrument in overcoming current structural problems. However, the development of a competitive industrial structure presupposes that the business sector be liberated from social policy targets, this also being a main prerequisite for successful privatization and increased direct investment from abroad. Sensible subsidies schedules have to be developed, including the subsidization of low-skill employment, preferably through a NIT system.

Obviously, industrial and social policy have to be closely linked. The maintenance of social peace is another important prerequisite. Consequently, the social acceptance of the planned reform measures is of the utmost importance. The success of the transformation process requires continuing social consensus, as was the case before, during and directly after the radical change in the CEECs. At that time, the social consensus was based primarily on the citizens' rejection of a state that insisted on making up their minds for them. Secondarily, it was based on the vague hope for creating greater opportunities to satisfy material needs, following a reorganization of the economic order and the incorporation of market system elements or the building of a free market economy.

Improved prospects for satisfying material needs are still a remote possibility for great sections of the population. Coupled with social equity problems caused by the spectacular increase in the incomes of particular groups in the population, this endangers social consensus, that is to say the acceptance of the transformation process. At the present moment, this loss of acceptance cannot be compensated for by the aversion to the old centrally-planned economic system which used to be shared by the great majority of the population, since a return to the old system is nowadays regarded as impossible or extremely improbable. It seems, then, that a crucial task for economic and social policy, essential for the successful conclusion of the transformation process, is to reinforce social consensus by setting up an efficient social security system.

The process requires (1) information about the societal attitudes towards the state in the course of the transformation process and (2) information about the possibilities regarding the introduction of a tax and income transfer system which would mitigate the hardships caused by the transformation process. Information concerning the allocative, accumulative and, especially, the distributive goals and consequences of various tax and transfer systems and about the trade-offs between these goals is also required.

If the state now attempts, within the constraints of its economic policy, to take into account the predominant desire for improved opportunities to satisfy material needs, people in the CEECs will be confronted for the first time with the conflict between efficiency and equity, a conflict that has been known for a long time in market economies. The measures to raise productivity, indispensable for increased efficiency, will lead to unemployment, inflation and a very unequal distribution of productivity gains. Already, some groups in the population have, by showing flexibility and a willingness to take risks as well as by luck, brought their present standards of living closer to Western standards. Other groups, however, will not be able to maintain their old level of prosperity and will possibly experience an absolute decline in their standards of living. These wide disparities in the benefits enjoyed as a result of the transformation process will lead to a decline in the (relative) losers' desire for transformation, a feeling initially shared by all citizens. The social consensus in favour of the transformation process will be lost. If there are no appropriate measures to compensate for the hardships of the transformation process, those called to finance these measures are not willing to do so, and the progress of the transformation will be endangered.

Distributional effects, for instance, which are connected with the operation of markets do face strong social rejection. Exploiting opportunities for speculative transactions and entrepreneurial risk-taking will inevitably seriously accentuate economic inequality in societies in which equality used to be regarded as the highest ideal. Moreover, unlike in Western states, this inequality is not made less severe by a tax and transfer system. On the contrary, it is made even worse by the old state institutions' apparent inability to ward off criminal practices. Furthermore, the wealth of the "nouveau riche" is openly flaunted and the discrepancy between "poor" and "rich" is, therefore, much more evident, while acceptance of inequality is much lower than, for instance, in the Federal Republic of Germany. Given the persistence of collectivist societal values in large sections of the population, it seems quite human that envy and social animosity are increasingly being manifested in the social life of the CEECs.[28]

The starting point for a reformulation of the role of the social state lies in the field of political philosophy. In this, we do not follow a liberal-anarchistic approach - as it is especially supported by Nozick -, but we assume that in the course of history state institutions have always played a decisive role, though the basic social values have always been subject to continuous change. Our starting point is,

28 See McKinnon (1991, pp. 107 - 122).

therefore, Popper's open society model, on the basis of which one can define the aims and instruments of the state and identify the value judgments connected with them.[29]

This starting point is time- and place-specific. This means that its validity for the Polish case is to be investigated and not taken as given. In this respect, the project's central theme concerns the identification of the difficulties and problems associated with changing values in the transformation process. An attempt will be made to introduce moral-ethical considerations in the issues currently discussed in Poland, primarily in academic and scientific circles but, hopefully, in broad public debate as well. This change in values occurring during the transformation process is best regarded as an evolutionary process.[30]

Based on these investigations, the main emphasis lies on the analysis of the functioning of the state's fiscal instruments. Without confidence in the state itself and without acceptance of the state's monopoly of power, the fiscal and redistributive instruments will fail. If tax avoidance, tax evasion and the obtainment of social benefits by devious means become the predominant behaviour, a social security system cannot be built. The immense income disparities will be maintained and glaring poverty will become an everyday phenomenon. This will severely try social consensus and endanger the transformation process itself. Political-philosophical and moral arguments are, therefore, intimately connected with the practical questions of how best to organize the tax and transfer system and determine the social acceptance and political feasibility of social policy measures.[31]

3.7 Some Public Choice Remarks

The feasibility of social reforms - even in the case of Western welfare states - mainly depends on the behaviour of politicians. It is quite obvious that the old nomenclature of the Eastern Bloc - which today is overwhelmingly still in office - has a philosophy which is characterized by paternalistic or even autocratic tendencies. Paternalism is also typical for a majority of Western politicians involved in social policy. The thinking of both groups is extremely conservative in the sense that "old (tax) systems are good ones". And such thinking is quite rational, since the old and tried systems can be exploited by experienced politicians to their own advantage.

---

29 For details, see Petersen (1993).

30 See Conference Papers of the Conference of the European Association of Evolutionary Politial Economy (1991) and Zon (1991).

31 See Müller and Petersen (1995).

Assuming that in social policy formulation politicians are the most important decision-making group, today a politicians' success depends on the prevailing picture which society has developed. A politicians' popularity mainly depends on whether he can maximize his interventions in public or, even worse, private sector activities. Even if politicians were fully aware of their character faults - an assumption which in view of the actual dramatis personae seems rather too optimistic - no rational incentives exist to abolish the failures of the system by fundamental reform. To the contrary, such behaviour would seem to them to be a serious mistake. On the one hand, politicians would have to intervene in the personal interests of voters, thus impairing their popularity. On the other hand, fundamental reform would destroy much of the rationale for their own jobs - the necessity of permanent interventions. From the politicians' point of view, then, it is rational not to cure the causes but the symptoms, and this strategy is in accordance with moral hazard theory.[32] Their expressed preference for market solutions is pure lip-service.

Instead of a fundamental market-oriented reform, temporary measures to decrease the costs of the social security system are much more promising. These, however, are only effective until all persons and groups involved have adapted their behaviour to the new regulations. Moreover, if these stop-gap reforms are coordinated with the re-election cycle, their positive short-term effects will ideally be realized at the right time to increase politicians' electoral attractiveness. The next budgetary cost explosion which will come several month later does not terrify an experienced politician, since it is possible for him in hearings, interviews, TV talk shows, etc. to demonstrate his importance, which strengthens his popularity anew. If such political behaviour is not due to lack of information, ignorance, indolence or simple stupidity - all not very attractive attributes for a politician - it must follow a certain logic of its own. And this seems to be that, by acting in this way, politicians are better able to exploit systemic failures for their own interests. Thus, efficient and frictionless tax and transfer systems are in their eyes counter-productive since they are detrimental to their self-interest.[33] To sum up: we are surrounded by moral hazard.

The integrated tax and transfer strategy connected with the NIT approach is in accordance with a revival of the „Ordnungspolitik" - namely, by a reformulation of the institutional settings to obtain a reduction of the discretionary interventions via a strategy of de-politicization. An improvement of the institutional framework also necessitates strengthening the ethical behaviour of those in charge. Institutional ethics have a higher degree of universal acceptance than personal ethics. Hence, politicians and bureaucrats, active in social institutions, should have a much stronger sense of their societal obligations than private persons. Unfortu-

32 See Petersen (1995).

33 Here, one has just to mention the discussions on the formula flexibility instead of discretionary interventionism in connection with the business cycle policy some decades ago which ended in favor of the latter.

nately, widespread corruption and scandals suggest that is this far from being the case. The logical solution to this moral hazard can only be: immediate reprivatization.

Is it time for such de-politicization strategies? Better still, is this feasible? Politicians are gradually facing the fact that, over the last few decades, they have taken over too many of the responsibilities formerly borne by the family or marketplace. The information explosion and growing political discontent mean that politicians are increasingly unable to solve complex societal problems. The arrogance of knowledge (Hayek) involved in this supposed knowledge of what is good for the people and what is supposedly unnecessary is recognized everywhere by well-informed citizens who point to the limited effectiveness of the political planning process. Any remaining euphoria should have been destroyed by the earth-shaking political changes of the last years, but still the political class is dominated by interventionists. Nevertheless, some politicians are becoming aware of the need to get rid of the ghosts they have summoned. The international discussion on privatization and a more efficient, reduced public sector is only one proof. The standard role of a successful politician should be changed from interventionism to causal therapy of today's imperfect institutions and policy instruments. Permanent and overwhelmingly blind activism is no proof of the quality of democratic leaders.

In view of these shortcomings within our own highly developed Western welfare states, Poland and the other CEE countries now have a historic opportunity to construct a much more efficient social security system in which personal responsibility will play a dominant role. The CEECs' low labour and other non-wage costs are an enormous competitive advantage which will lead to a re-allocation of capital in Europe in favour of these countries. In any case, competitive pressures on the European welfare states will steadily increase. Beyond that, one can only hope that the Polish system (as well as the reformed systems in the other CEECs) will become a yardstick for the reform of the tax and transfer systems within the EU member countries. Such challenges exist only in transitional periods and only in such periods are the chances for fundamental reforms realistic. In a settled, mixed economy with hundreds of effective interest groups, such reforms are much more difficult, if not impossible. To overcome these obstacles, competitive pressure from the East (in the form of effective tax and transfer schemes) would provide an additional argument to the reformers in Western Europe wishing to overcome the present welfare state sclerosis.

References

Belka, M. and S. Krajewski (1995): Polish Transformation After 5 Years - Some General Remarks. In: M. Belka and H.-G. Petersen (Ed.): op. cit., pp. 13-24.

Belka, M. and H.-G. Petersen eds., (1995): Economic Transformation in Poland. Reforms of Institutional Settings and Macroeconomic Performance. Campus, Frankfurt, New York 1995.

Bielawny, J., I. Bolkowiak, M. Majewicz, and W. Modzelewski (1991): Podatek dochodowny osòb fizycznych - Nowe przepisy i komentarz. (Personal Income Tax - New laws and legal commentaries) Instytut Finansow, Warsaw.

Bolkowiak, I. (1995): Tax System and Its Reform. In: M. Belka and H.-G. Petersen (Ed.): op. cit., pp. 165-181.

Calvo, G.A. and J.A. Frenkel (1991a): Credit Markets, Credibility, and Economic Transformation. In: The Journal of Economic Perspectives, Vol. 5, No 4, pp. 139-148.

Calvo, G.A. and J.A. Frenkel (1991b): From Centrally Planned to Market Economy. The Road from CPE to PCPE. In: IMF Staff Papers, Vol. 38, pp. 268-299.

Cassel, D. (1992): Inflation. In: D. Bender et. al. (Ed.): Vahlens Kompendium der Wirtschaftstheorie und Wirtschaftspolitik. Vol. 1, 5th ed, München, pp. 265-321.

Das Wirtschaftsprogramm (1991): In: BAK, H., P. Pysz, and R. Scharff (Ed.): Das Balcerowicz-Programm. Konzept, Realisierungsschritte, Zwischenergebnisse. Erlangen, pp. 9-31.

Dornbusch, R. and S. Fischer (1984): Macroeconomics. 3rd ed, New York et. al.

Golinowska, S. (1995): Public Social Expenditure. In: M. Belka and H.-G. Petersen (Ed.): op. cit., pp. 143-163.

Golinowska, S. and A. Ochocki (1995): Reforms and Social Conditions in Central and Eastern Europe 1989 - 1993. In: M. Belka and H.-G. Petersen (Ed.): op. cit., pp. 263-300.

Instytut Finansow (1991): Raport o stanie finansowym panstwa w roku 1991. (Report on Government Financial Situation in 1991).

Johnson, H.G. (1969): Beiträge zur Geldtheorie und Geldpolitik. Untersuchungen über das Spar-, Giro- und Kreditwesen, Vol. 18, Berlin.

Kramer, G. and J. Neneman (1995): The Effects of a Reform of Income Taxation in Poland. In: M. Belka and H.-G. Petersen (Ed.): op. cit., pp. 239-261.

McCinnon, R.I. (1991): Financial Control in the Transition from Classical Socialism to a Market Economy. In: The Journal of Economic Perspectives, Vol. 5, No 4, pp. 107-122.

Müller, K. and H.-G. Petersen (1995): Towards a Reformulation of the Role of the Tax and Social State in the Polish Transformation Process. In: M. Belka and H.-G. Petersen (Ed.): op. cit., pp. 131-141.

Nagel, T. and J. Neneman (1995): The Effects of a Reform of Private Consumption Taxation in Poland. In. M. Belka and H.-G. Petersen (Ed.): op. cit., pp. 205-237.

Petersen, H.-G.: Finanzwissenschaft II. Kohlhammer, Stuttgart et. al. 1988.

Petersen, H.-G.: Ökonomik, Ethik und Demokratie. Zu einer Theorie der Effizienz und Gerechtigkeit offener Gesellschaften. Nomos, Baden-Baden 1993.

Petersen, H.-G. (1993a): Finanzwissenschaft I. 3rd ed, Kohlhammer, Stuttgart et. al.

Petersen, H.G. (1995): Pros and Cons of Negative Income Tax. Paper prepared for the Egon-Sohmen-Smposium 1995 "Reforming the Welfare State", chaired by Herbert Giersch, August 31 - September 1, 1995, Prag (forthcoming).

Petersen, H.-G. and C. Sowada (1995): The Polish Success in Monetary Stabilization - New Insights into Monetary Policy in the Transformation Process. In: Supplements to Kredit und Kapital, Vol. 13, Berlin, pp. 385-411.

Portes, J. (1995): Economic Transformation in Central Europe and Eastern Germany. In: Zeitschrift für Wirtschafts- und Sozialwissenschaften, Beiheft 4, pp. 11-21.

Rapacki, R. and S. Linz (1992): Prywatyzacja w Europie Wschodniej: przypadek Polski. (Privatization in Eastern Europe: The Polish Case). In: World Economic Research Institute, Warsaw School of Economics, Working Papers No 70, Warsaw.

Sowada, C. (1993): Stabilisierung im Transformationsprozeß am Beispiel Polens. In: Integrated Tax and Transfer Research Group, Working Papers No. 9, Gießen.

Sowada, C. (1995): The Polish Stabilization Program: „Balcerowicz-Plan“. In: M. Belka and H.-G. Petersen (Ed.): op. cit., pp. 25-46.

Sowada, C. (1995a): Haushaltspolitische Konsequenzen steigender Staatsverschuldung in Polen. In: Finanzwissenschaftliche Diskussionsbeiträge Nr. 3, Universität Potsdam.

Zon, H.v. (1991): Alternative Scenarios for Central Europe (Poland, Czechoslowakia, Hungary). Commission of the European Community, Science, Research, and Development, Internal Paper FOP 226, Brussels.

Part III Transitional Economics: Macroeconomic and Monetary Policy

4 Macroeconomic Stability and the Transition Process

Nebojsa Savic
Economics Institute
Srpskih Vladara 16
P.O. Box 402
11000 Beograd - YUGOSLAVIA

Abstract

In 1994, after several years of recession experienced by all economies in transition, a significant number of countries recorded positive rates of growth. This shows that growth can be restored after the completion of the early phase of transition and after making the necessary adjustments.

The speed of further transition in the Central European countries in transition (CITs), which started with the efforts to achieve macroeconomic stability and, ultimately, the restoration of sustainable growth are directly related to the introduction of key microeconomic measures, especially the privatization and restructuring of enterprises, the financial rehabilitation of banks and the re-orientation of the government's role. This process is a transformation of an administered system to a market-based one and cannot be carried out by merely adjusting or improving on the existing system.

In 1994, after several years of recession experienced by all economies in transition, a significant number of countries recorded positive rates of growth. This shows that growth can be restored after the completion of the early phase of transition and after making the necessary adjustments.

The basic aim of this paper is, first, to point to the trends observed sofar in the transition process in all countries in transition, second, to identify macroeconomic stability as a precondition for further transition and, third, to suggest the future directions of the transition strategy as a key element in promoting economic growth in these contries.

4.1 The Results of the Transition Process So Far

Before beginning to analyse the results obtained so far, it is necessary to give a working definition of the three terms: development, transition and stabilization.

Development is the process of improving the standard of living of the population in all its key aspects, i.e. in terms of resource allocation, income distribution, education and health care, environmental protection, etc.

Transition is the process of transforming ex-socialist economies into market-based systems. As an opposite to an administered economy, economies in transition have been moving from the start of the transition process toward a new system of resource generation and allocation, coupled with a radical change in the role of the government and relevant institutions.

Stabilization is linked to the establishment of an appropriate relationship among macroeconomic variables including inflation, output, the balance of payments and unemployment. Economic stabilization is a vital prerequisite for the successful completion of the transition process.

It is evident that there are essential differences between the concepts of transition, stabilization and development and that they are highly interdependent.

Table 4.1 provides the main indicators of the share of the ***countries in transition (CITs)*** in the world economy.

Table 4.1 CIT share in the world economy

	World	CIT	Share of CITs
Population (bil)		0.4	7.3%
Area (mil. km^2)	133	35	19.0%
GDP (bil. US$)	23,060	815	3.5%
GDPpc (US$)	4,280	2,000	47.0%
Exports (bil. US$)	3,575	89	2.5%
Imports (bil. US$)	3,786	90	4.5%

Source: World Development Report 1995, The World Bank, 1995.

As the data show, average per capita GDP in the CITs is less than one half of the world average while export intensity, i.e.the share of CIT exports in world exports, is also below the world average, 11% against 15.5%. Their share in world GDP and the total volume of exports and imports is 3.5%, 2.5% and 4.5%, respectively.

In *Table 4.2* the key economic indicators for all *CITs* are set out. The first column in the table relates to per capita GNP in, as The World Bank likes to say, "international dollars", i.e. adjusted for differences between a currency's purchasing-power-parity (PPP) and its market exchange rate.

Table 4.2 CIT key economic indicators

	GNPpc (PPP)	GNPpc	Rate of growth (GDP)	Inflation (%)	Fiscal deficit (% GDP)
	1993	1993	1994	1994	1993
Albania		340	7%	16	-14.0
Tajikistan	1,380	470	-21%	5	-6.4
Georgia	2	580	-35%	7,380	-17.0
Armenia	2,040	660	5%	1,885	-16.1
Uzbekistan	2,510	970	-3%	423	-3.6
Azerbaijan	2,190	730	-22%	1,788	-18.0
Romania	2,800	1,140	3%	62	-3.5
Kyrgiz Republic	2,320	850	-27%	87	-8.4
Lithuania	3,110	1,320	2%	45	-1.5
Moldova	2,870	1,060	-22%	98	-8.0
Turkmenistan	3,950	1,230	-20%	1,100	-1.1
Latvia	5,100	2,010	2%	26	-1.7
Kazakhstan	3,710	1,560	-25%	1,160	-6.5
Poland	5,000	2,260	5%	30	-2.5
Ukraine	4,450	2,210	-23%	401	-9.1
Bulgaria	4,100	1,140	1%	122	-7.0
Estonia	5,250	3,080	6%	42	0.9
Slovak Republic	6,290	1,950	5%	12	-3.7
Hungary	6,050	3,350	2%	21	-8.2
Russian Federation	5,050	2,340	-15%	203	-9.9
Belarus	6,240	2,870	-22%	1,875	-1.5
Czech Republic	7,550	2,710	3%	10	1.0
FYR Macedonia		820	-7%	55	-2.6
Slovenia		6,540	6%	18	-1.0
Croatia		2,200	1%	-3	1.7
FR Yugoslavia		1,000	7%	0.00	0.00

Source: *World Development Report 1994*, World Bank and *Transition Report 1995*, EBRD, 1995.

It is customary to evaluate the success of a transition process by using three indicators: first, the extent of the role of private enterprises; second, market characteristics; and third, the development level of financial institutions. This is done in *Table 4.3*.

Table 4.3 Progress in transition

	Private sector's share of GDP in %	Enterprise privatization			Markets and trade		Financial institutions
		Large scale	Small scale	Enterprise restructuring	Price liberalization and competition	Trade and foreign exchange system	Banking reform
Albania	60	2	4	2	3	4	2
Armenia	45	2	3	2	3	3	2
Azerbaijan	25	1	1	2	3	2	2
Belarus	15	2	2	2	3	2	2
Bulgaria	45	2	3	2	3	4	2
Croatia	45	3	4	2	3	4	3
Czech Republic	70	4	4	3	3	4	3
Estonia	65	4	4	3	3	4	3
FYR Macedonia	40	2	4	2	3	4	3
Georgia	30	2	3	2	3	2	2
Hungary	60	4	4	3	3	4	3
Kazakhstan	25	2	2	1	3	3	2
Kyrgiz Republic	40	4	4	2	3	4	2
Latvia	60	2	4	2	3	4	3
Lithuania	55	3	4	2	3	4	3
Moldova	30	3	3	2	3	4	2
Poland	60	3	4	3	3	4	3
Romania	40	2	3	2	3	4	3
Russian Federation	55	3	4	2	3	3	2
Slovak Republic	60	3	4	3	3	4	3
Slovenia	45	3	4	3	3	4	3
Tajikistan	15	2	2	1	3	2	1
Turkmenistan	15	1	1	1	2	1	1
Ukraine	35	2	2	2	3	2	2
Uzbekistan	30	3	3	2	3	2	2
FR Yugoslavia*	30	2	4	2	3	3	3

* - author's estimate, Source: ***Transition report***, EBRD, 1995, p. 11-13.

Private enterprises are the central element of a market economy and presuppose the full development of ownership rights, including their sale and purchase. Thus, the share of private enterprises is used as one of the basic criteria for evaluating the success of a transition process.

Markets are the arena in which owners, entrepreneurs and managers do business. They provide information about the quality and availability of goods and services through prices. Price flexibility and inter-firm competition encourage creativity and innovativeness and improve efficiency.

Financial institutions, which are the essence of a market economy, link real and financial resources. They channel savings, secure an unhindered and efficient payments system and enhance financial discipline. This provides a basis for the imposition of hard budgetary constraints at the enterprise level and for the elimination of non-performing bank loans. In a market economy, financial institutions are free from governmental interference in providing credit to enterprises and can have recourse to enforceable bankruptcy laws.

A survey of the results achieved by individual countries is given in Table 3. The greatest progress in the transition process was made by the Czech Republic, Hungary, Poland, Slovakia, the Baltic countries and Slovenia. The middle group of countries comprises other East European countries, including Yugoslavia, Russia and Kyrgiz Republic, while the remaining countries have made very little progress.

Further evaluation of the CIT's progress can be based on two different but very useful analyses provided by *the Economist Intelligence Unit* (EIU), a sister company of the London *Economist* newspaper, and the European Bank for Reconstruction and Development (EBRD), respectively.

EIU analyzed the medium term prospects of the CITs using ten indicators (political stability, level of development, physical infrastructure, educational level, economic openness and indebtedness,etc.) considered as contributing to a country's capacity for growth. [1]

Probably the most prominent characteristic emerging from this figure is that the Central European countries are ranked higher than the countries of the former Soviet Union.

Poland's relatively low score in terms of development prospects could be explained by its huge foreign debt while the ranking of Albania and Belarus above Russia could be explained by the extensive changes already made in these two countries (in Albania real GDP rebounded strongly in 1993 and 1994 increasing by more than 10 percent thanks to the progress of structural reforms, especially in the agricultural sector, and the growth of construction and services).

In the EBRD report,[2] the CITs are classified according to the level of marketization rather than to the speed of change on the road to a market economy.

General examination of information provided suggests that all CITs could be classified, with respect to the transition progress in three groups.

The first group, which we named *advanced CITs*, consists of the eight countries where transition has progressed furthest (Czech Republic, Hungary, Poland, Estonia, Slovak Republic, Latvia, Lithuania and Slovenia). This group accounts for 11% of the CIT's total GNP .

The second group, which we named *middle CITs*, consists of seven countries (Croatia, FYR of Macedonia, Russia, Kyrgiz Republic, FR of Yugoslavia, Romania and Bulgaria) with 55% of total GNP generated in the CITs.

---

1 *The Economist,March 25, 1995, p.148.*

2 EBRD,*Transition Report - Investment and Enterprise Development,October 1994, p.p. 9-12*

The third group, which we named *low CITs*, consists of eleven countries representing 34% of the CIT's aggregate GNP.

The numerous differences observed among the economies in transition as well as the results achieved so far suggest that the aims to be attained in the near future will also have to be different.

In the countries that made the greatest progress in the process of transition - and those are the countries in which a significant improvement in the area of macroeconomic stabilization was made - the priority tasks include the restructuring of enterprises and the development of financial institutions, while at the same time preserving the gains achieved so far by stabilization and ensuring sound social walfare safety nets.

In the middle group of countries, one can point to the need to increase macroeconomic stability, intensify the process of privatization and introduce corporate management practices into enterprises.

Finally, essential to the countries in the early phase of transition are initial macroeconomic reforms, especially market liberalization and the progress of the transition process.

The economic performance of individual CITs is highly varied. The economies of the so-called advanced CITs, those which have achieved a reasonable measure of macroeconomic stability, have begun to grow again. On the other hand, those that have not yet implemented appropriate stabilization policies have continued to experience high inflation and substantial output losses.

Bringing down and controlling inflation has been a major policy challenge facing all countries in transition.

4.2 Macroeconomic Stability as a Precondition for Further Transition

Bruno (1994) points out that a sharp approach to stabilization was taken to a greater or lesser degree in all economies in transition, although there were differences in their ability to control the budget, credit expansion or the wage level and essential differences still remained in the area of macroeconomic reforms.[3]

The macroeconomic experience of economies in transition varies from a successful one - like that of the Czech Republic in which inflation and unemployment were maintained at a low level throughout the period of 3-4 years of a more care-

---

[3] See: Bruno, M., "Stabilization and Reform in Eastern Europe: A Preliminary Evaluation", in: O. Blanchard, K. A. Froot and J. D. Sachs, *The Transition in Eastern Europe - Vol. 1: Country Studies, NBER, 1994, p.p. 19-49.*, NBER, 1994, pp. 19-49.

fully thought-out transition - to that of some ex-Soviet republics which have fallen into deep crises after the disintegration of the Soviet Union.

The recessionary periods experienced by those economies in transition that launched their market reforms earlier are by- and- large over. In 1992, Poland became the first country in the region to record positive growth in its real GDP since the start of the transition process. In 1993, growth was also recorded in Romania, Slovenia and Albania and in 1994 in the Czech Republic, Hungary, Slovakia, all three Baltic countries and Yugoslavia.

The fact that most economies in transition now have positive growth rates reflects a structural change which resulted in the share of large enterprises in total production becoming much lower. The successful performance of the private sector, whose share in the creation of GDP exceeds 50 per cent in most economies in transition, has become the key determinant of economic growth, thus eliminating the major defect in the structure of ex-socialist economies: an overdeveloped sector of large enterprises and an underdeveloped sector of small and medium-sized enterprises.

Modern development theories treat the liberalization of foreign trade and foreign investment as the basis for encouraging growth in economies in transition.[4]

In the economies in transition, the flows of foreign trade have had the following characteristics:

(i) in the 1989-1993 period, trade among the COMECON countries was halved;

(ii) fast-reforming economies of the Central Europe an and Baltic countries shifted rapidly to Western markets and especially to the European Union;

(iii) the market structure changed significantly, since the main victims of the collapse of intra-regional trade were capital and manufactured goods, and

(iv) despite a significant volume of trade, total visible exports of these countries in 1993 did not exceed those of Korea alone.

Wage levels. - From a macroeconomic viewpoint, it is also important to compare wage levels, while at the same time not losing sight of the differences in purchasing power (see *Table 4.4*).

---

4 See: Rodrik, D., "Foreign Trade in Eastern Europe's Transition: Early Results", in: O. Blanchard, K.A. Froot, and J. D. Sachs, *The Transition in Eastern Europe - Vol. 2: Restructuring*, NBER, 1994, pp. 319-52.

Table 4.4 Average monthly wages in DM in 1994.

Bulgaria	178	Armenia	10
Croatia	390	Azarbaijan	44
Check Republic	345	Belarus	114
Estonia	133	Kazakhstan	186
Hungary	495	Kyrgiz Republic	19
Latvia	153	Moldova	48
Lithuania	101	Russia	155
Poland	303	Turkmenistan	84
Romania	128	Ukraine	31
Slovenia	657	Uzbekistan	39
Slovak Republic	314	FR Yugoslavia	140

Source: OECD and IMF.

Public revenues and expenditure. - Public finance is an important part of macroeconomic policies and a major element of the institutional framework of the economies in transition. The introduction of a modern tax system is crucial to transition and development. In an administered economy, the role of taxation differs from that in a market economy, where goods and services are generated primarily by the private sector.

In the economies in transition old tax systems were based on the taxation of the profit and turnover generated by state-owned enterprises. The process of transition increased competition, leading to a decline in the profit and output of state-owned enterprises and thus to a drop in fiscal revenues.

Tax revenues are usually classified into the following three categories: direct taxes, indirect taxes and taxes levied on foreign trade operations. *Table 4.5* provides a survey of the share of these three categories.

The table shows that in pre-transitional phases (in the late 1980s), the tax structure in industrialized economies and economies in transition was similar. Both groups of countries raised two-thirds of all revenues through direct taxation. This similarity in the structure of tax revenues 5-6 years ago can be explained by the high level of industrialization and the fact that industrial enterprises were the main source of taxation. In the 1989-93 period, the structure of tax revenues underwent a significant change geared to decreasing the share of indirect taxes and increasing the share of taxes levied on foreign trade operations.

Table 4.5 Tax shares in different countries (in % of total tax revenue)

Country group	Income and Social Security taxes (direct)	Domestic indirect taxes	Foreign trade and other taxes
Industrial countries 1987	67.6	29.3	3.1
Developing countries 1987	38.8	30.0	31.2
Transition countries 1989.	58.3	38.4	3.3
Transition countries 1993.	59.1	31.8	9.1

Source: Burgess, R. S. L. and N. H. Ster, "Taxation and Development", *Journal of Economic Literature*, XXXI, June 1993.

Empirical studies confirm that the level of taxation in the economies in transition was high in 1989 and that it declined in the period up to 1993. At the same time, however, expenditure remained the same. This led to an increase in the fiscal deficit which rose from an average 1.8 per cent of GDP in 1993 to 9 per cent in 1993, thus disturbing macroeconomic stability.

It is interesting to note that the highest public expenditures were recorded in those economies which were leaders in the process of transition(Slovakia 56 per cent of GDP, Hungary 55 per cent, Poland 50 per cent and the Czech Republic 49 per cent).

As for fiscal expenditure in the economies in transition, this did not decline although a change in its structure is apparent. In the 1989-93 period, a decrease was recorded in investment expenditure (from 6.1 per cent to 2.9 per cent of GDP), subsidies (from 8.5 per cent to 6.2 per cent) and social welfare transfers (from 14.9 per cent to 13.4 per cent), while other expenditure increased (from 7.2 per cent to 11.6 per cent).[5] The need to maintain social consensus in the face of strong resistance to a deterioration of living standards necessarily meant that in the economies in transition the role of public expenditure in protecting the general standard of living became a priority.

Convertibility and foreign exchange regimes. - Although underlying monetary and fiscal measures are more fundamental to macroeconomic stabilization than the exchange rate regime, it is interesting to see which kind of regime the CITs used. Convertibility has already been introduced in 16 countries while the others are aiming at it. Domestic convertibility introduced in these countries implies that an importer has the right to freely purchase the foreign currencies needed for his imports. However, he cannot hold them as assets either at home or abroad. In other words, there is an obligation to convert export earnings into local currency. An important issue that has arisen in this context is the choice of foreign exchange regime. The experience of the advanced group of countries suggests that an exchange rate pegged against a convertible currency can be an effective nominal

5 *Transition Report - ...EBRD, October 1994, p.p. 78-95*

anchor, although fixing the exchange rate is not sufficient to achieve lasting disinflation.

An exchange rate peg cannot survive long without fiscal discipline and the control of credit expansion by the central bank. Inflationary pressures stemming from these factors would quickly overwhelm the ability of the authorities to draw on foreign exchange reserves to stabilize the currency.

Two very important factors, that can also be useful in establishing the credibility of an exchange rate peg and of monetary policy in general, are a high degree of central bank independence, which reduces the possibility that the central bank will have to monetize future government deficits, and currency convertibility.

In order to reform their monetary system and to strengthen convertibility, eight CITs have introduced new national currencies (Lithuania, Latvia, Estonia, Slovenia, FYR of Macedonia, Croatia, the FR of Yugoslavia and the Kyrgiz Republic) while three of them have also established currency boards (Estonia, Lithuania and the FR Yugoslavia).[6] Fixed exchange rates have been introduced in eight CITs, in four of which they are pegged (Czech Republic, Hungary, Latvia, Poland and Slovenia). Floating exchange rates are used in eight other CITs (Bulgaria, FYR Macedonia, Romania, Russia, Kyrgiz Republic, Kazakhstan, Slovenia and Moldova).

Finally, for many CITs it is clear that the budgetary, credit and financial policies needed to allow the exchange rate to be pegged successfully are not yet in place.

The policies introduced so far in the economies in transition have focused on macroeconomic (monetary and fiscal policy) and microeconomic measures (liberalization of prices, wages and interest rates and antimonopoly measures). A summary review of the growth rates recorded by the different groups of countries is given in *Table 4.6*.

Most of the CITs started moving decisively toward a market economy a few years ago. As we have seen, performance has varied among countries, depending on initial conditions and on the economic policies implemented. Although many CITs are still experiencing huge output declines and high inflation (or hyperinflation), several countries in Central Europe and the Baltic countries have stabilized inflation at relatively low levels and have seen a turnaround in output. Structural change has often gone apace with successful stabilization efforts.[7]

---

[6] Corter-Douglas, H. and R. K. Abrams, "Introduction of a New National Currency: Policy, Institutional and Technical Issues", *IMF Working Paper, WP/93/49, June 1993.*, WP/93/49, June 1993.

[7] *World Economic Outlook, IMF, October 1994, p.p.65.*, IMF, October 1994, pp. 65.

Table 4.6 Growth of output and trade (annual rates in %)

	World output	CIT	Developing countries	Industrial countries	World trade
1986	3.6	3.6	4.8	2.9	4.3
1987	4.0	2.8	5.7	3.2	5.9
1988	4.7	4.3	5.3	4.4	9.1
1989	3.4	2.2	4.2	3.3	6.4
1990	2.2	-3.5	3.8	2.4	4.6
1991	0.9	-11.8	4.5	0.8	2.6
1992	1.7	-15.5	5.9	1.5	4.7
1993	2.3	-9.0	6.1	1.3	4.0
1994	3.1	-8.3	5.6	2.7	7.2
1995	3.6	-1.0	5.6	2.7	5.9

Source: *World Economic Outlook*, IMF, October 1994 (figures for 1994 and 1995 are estimates).

4.3 Transition Strategy in the Near Future

Analysis of past experience shows that there is no single ideal formula for carrying out the transition process and restoring growth. Early literature on transition concentrated on the sequencing of priorities with respect to stabilization, liberalization, restructuring and privatization. Today, the opinion prevails that there is no universal model because the starting points are different and so are the circumstances in which the process of transition is carried out. However, it is still possible to identify some elements which are essential for the success of every country and which fall primarily into the institutional sphere.

Generally speaking, optimism about the progress of the transition process is dwindling. No one country has so far implemented an extensive programme for winding up unprofitable firms. Instead, CIT governments often resorted to takeovers of these firms, thus transforming them into state-owned ones. Furthermore, the continuing financing of these firms under favourable terms is equivalent to implicit off-balance sheet subsidization. On frequent occasions, banks also granted credit to firms for paying out salaries regardless of their creditworthiness.[8]

[8] *Transition Report - ..., p.p. 45-50*

Macroeconomic Policy and Transition. - In the advanced countries that made the greatest progress in the transition process and achieved significant improvements in the area of macroeconomic stabilization, the priority tasks are the restructuring of enterprises and the development of financial institutions, while at the same time preserving stabilization aims and ensuring sound social safety nets. The middle group of countries need to increase macroeconomic stability and intensify the process of privatization and the introduction of corporate management into enterprises. Finally, essential to the countries in the early phase of transition are initial macroeconomic reforms, especially liberalization.

What Lies Ahead? - The role of government in transition is not eliminated. On the contrary, it is extremely important but must be radically transformed. Instead of channeling resources and output and intervening in the area of prices and foreign trade flows, the transformed government's role in economies in transition must be primarily to (i) establish a lawful state, along with the observance and enforcement of contracts and property rights, (ii) introduce an efficient tax system, (iii) provide social security, (iv) provide education and health care and (v) secure the relevant infrastructure, as well as law and order.[9]

Two important conditions for encouraging transition and achieving sustained growth in the near future are:

(i) setting in place the necessary legal infrastructure and transforming the government's role and

(ii) restructuring, privatization and financial deepening.

Legal infrastructure and a new role for government. - Under a market-based system, basic economic freedoms are safeguarded. The basis for this is provided by the legal system. In this connection, five areas to be observed are: ownership, contract, bankruptcy, competition and company law.

Clearly formulated property rights are essential for the introduction of a market economy and this part of the legal infrastructure is already in place. In a market economy, contract law sets a framework within which all contracts must be drawn up and executed.

Bankruptcy legislation aims at establishing financial discipline and imposing hard budgetary constraints. Loss-making enterprises and insolvent firms cannot legally survive, ensuring that the economy will employ their resources in a new way.[10]

---

9 On obstacles to a transition see: Buch, M. C., N. Funke, R. Heinrich and M. Raiser, *Overcoming Obstacles to Successful Reforms in Economies in Transition, Institut fur Weltwirtschaft an der Universitat Kiel, 1994..,*

10 For more detail on the methods of bankruptcy see: Aghion, D., O. Hart and J. Moore, "The Economics of Bankruptcy Reform", in. O. Blanchard, K., A. Froot, and J.d. Sachs, The Transition in Eastern Europe-Vol.2: Restructuring, NBER, 1994, p.p. 215-40.

Antimonopoly legislation should ensure competition and prevent enterprises from avoiding market discipline and taking advantage of unfair competition. Company law should identify business enterprises as legal entities and stipulate their rights, duties and functioning methods.

Restructuring, privatization and financial deepening. - After macroeconomic stabilization, the restructuring and privatization of state-owned enterprises are the key elements of an effective transition process. Here, the first step is to establish market discipline. Operational restructuring implies the adjustment of existing enterprises to a market-oriented environment by changing labour and capital inputs, as well as product design and mix. Financial restructuring should enable debt rescheduling and conversion. Market discipline implies the liberalization of prices and (foreign) trade, in addition to a tightening of budget discipline, reduction in fiscal subsidies, credit channeling and anti-monopoly legislation.

Vital prerequisites for achieving success in this process are the strengthening of domestic financial institutions and the encouragement of savings. The mobilization of savings and their efficient allocation are priority tasks that should be fulfilled by domestic banks and non-banking financial institutions.

The transition process should concentrate on vital macroeconomic and microeconomic reforms, in areas where so far too little has been done. It is especially important to start immediately with the restructuring of large enterprises and the recovery of the banking system, while at the same time encouraging the privatization process.[11] This is the only way in which it will be possible to ensure that the financial institutions will contribute to a market-based allocation of resources. Sustained growth will be possible only if the transition to a market economy is thorough.

4.4 Concluding Remarks

The sucess of transition in the Central European CITs, which started with the achievement of macroeconomic stability, is directly related to the introduction of microeconomic measures and, especially, to the restructuring of enterprises, the financial rehabilitation of banks and the transformation of the government's role. This process of transition from an administered system to a market-based one

---

[11] Without those elements of the stabilization process it seems that stabilization could be established without costs what is probably not possible. About costs of stabilization in previous inflationary episodes see: Solimano, A., "Inflation and the Cost of Stabilization - Country Experiences, Conceptual Issues, and Policy Lessons", *The World Bank Working Papers, WPS 226 July 1989.*

cannot be carried out merely by adjusting or improving on the existing system. Growth in the economies in transition can only be restored if the private-sector significantly increases its share in total output, while at the same time using extreme caution in implementing the bankruptcy legislation.[12]

References

Aghion, D., O. Hart and J. Moore, "The Economics of Bankruptcy Reform", in. O. Blanchard, K., A. Froot, and J.D. Sachs, *The Transition in Eastern Europe - Vol. 2: Restructuring*, NBER, 1994, pp. 215-40.

Bruno, M., "Stabilization and Reform in Eastern Europe: A Preliminary Evaluation", in: O. Blanchard, K. A. Froot and J.D. Sachs, *The Transition in Eastern Europe - Vol. 1: Country Studies*, NBER, 1994, pp. 19-49.

Bruno, M., "Stabilization and the Macroeconomics of Transition - How Different is Eastern Europe?", *Economics of Transition*, Vol. 1, No. 1, 1993, pp. 5-19.

Buch, M. C., N. Funke, R. Heinrich and M. Raiser, *Overcoming Obstacles to Successful Reforms in Economies in Transition*, Institut fur Weltwirtschaft an der Universitat Kiel, 1994.

Corter-Douglas, H. and R. K. Abrams, "Introduction of a New National Currency: Policy, Institutional and Technical Issues", *IMF Working Paper*, WP/93/49, June 1993.

The Economist, March 25th, 1995,

Rodrik, D., "Foreign Trade in Eastern Europe's Transition: Early Results", in: O. Blanchard, K.A. Froot, and J.D. Sachs, *The Transition in Eastern Europe - Vol. 2: Restructuring*, NBER, 1994,

Solimano, A., "Inflation and the Cost of Stabilization - Country Experiences, Conceptual Issues, and Policy Lessons", *The World Bank Working Papers*, WPS 226, July 1989.

Transition report - Economic Transition in Eastern Europe and the Former Soviet Union, EBRD,1994.

Transition Report - Investment and Enterprise Reform, EBRD, 1995.

World Economic Outlook, IMF, October 1994,

---

12 Bruno, M., "Stabilization and the Macroeconomics of Transition - How Different is Eastern Europe?", Economics of Transition, Vol. 1, No. 1, 1993, pp. 5-19.

5 Macroeconomic Stability and How to Avoid the Frequent Use of Stabilization Therapies

Goran Pitic
Economics Institute
Srpskih Vladara 16
P.O. Box 402
11000 Beograd - YUGOSLAVIA

Summary

All successful economic reforms start with a major stabilization effort. The basic monetary and fiscal theory of high inflation and sharp stabilization seems to apply more generally (budget deficits and money creation must be brought under control) and, to the extent that differences exist between groups of countries, these stem from problems in the ability to control the budget or the amount of credit or wage policy. The general lesson to be learned is that often macroeconomic adjustment cannot be achieved without at least some simultaneous structural reform and that the policy reform package has to place even greater emphasis on setting up institutions and rules of behaviour for the micro units. In order to diminish the costs of the reforms, the optimal sequencing of the reform measures is desirable. Countries that have experienced protracted high inflation need to achieve not only fiscal reconstruction by thorough budget balancing but also a far reaching institutional reconstruction that involves a financial system capable of providing efficient intermediation and a regulatory and trade regime that helps allocate resources in ways that maximize productivity. The efficacy of the financial system is a key determinant of the success of any economic transformation process.

5.1 Introduction

In discussions of reforms in Eastern Europe agreement is achieved on the desired end result of the process of economic reform but not on the most appropriate transition path. A clear understanding of what the end result of the economic reforms ought to be is important for the transition path for at least two reasons: The most obvious one is that certain reforms will be conditioned by the nature of the final objective; a second reason is that private sector responses are more likely to reinforce the reform process when there is less uncertainty about its final aims.

In very general terms, the objectives of the reforms in the Central and Eastern European Countries ($CEEC_s$) is to remove existing inefficiencies in their economies. In order to achieve this general aim some areas have been identified where changes are imperative. A list of the most obvious ones would include greater room for private ownership of land and capital, greater reliance on market forces in the determination of prices, decentralization of decision making concerning resource allocation and greater economic integration with the rest of the world.

A closely related issue is the speed of the adjustment of markets to changing signals and the credibility attached by agents to signals about future market environments, which are not yet evident in today's market.

There are at least three reasons why discussion about sequencing of reforms is of particular importance. First of all, it is administratively impossible to carry out all changes at once. Therefore, some distortions will remain in certain markets for some time. The theory of second best tells us that the removal of only one of a number of existing distortions in an economy may not lead to welfare improvements, due to the increased welfare costs of the remaining distortions. Secondly, speeds of adjustment to the reforms in different markets are not the same. Finally, it is possible that some reform sequences are more credible and as such are clearly to be preferred.

The $CEEC_s$, especially those that have experienced periods of high inflation or hyperinflation, are faced with a problem of time inconsistency of macroeconomic policies. In an environment where reforms create short-term costs to individuals and society as a whole, there will be the temptation to reverse or at least deviate from the initial course. Calvo (1989) analyzes a number of examples of non-credible reforms and establishes the general proposition that imperfect credibility implies the existence of intertemporal distortions.

The first part of the paper analyses the role of active economic policy management, - namely, fiscal, monetary and exchange rate policy management - in providing the desirable economic stability. The second part focuses on the banking and financial system reforms as key determinants of the success of the economic transformation process.

5.2 Active economic policy management

Although there are some exceptions, there is broad agreement that *macroeconomic stability is a prerequisite for the transformation and liberalization of an economy*. First, high inflation reduces the information content in prices and thus makes resource allocation decisions more difficult; second, the external consequences of excessive domestic demand will reduce the credibility of the liberalization measures. Stabilization in the CEEC$_s$, interpreted as removing the root causes of budget deficits (and in particular quasi deficits), requires certain economic reforms to accompany the stabilization effort. Successful stabilization in these economies involves removing subsidies to enterprises and tightening their budget constraints. Unavoidably, this entails important changes in the regime under which the enterprises operate and rationalization of the price structure. Clearly, it is not possible to design a satisfactory policy sequence in which stabilization comes first without being followed by at least some elements of structural reform.

Adjustment of the budget is the sine qua non of stabilization. This requires both the introduction of a productive tax structure (a broad tax base, without exemptions; a firm attitude toward tax compliance; moderate, preferably uniform, rates of taxation; absence of significant subsidies of any form, etc.) and a number of reforms on the expenditure side (efficient administration of public utility rates; cuts in public sector employment; privatization and closure of loss-making public sector firms; restoration, maintenance and investment expenditures on social and economic infrastructure).

Fiscal support to the stabilization programme, using the exchange rate as the nominal anchor, is of the utmost importance, especially if we bear in mind that money becomes an endogenous variable which depends on the mobility of capital.

The views about the *choice of the nominal anchor* for establishing price stability vary widely. The fixing of nominal prices may cause serious disruptions arising from considerable upsets in relative prices. Another option, targeting the expansion in money supply, raises the problem of growing demand for money should the stabilization programme be successful and inflation eradicated. At a given price level, growing demand for money will require a one-time expansion in the money supply which, in turn, may affect the credibility of the programme. On the other hand, if this expansion does not occur, real interest rates may rise. The third alternative to these targets is to fix the exchange rate. De facto indexation of all prices in the economy relative to a foreign currency implies that nominal contracts cease to be valid. This eliminates all practices of economic agents based on backward-looking behaviour and lies behind the idea of fixing the exchange rate in order to ensure price stability. A risk associated with this concept is that uncertainty about the ultimate outcome of stabilization may require high real interest rates in order to defend the exchange rate. Another related risk is that, should prices increase, a devaluation strategy may be required. However, implementing such a policy may raise concerns about credibility and further upward price movements.

Dornbusch (1990) and Sachs (1986) emphasize *the role of exchange-rate stabilization* in curbing hyperinflation in the economies characterized by dollarization of the goods and money markets and the use of the exchange rate as the price index of goods and services. These authors point out that exchange-rate stabilization leads to the convergence of the domestic inflation rate toward the world rate at a much faster pace than a stabilization programme based only on fiscal reform. In fact, as real tax revenue increases while exchange-rate stabilization brings down inflation, an improvement on the fiscal side makes it even more likely that the stabilization programme will be successful. The adoption of the exchange rate as an anchor restricts the government`s ability to surprise the private sector with unexpected devaluations. Some studies point out that in evaluating an exchange-rate system (whether fixed or flexible), one should bear in mind that the state authorities are "inclined" toward inflation. In other words, if the rule of discretion is to be applied to an exchange-rate adjustment, it is important to know how this discretion can be abused. As is well known, it is impossible to sustain a fixed exchange rate if fiscal imbalances are financed by money issuance. In order to sustain a competitive exchange rate, a number of high-inflation countries resorted to a crawling peg system, whereby the nominal exchange rate is occasionally adjusted to inflation rate differentials. In such scenarios, economies usually adapt to living with relatively high inflation and institutionalize general indexation. It is also evident that a peg to a stable monetary unit can only be used as an instrument of domestic macroeconomic stabilization if restrictions on foreign trade are abolished. Although some IMF studies show that the countries with a fixed exchange-rate system are superior to those with a flexible exchange-rate system in bringing down inflation, the unclear direction of causality poses a serious problem: whether the countries with a fixed exchange-rate system sustain a low inflation rate over a longer term or whether the countries with low inflation sustain the fixed interest rate. Edwards (1992) suggests, on the basis of empirical evidence, that a fixed exchange-rate system relies to a greater extent on financial discipline and a lower inflation rate.

If disruptions occur on a goods market, output will be less stable if the exchange rate is fixed, while prices will be less stable if the size of the money supply is fixed. It should be noted that a fixed exchange-rate system is more appropriate from an economic policy aspect if disruptions occur primarily on the financial market. The stabilization of the key price in an economy (i.e. an open economy where tradeable products are an important price-level component), which can be monitored from day to day, gives a better signal to economic agents than the money supply with its indirect signals. Likewise, the instability of monetary targets, especially during a disinflationary period, affects their validity as nominal anchors in stabilization programmes. Meeting any monetary target has proven difficult because of the inability to forecast the development of structural parameters underlying the transmission of monetary impulses.

Bofinger (1990) argues that in transition economies part of the money supply is endogenously determined by the need to keep insolvent firms liquid. It is assumed that the central bank cannot credibly commit itself to the announcement of a monetary target which disregards the financing needs of insolvent firms. There are essentially two different, albeit related, channels through which the money supply can become endogenous. The first channel is the direct financing of insolvent firms by the monetary authorities. Hence, these credits are indirect subsidies - or part of the quasi fiscal deficit, which undermines the independence of the monetary authorities and weakens the traditional role of commercial banks. A second channel emerges if insolvent banks are kept liquid through refinancing facilities of the central bank even if the quasi-fiscal activities have been fully consolidated in the budget. The greater the share of insolvent banks which is dependent on central bank refinancing, the larger is this endogenous component of the money supply. On the other hand, shifts in the demand for money can have two different causes. One-time structural shifts occur if administrative restrictions are abolished. Since decisions of banks and non-banks in the socialist banking system were highly regulated by direct controls on the holdings of certain monetary aggregates and on interest rates, agents are likely to adjust their portfolios to the desired composition after these controls are lifted. This implies that the money demand functions that could be estimated for the pre-reform period are unlikely to reflect the true preferences of the market participants, implying that the elasticities of the demand for money with respect to income or interest rates will change. Once a target has been set and money demand increases in an unexpected, yet permanent way, sticking to the original target would lead to an overly restrictive monetary policy, and vice versa. Measurement of velocity is, in addition, complicated by two transformation-specific factors. In general, because the magnitude of the underestimation of GDP and the amount of interenterprise debt are unknown, monetary authorities may react to a perceived change in the demand for money while the true structural parameters have remained unchanged.

The lesson to be learnt from the recent stabilization programmes being implemented in the $CEEC_s$ is that fixed exchange rates are not a shortcut to price stability. Monetary stability and credibility is not easily imported; it must be built at home. The way to build monetary stability and credibility includes an institutional reform of the central bank, with (1) price stability as the goal of monetary policy, (2) sufficient central bank independence to achieve the goal, and (3) central bank accountability for achieving the goal. It also includes pursuing a fiscal policy that is consistent with full employment and price stability. All this also requires political support. The public and policy makers need to be convinced that price stability is desirable and that institutional reform is necessary for credibility.

The lower the credibility, the higher the *expectations*, which affect the inflationary process in several interconnected ways. Expectations of high inflation can become self-fulfilling through a number of channels. In particular, expectations of high inflation can lead to: a high velocity of money, a flight from the currency, and a large budget deficit, as high inflation leads to high nominal interest rates, which in turn raise the cost of public debt servicing. As a result of the effects of inflationary expectations, there are direct gains (in terms of reduced output loss and quicker price stabilization) to derive from policies and institutions that raise the credibility of stabilization. Such policies and institutions bolster the demand for money and reduce nominal interest rates, thereby reducing the public sector budget deficit.

It is not just conventional adjustment costs that block a quick move to one of the many Pareto-much-superior allocations. The transformation process will require time to establish a credible new framework for economic decision-making. It is essential to coordinate expectations around a relative price structure radically different from the pre-reform one. Discontinuities in history - overriding hysteresis -, however positive, may create a serious disequilibrium while a new set of consistent expectations evolves. A comprehensive change of regime occurs when expectations and real economic variables shift in mutually reinforcing patterns to establish a new economic environment that alters the economy`s dynamic path.

5.3 Banking and financial system reforms

While monetary policy is concerned with the provision of the optimal money supply to an economy (given the structure of money demand), *banking system reform* has important implications for both, the structure of the demand for money as well as the transmission of monetary impulses. The conduct of a successful monetary policy depends on the stability of structural parameters that are at least partially being determined through the financial system. At the same time, the success of banking system reform, i.e. the improvement in the efficiency of financial resource allocation, is affected by the stability of the monetary system. Monetary stability is crucial for an efficient allocation of resources because price signals should not be disturbed by high and volatile inflation rates which make it difficult to separate shifts in relative prices from movements in the general price level.

An essential obstacle that has to be overcome in order to set up a market-oriented banking sector in reforming economies is the absence of a clear monetary authority. It is true that state or national banks have been converted into central banks in the image of those that exist in market economies. But most reforming economies have yet to ensure that those central banks represent genuine monetary authorities. In essence, what central bank independence entails is the establishment of appropriate checks and balances in the exercise of economic policy in the monetary sphere. Operationally, central bank independence means that the monetary authorities are free to pursue their own objectives without government interference. A corollary of this freedom is, despite its character as banker of the government, the central bank's ability to deny to the government recourse to its financial resources. In an institutional setting where the central bank is just being established and, more broadly, the monetary authority is just being installed, clear and simple policy rules can be instrumental in filling the institutional vacuum. This is one of the strong reasons behind the current renewed interest in the concept of currency boards, which can be viewed variedly as a central banking principle, as a central bank substitute or as a first step toward a central bank.

A major problem in any attempt to achieve a non-inflationary policy in a CEEC is the low credibility of the central bank's monetary policy in the transition phase, the important reason for that being its insufficient control over the asset side of its balance sheet. This can be changed only if large parts of the enterprise sector are privatized - which is identical with a substitution of soft budget constraints by stringent bankruptcy laws - and if the high degree of monopolization is reduced by more liberal foreign trade regulations. As the work of Barro and Gordon (1983) demonstrates, a non-inflationary policy which is not regarded as credible by the private sector is associated with output losses. Depending on the social welfare function of a country, this outcome can be worse than an inflationary policy which is fully anticipated. The credibility problem of non-inflationary policies in the $CEEC_s$ calls for far-reaching real sector reforms.

A second class of problems for monetary policy, which are associated with the transition process, arises even if the central bank were absolutely independent and its policies perfectly credible. As we have already mentioned, operational difficulties are caused by the high instability of almost all the parameters needed to determine domestic targets for monetary policy and to assess their actual stance.

The efficacy of the financial system is a key determinant of the success of the economic transformation process. Three immediate steps are needed. First, high priority should be given to the restructuring and modernization of the banking sector - involving the strengthening of the capital base of banks, the establishment of more effective competition within the banking system and the creation of an efficient payments settlement system. Second, the creation of a financial sector should be front-loaded with a strong and effective bank supervisory framework and other regulatory measures to minimize moral hazard problems, to foster sound borrowing, lending and management practices, and - more generally - to enhance the confidence of market participants, most of whom are relatively inexperienced. Third, efficient financial intermediation requires a stable macro-economic environment. There are important interactions between the creation of a market-based financial system and establishing the structural conditions for macro-economic control.

Financially repressed economies are characterized by distorted real deposit and lending rates, excessive reserve requirements, administratively determined credit ceilings and the inevitable development of a large number of "privileged" financial circuits. Quite often, real interest rates are negative, with adverse consequences for the development of financial markets. However, the development of a stable and competitive financial system is not simply a matter of liberalizing financial market rates. On the contrary, if the macro-economic environment is unstable and bank supervision and other financial market regulations are out of touch with the realities of the market place, financial liberalization is likely to result in increased macro-economic instability and in a higher degree of financial fragility. Financial liberalization should therefore not only be accompanied or preceded by strong macro-economic policies to stabilize the economy but also by the elimination of institutional and structural obstacles. Sound banking regulatory and supervisory policies are very important for minimizing moral hazard in the financial system, in particular if the macroeconomic environment is unstable. The recapitalization of the banking sector and the restructuring of inherited substandard loans are key elements of the reform of the financial sector. Second, pressure on the banks to behave commercially without first restructuring their balance-sheets might be ineffective or even counter-productive. Indeed, such a policy might induce under-capitalized banks to continue to provide new high-interest loans to customers with large outstanding debts that are difficult to collect, thereby perpetuating the misallocation of credit. This rolling over of credits and capitalization of interest would imply that the weak banks remain captives of their large non-creditworthy customers. At the same time, viable enterprises may be crowded out from access to funds because distress lending moves the cost of external funds to unacceptably high levels. Promising investment projects of the latter enterprises might be denied funding while investments by unproductive state-owned enterprises continue. Third, it is necessary to increase competition between financial institutions. Lack of competition is also an important reason why administrative arrangements by central banks continue to dominate the setting of interest rates in the interbank markets as well as in the credit and deposit markets. Fourth, the requirement that interbank clearings be settled in central bank funds is essential for money market development and better monetary management.

One of the priority aims of the reform process must be the reconstitution of an efficient capital stock. To this end, it is urgent that institutions be established capable of mobilizing savings and channeling them toward activities that are viable in a market setting.

A common major difficulty faced by banks in these economies is the low quality of their loan portfolios and the existence of a liquidity overhang, that is, the existence of an excess supply of bank liabilities. The banks are not in a position to do much more than roll over their maturing loans and capitalize their accrued interest. This, together with a general policy trend to introduce the financial discipline required by the reform effort, has tended to restrain credit flows in reforming economies. Such credit restraint has contributed to the emergence and rapid growth of inter-enterprise arrears, which have thus become an involuntary source of finance that has permitted enterprises to circumvent credit stringency. This process, however, further weakens the banks, since the enterprises that run arrears cannot and do not pay while those that, as a consequence, are not paid find it correspondingly harder to service their debts. Thus, even though there is no bank credit expansion, accruing unpaid interest obligations are capitalized, adding to the banks' impaired assets, and nonperforming loans and financial discipline remains elusive.

Instituting a price system through the decentralisation of resource allocation and the deregulation of enterprises and instituting private enterprises through legalization of private share owning and mass privatization are necessary but far from sufficient to achieve the potential of a capitalist market economy[1] . The step that is so far missing in the privatization plans of most $CEEC_s$ is the creation of an *appropriate mechanism to control private enterprise.*

Taking into account present-day conditions in the $CEEC_s$, one class of mechanisms, namely, outsider control by banks and other financial intermediaries, is well designed to promote enterprise performance. In the course of mass privatization by voucher, one or two large blocks of shares of an enterprise could be placed with the financial intermediaries set up to hold shares and receive vouchers from the public. The other device for outside financial control is an appropriate kind of bank or other financial intermediary.

Among the critical issues facing the emerging economies of Central and Eastern Europe is the choice of linkages between financial institutions and a privatized productive sector. The development of a competitive financial market based on private property rights is of crucial importance for the transformation of these economies.

---

[1] There are two main sources of political constraints related to privatization. One is related to the redistributive effects of privatization and the other is related to restructuring. One must distinguish between *ex ante* and *ex post* political constraints. *Ex ante* constraints are feasibility constraints. Proposals may be blocked. *Ex ante* constraints also mean that important coalitions may be pushing some forms of privatization that are economically not sensible but politically difficult to avoid. Ex post political constraints concern the danger of backlash and reversal of given policies. With respect to the distributive effects, this may be the case, for example, of a program advertised as very egalitarian that in fact induces a high concentration of wealth in the hands of a small number of people, or of a policy advertised as being in favor of the domestic population, but ends up favoring foreign capital. The more serious political constraints are related to the serious income risks related to restructuring. It is obvious that there will be a massive shift from heavy industry to services, from big to small enterprises, but in most cases, nobody knows in advance which enterprises will survive and which will die. These risks related to restructuring are probably the most important source of political constraints in the transition period.

References

Barro, R. and D. Gordon, (1983), " A Positive Theor`y of Monetary Policy in NaturalRate Model", Journal of Political Economy, Vol.91.

Bofinger, P., (1990), "The Role of Monetary Policy in the Process of Economic Reform in Eastern Europe", Discussion Paper, Centre for Economic Policy Research, London.

Buch, C., (1995), "Monetary Policy and the Transformation of the Banking System in Eastern Europe", Working Paper, The Kiel Institute of World Economics.

Calvo, G., (1989), "Incredible Reforms", IMF Staff Papers.

Dornbusch, R., (1990), "Policies to Move from Stabilization to Growth", Discussion Paper, Centre for Economic Policy Research, London.

Dornbusch, R., (1990), "Credibility and Stabilization", Discussion Paper, Centre for Economic Policy Research, London.

Edwards, S., (1992), "The Sequencing of Structural Adjustment and Stabilization", Working Paper, International Centre for Economic Growth, San Francisco.

Edwards, S., (1989), Exchange Rate Misalignment in Developing Countries, John Hopkins Press, Baltimore.

Portes, R, (1991), " The Path of Reform in Central and Eastern Europe: An Introduction", Discussion Paper, Centre for Economic Policy Research, London.

Roland, G., (1994), "On the Speed and Sequencing of Privatization and restructuring", Discussion Paper, Centre for Economic Policy Research, London.

Sachs, J., (1986), "The Bolivian Hyperinflation and Stabilization", N.B.E.R. Working Paper.

6 Problems of Transition in the Monetary Sector: The Bulgarian Experience

Mileti Mladenov
Bulgarian National Bank
1 Al Battenberg Square
1000 Sofia - BULGARIA

Summary

The development of the reforms in Bulgaria in controversial. Most of the new private companies don't have enough capital and their access to credit is difficult. Though foreign companies have entered the Bulgarian market, the flow of foreign investments is still comparatively low. Privatization in the public sector has been very slow up to now.

Economic growth in 1994 and 1995 was modest. However, the uncompleted structural reform, the increasing losses of the government enterprises and loss of confidence in the banking system, created conditions for financial crisis and for a significant decrease in production in 1996. The budget deficit and the rate of inflation have risen and the lev is greatly depreciated.

Fiscal and monetary policies are important elements of macroeconomic stabilization policy. In Bulgaria, the policies followed by the authorities have signally failed to prove successful. Stabilization of the banking system is also a major and urgent priority.

In the beginning of 1997, Bulgaria is on the edge o hyperinflation. Fortunately enough, the political crisis, which started in December 1996, has been resolved and parliamentary elections are expected to take place in April 1997. The IMF has made a proposal for the introduction of a Currency Board in Bulgaria, expected to come into effect in the beginning of Summer.

6.1 Private sector developments and prospects

Bulgaria, like the rest of the former communist countries, is in a process of transition from a centrally-planned economy to a market-oriented one. But, whereas in other CEEC countries the number of small private enterprises operating in the services sector, agriculture, etc., was substantial even before the beginning of reforms in 1989, the private sector in Bulgaria, prior to that date, was contributing less than 5% of GDP and private enterprises were not even legal before the end of 1988. Since 1989, Bulgaria's private sector has been developing rapidly. At present, the latter contributes about 50% of GDP and statistics show that approximately another 20% of incomes are generated by informal activities. Since 1990, the private sector is the main source of growth in output and employment. The Bulgarian Parliament has voted many new laws in order to establish a basis for the development of the private sector, but the process of forming a legal framework for entrepreneurial activities is still unfinished. Land and some buildings were given back to the descendants of their former owners. A number of small enterprises were created and found their market shares. Currently, the private sector is concentrated on agriculture and the services. Joint ventures are being established between foreign and domestic companies. Foreign companies have become active in the Bulgarian market but the flow of foreign investment is still comparatively low. Admittedly, privatization in the public sector has been very slow up to now. However, the need to avoid a financial crisis caused by the losses accumulating in the inefficiently working state-owned enterprises and the need to seek the support of international financial institutions are exerting pressure on the government to carry out wide-ranging programme with the emphasis on faster privatization of state-owned enterprises and the closure of the biggest loss-makers among them. A key instrument for fostering large-scale privatization is the mass (voucher) privatization program.

The process of privatisation is speeding up. One of the benefits of privatisation is that it promotes efficient financial institutions and capital markets. The methods used for privatisation include: public sale of shares, public tender, public auction, direct negotiation with potential buyers, lease and buy-out and debt-equity swaps. The institutions to direct and control the privatisation process are already in place.

In 1995, the country's GDP was about USD 13 billion (at the average 1995 rate of exchange of 68 lev/USD) , or USD 1450 per capita. GDP has shrunk significantly in real terms since 1989. The first year positive economic growth was 1994, when GDP increased by 1.4% in real terms while it rose by 2.6% in 1995.

At the beginning of 1996, however, the incomplete structural reform and the increasing losses, both in the real and the financial sectors, created the conditions for a new financial crises and massive loss of public confidence in the national currency and the banking system. The crisis is evident in the negative evolution of the main macroeconomic magnitudes (exchange rate, foreign exchange reserves, inflation, unemployment, production, imports, exports). Following negotiations with the IMF and World Bank, a new stand-by agreement and a new SAL (Structural Adjustment Loan) were reached. In order to receive this new financing, Bulgaria must satisfy certain strict conditions, namely to complete the structural reform, especially to proceed with broad privatization, to raise administered prices to realistic levels and to continue to discharge properly its international financial obligations.

Undoubtedly, the Bulgarian economy is currently facing a difficult situation. The level of direct foreign investment remains low at about 100 million USD per year but hopefully the completion of the arrangements with the IMF and the World Bank and the speeding up of reforms will attract more foreign investors. In this respect, the privatization process will offer good opportunities for profitable investments. A number of joint-ventures have already been established, and certain important deals are in the process of negotiation. For example, there are several active joint-ventures in the telecommunications sector, where negotiations are in progress, aiming at the sale of a big part of the national telecom operator.

Bulgaria has 8.5 million inhabitants. The total labour force is about 4 million, of which 3,2 million are employed. Thanks to the growth in the private sector, unemployment, measured as a ratio of the registered unemployed to the labour force, has decreased in 1995 and has stabilized at about 12%. The agreement reached with the international financial institutions in 1996 to close the biggest loss-makers and to undertake rehabilitation measures for the remaining lame duck enterprises will result in increased unemployment and will inevitably cause further decreases in real incomes, although this should only be a temporary development.

6.2 Fiscal policy

In compliance with the overall anti-inflation economic policy, fiscal policy is restrictive. It aims at bringing down the budget deficit to the lowest possible level and at achieving a primary surplus, given the huge government debt and the financial burden of servicing it.

After 1989, tax reforms resulted in the reduction and simplification of the previous complex rate structure, broadened the base and introduced modern tax instruments, such as VAT. Severe problems with tax administration and collection make it difficult to reduce the government budget deficit. The aim of the policy-makers is to improve tax collection and establish a modern tax system, which will help create an investor-friendly business climate and, at the same time, optimize revenues while striving to cut public expenditure.

In spite of the fact that in 1994 and 1995 there had been a primary budget surplus, representing about 7% of the GDP, Bulgaria's overall budget deficit remained high. In 1994 and 1995 it represented 5,8% and 5,7% of GDP respectively, mainly because of large interest payments on the internal debt (about 12% of the GDP). The volume of government revenue and expenditure decreased significantly and efforts were made to decrease the budget deficit by means of cash privatization programme.

6.3 External developments and foreign indebtedness

Economic growth in 1994 benefited the current account, which had been negative since the beginning of the reform with its deficit reaching 1098 million USD in 1993, or 10.2% of GDP. The current account was balanced in 1994 and ran a surplus of USD 335 million (about 2.5% of GDP) in 1995.

Bulgaria's capital account, which was positive in 1994 in spite of the front-loaded payments after the completion of the deal with the London club, became negative in 1995. This was due mainly to bigger principal repayments, capital outflow and a decrease in short--term lending from abroad. In spite of these shortfalls, the overall balance of payments was in surplus with more than 400 million USD.

Bulgaria's official foreign debt was larger than the country's GDP. In 1993, the debt-to-GDP ratio was 115%. The successful completion of the Debt Service Reduction Deal with the London club creditors in 1994, however, drastically improved the country's international creditworthiness. On the other hand, Bulgaria's debt service burden reached 7% of GDP in 1995 and is expected to increase further, contributing to a decrease of country's official foreign indebtedness, which dropped to 76% of GDP in 1995. After the virtual depletion of Bulgarian foreign reserves to 100 million USD (monetary gold excluded) in the beginning of 1996, international financial institutions committed themselves to support the Bulgarian authorities in their efforts to speed up the reforms and to make regular payments on the debt.

6.4 Monetary policy

BNB's task as a central bank is to bring down the rate of inflation and to maintain the stability in the financial sector and in the overall economy through implementation of the appropriate monetary policies. It is also authorised by law to regulate and control the activity of the commercial banks, i.e. it is the banks' supervisory authority.

BNB's primary monetary policy goal is to subdue inflation. For this purpose, BNB has set specific money supply targets. Given the factors which were responsible for run-away inflation, the only way to consistently subdue inflationary pressures is through radical changes in the general economic conditions. Monetary restriction could play a positive role only in combination with extensive structural reforms, primarily privatisation, political stability and the maintenance of tight fiscal and incomes policies. The accomplishment of these objectives will ease monetary constraints and accelerate economic growth.

In pursuing its money supply growth targets, the BNB has applied a variety of monetary policy instruments. The major goal has been to discontinue the use of direct instruments and move to market-based ones to control the monetary base.

At the beginning of the financial sector reform, from 1991 until 1994, direct credit ceilings were adopted as an intermediate target for money supply control and as the main instrument of BNB's monetary policy. Since then, open market operations have begun to play a major role as an instrument of liquidity control in the banking system.

Commercial bank refinancing, as an instrument of BNB's monetary policy, takes several forms: lombard loans, discount loans, short-term BNB deposits with commercial banks and overdraft facilities. Minimum reserve requirements have also been used by BNB as a monetary policy tool.

BNB's foreign exchange policy, an integral part of its monetary policy, has been directed at maintaining the external stability of the lev. A floating exchange rate system was set up at the beginning of the reforms and the foreign exchange market developed.

The dramatic fluctuations observed in the lev exchange rate, however, clearly revealed the difficulties of pursuing a foreign exchange policy under unbalanced demand and supply conditions and with reduced foreign financing. In turn, foreign exchange policy requirements substantially limited the scope for conducting a consistent anti-inflationary monetary policy and underlined the need for closer coordination of monetary policy goals and instruments in order to maintain the external and internal stability of the lev.

At the beginning of 1996, the central bank forex reserves had dwindled to 100 million USD. Even worse, the exchange rate crisis was combined with decreasing confidence in the banking system. Thus, it was important for the BNB to work in the direction of restoring confidence in the national currency. For this purpose, a set of measures were agreed with the IMF and the World Bank, including replenishment of the foreign exchange reserves through their support, thus restoring confidence in the lev and the banking system. This is properly seen as a sine qua non for achieving monetary policy goals, since decreased demand for levs had been impeding the implementation of monetary policy and was fuelling inflation.

Consistent application of tight fiscal and incomes policies has limited the lev bank credit to the State sector. Credits to the real sector have decreased in real terms, too. Any additional need for direct budget financing will crowd out the real sector from the credit market, with negative effects for the economy. Only if financial stability is achieved and monetary discipline vastly improved will there be further increases in the rate of economic growth. The additional credit resources made available thanks to reduced bank financing of the State budget deficit should be channeled to the nonfinancial sector to support the economic recovery.

Another key determinant to the success of BNB's monetary policy, especially after the crisis in 1996, is the coordination of intentions and activities between the BNB and the Government, for financial stability can only be achieved through consistent monetary and fiscal policies. In this context, more extensive nonbank financing of the budget deficit will be decisive if monetary policy is to overcome fiscal policy pressures.

6.5 Structure and legal framework of the financial system

Bulgaria's transition to a market-oriented economy was accompanied by drastic changes both in the real economy and the financial sector. In regard to the latter, the first step was to create a sound legislative basis for the development of the banking system. To this effect, the Bulgarian National Bank (BNB) was established as the country's central bank while a Law on Banking and Credit Activities (1992) and a number of BNB regulations have also been adopted, providing the operational framework in which Bulgarian Credit institutions are to function. Following the creation of a two-tier financial system, a large number of commercial banks and non-bank financial institutions have been granted licenses to operate.

The Law on Banking and Credit Activities determines the scope of banking operations and the basic requirements for conducting banking and institutional lending activities in Bulgaria, while the BNB's regulations spell out in detail the terms and conditions under which banking may operate.

The regulations governing BNB's crucial supervisory task have been formulated on the basis of the documents adopted by the Basle committee as well as of the European Union's banking directives. Recently, the legal framework was broadened in order to establish a more appropriate basis for closing down banks and guaranteeing bank deposits.

At present, there are over 30 universal commercial banks in Bulgaria and one special financial institution - the State Savings Bank (SSB). The SSB operates under a separate low, adopted many years ago. It has no equity capital and provides full state guarantee on the deposits in attracts. SSB's deposits are the main source of loanable funds for the interbank money market. There are plans to transform the SSB into a commercial bank.

More than ten commercial banks are still state-owned. At present a "state-owned bank" means a bank in which another state bank, state-owned company or the Bank Consolidation Company (BCC) have the majority of the shares. The BCC is a holding company, established by the government in 1992, to which the State's and BNB's shares in the banks were transferred. The aim of the BCC is to consolidate the small state-owned banks, to improve the financial health of the state-owned banks and to take steps for their recapitalisation and eventual privatisation.

The private sector in the Bulgarian banking system has developed rapidly with over twenty five private banks already in operation. The minimum capital requirement for establishing a bank is 1,4 bln BGL (about o.5 million USD at the rate $1=3 000 lv.) and 2,2 bln. BGL (about 0,7 million USD) for a full license (including international operations). Presently, there are six foreign banks licensed for operations in Bulgaria: ING, Reiffeisenbank, BNP-Dresdner Bank, Xiosbank, the National Bank of Greece and Ionian Bank.

The Law on Economic Activity of Foreign Persons and on Protection of Foreign Investments allows for the establishment of foreign banks and for the equal treatment of Bulgarian and foreign investors establishing a bank. EBRD holds shares in the Bulgarian Investment Bank (BIB) and in BNP-Dresdner Bank. The Commercial Bank of Greece has a share in BIB, too. Finally, some Russian banks have shares in the Corporate Commercial Bank and in the Bulgarian-Russian Investment Bank.

BNB also licenses non-bank financial institutions - financial and brokerage houses and foreign exchange bureaux. At the beginning of 1997, there were 135 financial brokerage houses, 27 brokers and over 740 exchange bureaux.

Investment fund companies are still small institutions in Bulgaria and stock exchange activities are still marginal. The two largest stock exchanges are the Bulgarian Stock Exchange and the Sofia Stock Exchange. In order to regulate these activities a law on Securities, Stock Exchanges and Investment Funds was enforced and a Securities Committee was formed. A Central Depository was also established. In order to serve the voucher privatization, a law on the privatization funds was passed and special financial intermediaries, whose liabilities are the privatization vouchers, were created.

Despite the fact that a number of insurance companies are operating in the market, the insurance market and institutions have not yet been provided with an adequate regulatory framework.

6.6 Problems of transition

The Bulgarian bank's problems with non-performing loans received by State-owned enterprises had appeared before the beginning of the economic reform and intensified thereafter. Most of the banks assets are of low quality and are the root cause of the big losses incurred by the entire banking system. Measures taken to clean bank balance-sheets from inherited bad debts proved an inadequate solution to the problem. Repeatedly, the central bank, being the lender of last resort, has been forced to ease its monetary policy in order to provide liquidity to the banking system. Several of the biggest State-owned banks have the worst portfolios. Too fast and unsound expansion of some private banks led to severe liquidity problems and insolvencies.

The capital adequacy of some banks had become negative. Even more, despite the fact that the BNB took control over two insolvent private banks, the liquidity crisis in the banking system intensified. Implementation of a consistently tight monetary policy under these conditions became unfeasible because of BNB's obligation, as a lender of last resort, to pour liquidity into several problem banks and because arrears in interbank payments were asphyxiating the settlement system. Eventually, some banks with the exchange rate crisis, ruined public confidence in the banking system and led to a run on deposits and large-scale currency substitution.

Given this critical situation, the laws concerning bank insolvency and bank deposits guarantee were amended. Depositors received a guarantee for the money then put into banks, while legal insolvency proceedings began for fifteen insolvent state and private banks. These banks have about 50% of the assets of the banking system. A broad set of measures was also prepared in order to place the whole banking system on a sound footing. The stabilisation of the banking system is vital for effective monetary policy. Once these challenges are overcome, fast and constructive actions can be undertaken, such as conservatorship, closure, rehabilitation, mergers, financial performance targets for individual banks and for the capital adequacy of the system as a whole, as well as direct recapitalization of some state-owned banks with liquidity and capital shortfalls.

6.7 Concluding remarks

Bulgaria started the process of transition to a market economy having an almost 100% state-owned economy and huge foreign debt. Recent economic policies have been aiming at decreasing inflation and restructuring the economy in order to normalize the situation in the country. Structural reforms were partly implemented and this led to modest economic growth, but some major problems remain unsolved. The need to avoid financial collapse, brought about by the huge losses accruing in the inefficient state-owned enterprises, and the need to obtain the support of international financial institutions have spurred the government to carry out an emergency economic stabilization programme, the ultimate goal of which is to restore public confidence in the banking sector, impost financial discipline on the enterprises, decrease inflation, build adequate foreign exchange reserves, ensure fiscal and external viability and complete the structural reform. To achieve macroeconomic stability, the government must also carry through fiscal adjustment and bank-rehabilitation. Finally, fast privatization, enforcement of an appropriate legal framework for business, raising administered prices to realistic levels and calling for the scheduled management of foreign debt payments are also of vital importance in achieving lasting positive results.

Needless to say, the success of the programme will crucially depend on the consistent and coordinated implementation of these policies.

The postscript government emergency stabilization programme, however, was not efficiently implemented and the country plunged into a deeper crisis in the second half of 1996. According to estimates, GDP dropped by 10% in 1996, the inflation rate rose to above 300%, the lev depreciated more than sixfold and the budget deficit went up. As a result, the fourth stand-by agreement with the IMF was interrupted in the autumn of 1996. A political crisis, accompanied by mass demonstrations in Sofia and other Bulgarian cities developed in December - January 1997 and led to the fall of the socialist government and a decision to hold parliamentary elections in April 1997. Meanwhile the IMF proposed a new option for negotiations and support, namely the establishment of a Currency Board, given the loss of monetary and fiscal control and the collapse of the Bulgarian currency. By January 1997, the monthly rate of inflation was about 50% and there was massive dolarization of the Bulgarian economy, while real incomes went down drastically. In order to stop these destructive developments Bulgaria needs radical solutions and actions both on the political and economic front.

Part IV Competition Policy, Internal Market and Trade Policies in the CEECs

7 Competition Policy and Integration: Levelling or Tilling the Playing Field?

Peter Holmes
University of Sussex*
Arts Building
Falmer, Brighton BN1 9QN

Abstract

In the early years of the Common Market, competition rules played a vital role in promoting the integration of the west European economy. Now, the EU is calling on the Central and East European Countries (CEECs) to harmonise competition laws much more tightly than has been required for founder or newly acceding member states, such as Greece, even after accession. The Europe Agreements indicated the general obligation and the recent White Paper spelled it out in more depth. The justification is that the Internal Market *acquis* is implicitly enforced by the European Court of Justice for member states but has to be made explicit in the case of Europe Agreement partners, who do not have obligations of harmonisation under the Rome Treaty. But the asymmetry requires the CEECs to accept all the rules of the Internal Market before accession, with the rest of the *acquis communautaire* after accession.

The fundamental question is how far the CEE's must harmonise their rules before wholly free trade is possible. Although the EU is asymmetrically abolishing conventional measures of protection, it retains contingent protection on industrial goods as well as agricultural protection. Some have argued that once the CEECs adopt competition rules akin to those in the EU, it will be possible to abolish all anti-dumping duties as the competition rules can then be used to deal with "unfair competition". This paper argues that the alignment of competition laws should be part of an accession strategy, not a condition for free trade in industrial goods.

---

* The research reported on here is supported by grants from the Single European Market and Global Economic Institutions initiatives of the UK Economic and Social Research Council, whose generous support for a conference in Prague in March 1995 is greatly appreciated, along with that of the ACE and COST programmes. Earlier versions have been presented at workshops in Prague, Athens and Florence and I am very grateful to discussants including Sally Vansiclen, Ferenc Vissi, and Giuliano Amato.

7.1 Introduction

The central theme of the present paper is that the adoption of EU style competition laws in the CEEC region is a good thing, but the pace and tightness of the harmonisation should be geared to the internal needs of the CEECs themselves and not used as a condition of market access to the EU. In particular, the link that can be made between adaptation of competition rules and an end to anti-dumping is complex. The scope for trade arrangements like those in the European Economic Area for the CEECs appears strictly limited since the politics of trade policy are such that the EU can only guarantee totally free market access to the CEECs if they concede almost as much sovereignty as members must.

In the May 1995 White Paper on *"Preparation of the Associated Countries of Central and Eastern Europe for integration into the internal market of the Union,"* the European Commission outlines the measures in the *acquis communautaire* that constitute the Internal Market to which, of course, the rules of competition policy are central.

The White Paper identifies the alignment of the CEE Countries (CEECs) with the rules of the internal market as a crucial step in the pre-accession phase. This is to be distinguished both from the establishment of a customs union and the application of the full *acquis communautaire* which would be associated with full membership. In particular, while the adoption by the CEECs of the Internal Market rules would seem to put them in a position to have the same relationship with the EU as that of the European Economic Area countries, the White Paper does not make explicit the status of the relationship that would be implied if the Internal Market rules were applied. The White Paper states that it does not intend to create demands for the CEECs, but merely to list the internal market rules for the convenience of the CEECs that will eventually have to adopt them if they are to be members. The text suggests that it is up to the CEECs to respond as they see fit.

The White Paper indicates the distinction between what is an internal market matter and what is the rest of the *acquis communautaire*: measures that are designed to lift standards in order to equalise costs are part of the internal market process, while measures that serve exclusively to benefit the citizens of the countries where they are applied are part of the wider definition. It is the former that must be adopted first.

The White Paper does not therefore in itself map out a response on the part of the EU to adoption of the Internal Market rules by the CEECs. However, the conclusion (para 6.6) restates the Commission's communiqué of July 13th 1994:

> " once satisfactory implementation of competition and state aids policies (by the associated countries) has been achieved, together with the wider application of other parts of Community law linked to the wider market, the Union could decide to reduce progressively the application of

> commercial defence instruments for industrial products from the countries concerned, since it would have a level of guarantee against unfair competition comparable to that existing inside the internal market."

The centrality of competition policy in the process of reciprocal market opening is highlighted by the fact that in the Council's subsequent declaration at the Essen Summit of 9/10th December a similar but not identical wording is used specifically in the chapter on competition policy:

> "As satisfactory implementation of competition policy and control of state aids are achieved, together with the wider application of other parts of Community law linked to the internal market, providing a level of guarantee against unfair competition comparable to that existing inside the internal market, so the Union should be ready to consider refraining from using commercial defence instruments for industrial products." (p.14).

Although the sequence of tenses is a little odd and ambiguous, a generous interpretation of the Commission's wording is that "could" means "would be able to".But the Council's "ready to consider" really spells out that it means "we may think about it. "Obviously, what matters is what the EU does, not what it says. Nevertheless, the unwillingness of the Council to adopt even the ambiguous form of words used by the Commission indicates that even though the Commission and many members of the Council have strong goodwill towards the CEECs, they are subject to real political constraints which limit even the gestures that can be made.

The texts cited appear to signify the following. Competition rules are a vital part of the trade policy relationship between the EU and the CEECs, just as competition policy was the primary integrating device in the early years of the Common Market. Nevertheless, before the EU can *consider* dropping its last commercial policy instruments against the CEECs it will want to see a full set of Internal Market rules applying, not just competition rules. Even after the CEECs go this far ("once satisfactory implementation.. has been achieved"), the EU can do not more than say that it might gradually "reduce" (not necessarily eliminate) all remaining trade barriers.

We could thus see an entire "internal market" between the EU and the CEECs with every feature except those characterising the Internal Market, namely the free movement of goods, persons, services and capital in an area without frontiers, very much the grin of the Cheshire Cat but no cat. It is not being argued here that the Commission intend such a bargain, but merely that it is very hard to make sure that the good intentions of the Community give real assurances to the partners[1] .

The relationship between trade and competition policy has taken on a significance in relations between the CEECs and the EU that has not been the case in

---

[1] It is worth remembering that the Customs Union with Turkey allows for anti-dumping action within what is ostensibly a common customs zone.

other trade negotiations, apart perhaps from the European Economic Area (EEA) experience.

There are several reasons why harmonisation of competition policy as required in the Europe Agreements is a good idea:

- the rules themselves are tried and tested and provide an excellent off-the-shelf model for the CEECs for which expertise in implementation is readily available;
- the existence of an external obligation to apply these rules assists the authorities enforce rules which may be in the national interest but which sectional interests oppose;
- these rules were developed with the promotion of trade and integration in mind;
- fuller harmonisation of these rules will lessen the need for commercial policy measures by the EU ;
- adopting the rules as soon as possible helps anticipate eventual EU accession.

And yet there are reservations that need to be expressed. Disinterested assistance to the CEECs is not the only motive of the EU in this matter. Lester Thurow (1992) has argued that the EU can force its neighbours to play by its rules if it wishes to do so. In effect, there is also a mercantilist agenda. EU firms are seeking maximum market access to their neighbours and are seeking to minimise what they perceive as unfair competition from their neighbours. The harmonisation process contains two elements: one is assisting partners to develop efficient economies but the other is to lead them to adopt rules familiar to, and possibly favourable to, EU firms. Excellent as EU rules have proved to be for the EU as it is now, there is genuine room for debate whether the same rules can be applied in countries with such different economic conditions. The EU is calling on its neighbours to adapt national competition rules to the EU's standards much more rigorously than is the case with the existing member states.

There is clearly a political will on the part of the Commission and many member states to pursue free trade and eventual accession, but it would be a mistake for the CEECs to ignore the political barriers to the full realisation of the promises.

7.2 Competition and integration

Competition policy is one of the most valuable parts of the *acquis communautaire* that new members might wish to take over; it has had extremely powerful effects. Firstly, it has been a force for the promotion of economic efficiency in the sense that anti-trust policy has done in the USA. Moreover, it has been one of the key instruments that opened up trade between the member states, and so played a role equivalent to the US interstate commerce rules as well as to the anti-trust authorities. Commercial policy has been abandoned within the EU because competition policy allows market access barriers to be corrected at source and so does not require provision for retaliation.

However, the adoption of all the EU competition rules may not be an unalloyed benefit, and there could be problems for the partner countries. There are two possible sources of problem. The first is that from an efficiency viewpoint the same rules may not suit countries at different stages of development. The second point is that the EU's competition rules are not only meant to enforce economic efficiency but are also designed to promote "fairness".This notion of fairness involves the upholding of rights of producers and the structure of rights embedded in EU competition rules is not always consistent with interests of consumers and producers in the CEEC partners.

The White Paper makes this point quite clear when in para 3.3 it goes through what part of EEC legislation is internal market and what is not. On social policy, it makes clear in 3.8 that "An uneven approach in national legislation concerning workers' rights or health and safety in the workplace could result in unequal costs for economic operators and threaten to distort competition." It notes that Article 100 of the Rome Treaty was used as the basis for much social legislation pre-1985.

7.3 Principles of competition policy: Levelling playingfield vs efficiency

The Rome Treaty stated that one objective of the EEC was "balanced trade and fair competition". Articles 85 and 86 come closer to enshrining a more US style efficiency objective, but it is a common theme of American commentators (eg Hawk, 1987) that EC policy does not give sole priority to consumer welfare and at the same time EC policy has never been wholly influenced by the Chicago approach.

A close analysis of EU competition practice shows that the aspect of fairness is far more significant than economists would normally suppose. The favourable treatment given to SMEs reflects social priorities other than efficiency. Detailed analysis of the role of competition policy in the car industry shows that it has been tailored to meet the needs of a trade policy regime which is itself a complex compromise of political and economic interests. Here, as elsewhere, the state aids rules seem to be mostly concerned with fairness among producers than with economic efficiency.

Although EU competition law refers to the interests of consumers, this has never been a paramount pre-occupation either in principle or in practice. In practice consumer groups have only made very limited headway in using competition law. Consumer groups have been given standing to make complaints to DG IV, the Court of First Instance has rarely allowed a complaint against the Commission's refusal to investigate a complaint. On the other hand, in competition cases, the rules on evidence and the burden of proof give strong protection to firms accused of violations. This fits in with the notion of competition law as a system where the playing field is to be levelled by giving equal rights to all producers. By setting up such an even contest between producers, it can be reasonably hoped that the interests of consumers will be upheld. But whereas consumers have general interests, the system is geared to protecting individual producers' rights. It is interesting for economists to hear lawyers debating such matters as the rights of confidentiality vs access to information in competition cases. These debates are almost always in the context of the individual rights of the complainant vs those of the accused, rather than in terms of what is in the public interest to reveal.

It is sometimes overlooked by economists that competition laws are as frequently used by firms against other firms as they are spontaneously employed by the public authorities against abuses. Lawyers frequently call for user friendly competition law, by which they mean laws which are convenient to their clients. If all producers have equal rights and standing, the consumer will end up benefiting. The problem comes when there are no entrants to complain about the monopolist or some producers are excluded from the game because they are foreign.

The significance of producer rights emerges most in the contrast with anti-dumping law. This was in some sense once an offshoot of competition law (notably the US 1916 anti-dumping law), but it is now an offshoot where only one set of producers have rights, namely the domestic competitors of imports. The onus of proof is very different in anti-dumping cases and competition cases. Foreign firms are more or less guilty till they can prove themselves innocent and consumer interests are invariably secondary. It would be unthinkable for the Commission to impose "provisional fines" of 20 to 40% of the value of turnover of the item in question, and to determine what is a fair price, just because a *prima facie* case had been established of unfairness in a competition case! In anti-dumping law, domestic producers have rights that other actors do not have, while in competition law all producers have equal rights at the outset and consumer interests are written into the Treaty.

The symmetry of producer interests and the tougher standards of proof before action can be taken makes competition law more appealing to liberal economists than trade law as a way of regulating international competition, though as we shall see the case for this is not as straightforward as it appears.

7.4 Applications to the CEECs

7.4.1 Asymmetry of rules

The 1991 Europe Agreements (EAs) required that the Associates within 3 years align their competition laws to those of the EU. The White Paper spells out what the Commission thinks those obligations mean, though. from a legal perspective the texts of the original European Agreements are definitive. The White Paper contains two distinct elements. It is the European Commission's interpretation of what is implied by what has already been agreed in the EA's. In addition, there is a description of a further set of steps that would have eventually to be taken if Internal Market conditions are to be applied. These are not presented as specific requirements but as a road map for the future. Nevertheless, as the citation at the start of this paper indicates, the EU implies that what is in the White Paper may represent political conditions for the abandonment of commercial policy instruments by the EU..

The most striking aspect of the proposals in the White Paper is its argument that the Europe Agreements create obligations on the CEEC partner countries to adopt competition rules broadly comparable to those of the EC's provisions in stricter terms than is the case for existing member states of the EU! At several points, the White Paper uses the formula, as in for example:

> " A legal obligation for Member states to align their legislation to the Community state aid control system does not exist and would indeed be superfluous because of the Commission's role of the controlling authority under the EC Treaty.
>
> For the CEEC, the situation is obviously different. Taking into account their obligations under the Europe agreements, it is indispensable that they adopt a system similar to that of the Community with a national authority endowed with monitoring powers." p.53.

Similar paragraphs cover the other areas of competition policy.

There are major differences between these proposals and those affecting the states of the EEA . There is no multilateral equivalent of the ESA surveillance authority, all arrangements being between the EU and individual states, though the obligation to conform to EU rules at the national level seems to be similar. At the same time, the nature of the trade arrangements to which these competition rules are linked is very different. The EEA offered considerably greater security of market access than the Europe Agreements at the same time as requiring acceptance of all the internal market *acquis*. .Perhaps even more important than this was the fact that almost as soon as the EEA agreement was signed, membership negotiations began. It was clear that the incentive for the individual states to comply with EU-dictated rules, without having any say in them, was a very high probability of rapid accession. The Europe Agreements, apart from the competition provisions, effectively involve slightly looser commitments on both sides.

In the case of the CEECs, not only is there no absolute guarantee of EU membership if they adopt EU competition rules, there is no guarantee of totally free trade. Many economists have proposed that in this area, as with the EEA, anti-dumping rules should be replaced by competition rules. But the Commission argues that until the whole internal market *acquis* is adopted, the CEECs could have asymmetric advantages that would allow them to sell on unfair terms into the EU market, as the citation from para.6.6 indicates.

According to the Commission and the Council, the EU *might* end the use of commercial instruments if the partner countries adopt EU competition rules *and* the rest of the internal market principles.

However, until full membership has occurred it is hard to see how a genuine intention to do this can be credibly believed by the CEEC partners in the face of internal pressures from EU producers who feel threatened by the consequences of some of the distortions surviving in the CEECs from the pre-1989 era. From the point of view of economic efficiency, it is indeed arguable that the EU should import any cheap steel from the CEECs regardless of why the steel is cheap. But experience suggests that steel producers in the EU can make a politically convincing case that they have made expensive commitments to sink capital in this sector in pre-1989 market conditions which cannot be easily transferred to other sectors. They question why they should have to bear a disproportionate share of any costs of a policy of openness to the east?

7.4.2 National divergences

Many national competition regimes within the EU do have some principles that are quite different from EU law and to the extent that they are effectively applied in cases that do not involve distortions of intra-EU trade they may be quite important. British rules on monopolies and mergers allow much more freedom for the government to apply its idea of the public interest. In recent years, the UK government has at various times declared that it would view with suspicion take-overs by firms owned by foreign governments or that it would only refer to the Monopolies and Mergers Commission cases where competition was directly threatened. In certain cases, critics of the government have unsuccessfully urged it to take account of other aspects of the public interest (such as the perceived importance of a certain enterprise's links with a particular locality - for example in the Pilkington-BTR, Guinness-Distillers, and Nestlé-Rowntree cases). Although the Conservative government chose not to do so, another government might. At the same time, the government has been accused of ignoring the competition criteria laid down in the national merger rules in order to permit concentrations of ownership of newspapers in favourable hands, a one-sided but in practice legally unchallengeable view of the public interest. The Commission suggests in the White

Paper that a public interest clause should be added into the merger rules for CEECs. This would represent quite an important difference from the EU's own rules. The question arises, however, why if that important principle can be conceded there, the same cannot be applied in other areas.

7.4.3 Optimal intensity of competition

Once we are in markets that are not purely contestable, there are no clear yardsticks about what kinds of behaviour really are more or less competitive (can predatory price-cutting ever actually occur? can it be proved?)

In addition, in inherently imperfect markets the optimal intensity of competition is always debatable. Is there really a danger of "destructive competition"? The real interests of different economies may well differ.

A striking example of this concerns the case of the public utilities. The EU has recently taken gradual but bold steps to liberalise the provision of telecommunications services in the EU. This follows a long period of state monopoly and the liberalisation of voice telecommunications is still to come. Special provisions were made for Greece, with the reasons given including the need for monopoly rents to be garnered in order to facilitate the rapid expansion of the network. Telecoms experts in the Commission seem almost unanimous that the CEECs should "do as we say but not as we do". Do not make the same mistake as we did by allowing monopolies to remain too long, is the very sensible advice given. But while this proposal seems eminently sensible, who is to have the last say on its adoption? The EU's position is not wholly disinterested in this matter since more liberalisation means easier access for EU firms.

7.4.4 State aids

A critical example of the EU's wish for conformity with EU rules is in the area of state aids. Although the Europe Agreements allow the partner countries to be treated as covered by article 92(3) - which gives them more discretion than most of the EU member states - nevertheless, the EU is asking in the White Paper for the partner countries to adopt a form of control that parallels that of the member states, with pre-notification of aids to a national body set up for this purpose. There is an *implicit* expectation that there may be ex ante consultations between the Community and the national surveillance authorities to ensure that the surveillance authority concerned does not authorise an aid that will later be contested by the Community. This would give the Community far more power over the CEEC trading partners than it would have vis-à-vis other GATT/WTO partners. Moreover, the community could use this power in an asymmetric way. It seems very likely that the Community would complain to one of its partners if aids had been given within a CEE state in such a way as to appear to discriminate against or between EU based firms. Thus, it would be entirely normal for complaints to be made and even upheld if Hungary were perceived to be supporting Suzuki in a way that could be construed as harming EU-based firms. On the other hand, even if only because of the need for DG IV to choose priorities given its limited resources, it seems very unlikely that state aids which discriminated against Japanese firms would be a source of pressure. This would, however, undermine one of the most valuable aspects of EU state aid policy, which is to avoid inefficiencies by distorting the profitability of investment by one economic agent rather than the other. J-F Marchipont has argued that even within the EU the main goal has become that of providing symmetrical conditions (a level playing field) for the different firms within any given industry rather than between industries. In practice, state aid rules allow different levels of subsidy to be given to different industries, cars and electronics being favourably treated in this respect. Marchipont argues that the EU needs rules that avoid distortions between industries. Similar considerations apply in the CEECs. From the point of view of economic efficiency and the avoidance of distortions in the partner countries, it is, however, important that they should avoid favouring certain sectors or investors more than others, except where there is a clear case that one type of investment brings more positive spillover effects than others. Reading Commission decisions on subsidy cases, the general tenor of the reasoning does not go in this direction. The use of the EU's existing procedures would lead the national authorities to be more concerned with the level playing field aspects rather than the efficiency aspects, and one suspects that the avoidance of unfavourable effects on EU firms would dominate the agenda. Commission decisions on subsidies typically take account of industrial policy considerations such as the amount of capacity in the sector and the likely growth of the demand for the item in question. It would be natural for such considerations to end up being taken account of in state aids cases in such a way that the CEECs might be deterred from promoting investment in areas where it had a genuine comparative advantage but where this might replace capacity existing elsewhere in Europe.

Some observers doubt the realism of mimicking EU procedures at all. Where the state is still a very major shareholder and fledgling capital markets are little developed, it is difficult to really apply the criteria used in the EU itself. Moreover, the notion of a national surveillance authority within the state apparatus with the credibility to dispute subsidy decisions given by the rest of the public authorities is far removed from the public administration traditions of the countries concerned. Doubts have been expressed by the authorities in both Hungary and Poland about the suitability of the detailed rules of the EU.[2]

---

[2] Mr Sopocko, Chairman of the Polish Anti-Monopoly Office told an EU -sponsored conference in 1995: "The EU state aid rules were basically created for the comparatively rich countries with strong and efficient private sectors to help developing some backward tregions or enterprises and sectors during times of temporary difficulty. But this is clearly not the case in countries in the process of transformation." (p.35) At the same meeting,

This is one of the most sensitive areas and, given the difficulties of the Commission in disciplining the member states, it is somewhat utopian to suppose that the mere creation of national monitoring agencies will be an effective instrument of control - as opposed to a chain of influence for the EU. Attention surely needs to be given to the EEA surveillance authority experience where genuine independence was ensured by having a multinational agency as well as the supranational pressures of the EU relationship. In any case, no purely mechanical transposition of previous experience is likely to be very effective.

7.4.5 Intellectual property

Another area where the enforcement of EU competition rules may be unfavourable to the partner countries concerns the competition aspects of intellectual property. Within the EU, there are rules restricting the ability of owners of intellectual property rights to abuse these in anticompetitive ways. Some would argue that these rules (and rules on trade marks) are not as tough as they ought to be (see Frazer). But it is clear that outside the Internal Market the rules offer no help at all. Under the doctrine of "exhaustion", if a firm in one member state licenses a patent to a firm in another, it cannot restrict to whom output is sold within the EU. On the other hand, an EU firm can impose restrictions on, say, licensee Polish firms preventing them exporting from Poland at all. The European Court of Justice (ECJ) has in several cases ruled that copyright protection can be used to prevent parallel imports into the EU.

The nature of patent protection is itself an area where international competition rules need to be thought through. From the point of view of economic efficiency, the retrospective enforcement of EU definitions of the scope of patents can have no effect other than reinforcing monopoly power. In fact, it has been argued by some observers that this has caused severe problems for the Polish pharmaceutical industry which could not be resolved through the application of competition law within Poland.

With the insistence on acceptance of EU intellectual property and patent rules by the CEECs, the scope for abuse by EU firms has increased. Thus, it would seem reasonable to try to achieve greater symmetry in the law, with EU authorities banning practices in CEECs that would be illegal if undertaken within the EU. Reciprocity is called for.

Ms Ivanics of the Hungarian Finance Ministry questioned the need to comply with the letter of EU secondary legislation on state aids, (p.69). See European Commission 1995a.

7.4.6 Legal concepts

The White Paper implies that taking on board EU competition law implies accepting the full jurisprudence of the European Court of Justice as legal precedent. Where the ECJ has interpreted a notion in a certain way this is the way the CEECs must interpret it. The CEEC courts will be free to make their own decisions only in cases where there are no precedents. As a matter of pure logic, the CEEC courts could decide to ignore EU precedents only in cases where there is no possibility of trade being affected, although this would be impractical as well as confusing for economic actors.

Perhaps the most controversial area is that of vertical restraints, where case law is very important. Here, the Commission is insisting that the partners exactly parallel the system of block and individual exemptions. The Commission is arguing that CEEC practice must exactly parallel that of the EU, so that where the Commission has chosen to require agreements of a certain kind to seek individual exemption under Article 85, the partner countries must deal with each case individually, even where it appears that exemptions are always granted and so a block exemption would be simpler. Vissi (1996) has argued that it would be more convenient for Hungary to operate a simpler set of rules which he argues would have the same effect. On the other hand, he claims that the inconveniences to be anticipated by close harmonisation of laws are limited. And Polish experts argue that the experience generated by having identical rules to the EU will benefit Polish firms. It would appear that the EU's proposals in the White Paper in this area go somewhat further than the Europe Agreements themselves, and it is only the latter which are legally binding.

The bottom line is that the CEECs should be allowed to interpret the idea of adopting the core principles of EU competition law in a flexible way. It seems very unlikely that any divergences that might be chosen would be with protectionist aims. Besides, if by any chance there were adverse consequences on trade because of approximation rather than 100% harmonisation, there are mechanisms for dealing with this ex post. Fingleton et al (1996) argue that the kinds of discrepancies that might arise from allowing maximum leeway to CEECs in the adoption of EU competition policy would lead to few serious distortions of trade.

7.4.7 Reciprocity and the wider International Competition agenda

One asymmetry in the system concerns cartellistic and monopolistic practices by EU firms in CEECs. It would appear that, at present, abuses that are undertaken in the EU with an effect in the partner countries are the responsibility of the partner country, and vice versa. That is to say, if an EU firm abuses in Poland its dominant position in the EU, it is for the Poles to deal with it. Any kind of market sharing arrangement involving Eastern Europe, would, like other export cartels, be exempt from Articles 85 and 86 unless it could be shown that there had been an effect on intra-EU trade. A determined DG IV could, if it put its mind to it, find a risk that a concerted practice in one area would spill over into another, but we know that there is a vast area of discretion here. In the instance of the case brought by the European consumers' group BEUC against the privately negotiated restrictions on car imports to the UK from Japan, agreed between the UK and Japanese car producers, the Commission responded to BEUC that they could not see any effect on intra-EU trade. This was an extremely disingenuous response since it is widely agreed that if one part of the Common Market has a different level of trade restrictions there will either be trade deflection or the need for measures to stop this happening (as envisaged in Article 115). If cartel-type arrangements on imports, which are definitely covered by European law, are not automatically investigated, there is even less guarantee that export arrangements will be addressed. (See Frazer and Holmes, 1995).

P.Vigier (1992) warns of the danger that European car manufacturers might carve up the East European markets into separate fiefdoms, Poland for FIAT, the Czech Republic and Slovakia for VW etc. If this did happen, there would be very little that the local authorities could do to discipline powerful foreign firms who could make the threat of pulling out. The experience of VW in the Czech Republic raises a number of doubts. It is believed that the firm pressed the former Czecho-Slovak authorities to grant increased tariff protection as a way of making investment in Skoda more attractive. VW strengthened a quasi-monopoly in the Czech Republic and Slovakia and were able to raise prices by amounts which only a very sophisticated analysis could really determine the fairness of. The main concern of the Community authorities seems to have been, however, whether there was any unfairness towards firms in the EU. Renault felt aggrieved that its bid was rejected but could not do anything. Doubts were also raised about whether there might be a risk of cross subsidy from what seemed to be becoming a profitable Czech operation to the rest of the EU. As things stand, the Community's concern seems essentially to be whether or not other EU firms are being disadvantaged.

There is also the question of exports back to the EU. With wage levels as low as they are in CEECs, the fear exists of low price competition from E.Europe into the EU. The natural response is safeguard duties or, in extreme cases, anti-dumping duties. This would be against the interest of EU consumers and the partner country economies. On the other hand, the same problem can be resolved by firm behaviour. Multinational investment in Eastern Europe is capable of internalising the adjustment cost, in the sense that there is an incentive to moderate any rise in exports to take into account the adjustment costs incurred within the EU by substitution of non-EU for EU production. This is rational behaviour for firms and socially desirable as far as EU workers are concerned, but it is not in the interests of the CEECs.

Such questions arise in the steel industry. Rollo and Smith [1993] note findings of an incipient cartellisation of E.European steel markets, with discussions taking place between EU and the then Czechoslovak steel producers. The iron and steel industry has something of a history of cartelisation (not entirely discouraged by the ECSC arrangements) and DG IV has had recent occasion to investigate action by the EU producers, (see Hoekman and Mavroidis).

There are a number of reports emerging (e.g. on the glass and car industries) of foreign investors seeking additional protection for their new market, which might have the effect of consolidating a monopoly position.

7.4.8 The EU Trade and Competition Interface

The signals sent out by the EU authorities in the past have been mixed regarding private import restrictions. In the original Franco-Japanese ball bearings case, the Commission made it very clear that only the public authorities could control imports. However, having condemned the private arrangements, the Commission did indeed set about controlling ball bearing imports with anti-dumping duties. In the case of Aluminium from Eastern Europe (1985), even under the old regime, the Commission asserted its right to condemn agreements between western producers and the state trading organisations to limit sales in the EU. However, no fines were imposed. In the case referred to above, where the consumer group BEUC challenged the Commission's refusal to investigate a privately operated import restriction on cars between Japan and the UK, the Commission declined to investigate and the Commission's submission to the Court of First Instance led the judges in the oral hearing to enquire whether the Commission was seeking to reverse the doctrine that went back at least to the ball bearings case, (see Frazer and Holmes, 1995).

In the present circumstances, it is most desirable that the Commission should reactivate its earlier vigorous pursuit of private import restrictions to give a signal to CEEC partner firms that no arrangements will be tolerated under which EU producers regulate the flow of competing imports home. It is vital that the EU move closer to bringing together its own trade and competition interface. Where anti-dumping complaints occur, DG-I should investigate allegations that the anti-dumping complaint is being directed at sustaining an EC cartel. Messerlin has claimed that in the past the Commission has allowed chemical firms to sustain intra-EU cartels by the use of trade measures, with special consequences for E.Europe. More recently, in the case of paintbrushes from China and Calcium Metal (Nolle, and Extramet), the ECJ found procedural grounds for rejecting anti-dumping decisions in cases where it was alleged that the complainant was abusing a dominant position inside the EU.

It is important that the EU should forge closer links between its own trade and competition policies and relations with CEEC's are an ideal opportunity to put into practice some of the more general principles the EU has been advocating.. In the context of the EU's desire to introduce international competition policy issues into the WTO, as advocated by the Commission, it would make considerable sense to apply the same principles to relations with the CEECs, and to go beyond the looser rules of comity. The EU should undertake to make illegal, - and, where appropriate, to pursue in the EU - abuses originating in the EU which have their impact on the partners.. It is reasonable to expect reciprocity, in the unlikely event that CEEC firms would be able to act unfairly in the EU. To make such a policy work, however, would require not merely an agreement to make export cartels etc illegal but also an undertaking to enforce. The Europe Agreements provide for "positive comity", which means that CEEC and EU competition authorities agree to take into account the impact of their actions in the other region, but this falls short of an obligation on the EU's side to prevent restrictive practices by EU-based firms that have harmful effects in the CEEC markets.

7.5 Competition rules and free trade

Clearly, one aim of the full harmonisation of competition law is to replace trade regulations by competition measures, as discussed in the work of Marceau (1994) and Hoekman and Mavroidis (1995). But it is hard to see that this is entirely feasible for the EU-CEEC relationship until the CEECs have adopted the full internal market *acquis*. Indeed, the absolute guarantee of mutual access can really only exist within the EU, where in response to market closure EU law offers scope for enforcing opening rather than allowing retaliation.

The strategy of harmonisation of competition laws between the EU and CEECs must surely be welcomed at the broadest level. It is likely to make eventual membership easier and in the meantime it will facilitate the economic integration process. Harmonisation of competition policy is a necessary condition for the replacement of commercial instruments by competition rules, though it seems very unlikely that in this case the policy alignment will be enough by itself to make this possible.

The Commission has gone as far as it can in offering a political commitment to curtail the use of anti-dumping, but EU businessmen consider this a violation of their rights under the legislation as it stands. Indeed, until the EU makes a formal political commitment more binding than those contained in the declarations cited at the start of this paper, there cannot be a binding commitment to the cessation of all use of anti-dumping measures. In fact, since 1991 there has been a sign of curtailment of anti-dumping action, although steel and chemicals continue to pose problems. There is no indication of a reduction in the number of anti-dumping complaints between 1991 and 1995. By the end of 1995, there were fewer measures in force than two years before against the CEECs in general, with Poland having the same number of measures as in 1993.

The amount of trade directly affected is very small. It is estimated by Commission sources at under 0.5% of all imports from the countries concerned in 1995. The figure, of course, represents a higher pecentage of the total exports of the CEECs but a lower percentage still of related EU output. The protection given to EU producers is thus minimal in comparison to the salience of the instrument and the uncertainties that may be created for CEEC exporters by the possibility of its use.[3] It is not that the EU deserves criticism for using anti-dumping policy on a massive scale. On the contrary, the small extent of the measures indicates that the overall impact on the EU of renouncing the use of measures would be very limited indeed.

Rollo and Smith have argued that the prospective adjustment problems that could be created by likely growth of EU imports from CEEC partners is modest relative to other shocks that the EU economy and its sensitive sectors have absorbed. At the same time, as they point out, the main economic interest of the EU economy as a whole from a mercantilist point of view lies in its exports to the region. The CEECs have begun to run current account deficits again. With the EU as the main trading partner still in recession, it is in the EU's macro-economic interest to ensure continuation of growth among its neighbours. Any increase in imports from them is likely to be recycled back to the EU as additional export demand. At a micro-economic level, additional low cost imports from its partners improve living standards and, by lowering the cost of living, ease wage pressure on business in general and hence improve EU competitiveness in third markets.

There are protectionist pressures emanating from EU producer interests vis-a-vis the CEECs, some of which can be legally justified within the framework of anti-dumping rules. Such pressures will not be quelled simply by the harmonisation of competition rules. EU policy makers will have to make a political choice between a rapid integration of the CEECs and either overriding particular interests in the EU itself or else dealing with adjustment problems some other way. Economic theory suggests that the use of social and industrial policies in the EU are superior to trade instruments in dealing with any ensuing problems on the EU side, though these may be hard to apply.

The EU's pressure on its partners to adopt its own rules should not go beyond what is in their interest. This makes sense from a number of points of view. If they are to become members of the EU, it is best that they be in as healthy and contented a state as possible. If they are not guaranteed membership, there is no economic or political case for rule harmonisation beyond what is in the partners' own interest, apart from the mercantilist case which is flawed.

The obligation to enforce EU competition policy rules in the partner countries places them in an asymmetrical situation which is acceptable as long as these rules

---

[3] Clearly the uncertainty created by residual non-commercial behaviour by CEEC exporters is a counter balancing factor. However, it can be argued that EU firms are better placed to predict and resist the behaviour of CEEC enterprises than the latter are to predict the policy of the EU and that it is efficient to minimise that risk.

are desired for their own sakes in the sense that their credible application will generate efficiency gains for the partner countries. But if the EU's monitoring takes the form of vigilantly pursuing the rights of EU producers in these markets, whilst leaving the local authorities to pursue any malpractices by EU firms in those markets, the benefits will be one-sided.

There is a risk of a Catch-22 situation. If the EU does not unilaterally dismantle its commercial instruments, the CEEC partners may find it difficult to apply EU rules, especially with respect to state aids, since the ability to allow superseded activities to shut down very much rests on the ability to increase exports wherever there is scope. On the other hand, if access to EU markets has been made conditional on rapid harmonisation this may be problematic.

7.6 The Prospect of accession

The adoption of common competition laws is clearly related to accession. The problem is that the link is not made explicit. It seems very likely that an extremely long transition period will be needed for membership. Richard Baldwin has argued that membership of the EU is not imaginable for the foreseeable future. He suggests gradual alignment of policies and a form of European Economic Area. There is a lot to be said for this idea, but it has disadvantages. It does not overcome the Catch-22. Some adjustments will not be possible until absolutely guaranteed access to EU markets can be promised; this cannot be ensured without full membership and full membership cannot be guaranteed without all structural adjustments. The problem is that guarantees given by the EU to non-members are not normally legally enforceable in European Courts. Nor are guarantees given by partner countries. Thus, it is hard to see the industrial interests in the EU accepting that the EU adapt its own internal legislation to rule out anti-dumping or safeguard measures until there is an absolute legally-enforceable guarantee of no "unfairness" on the other side! The actual EEA waiting room required the members unilaterally to accept all EU rules with no political voice. It did not prove a sustainable situation.

An alternative scenario can be envisaged, however, in which legal membership of the EU takes place quite soon, not when the structural adaptation (including the full implementation of competition law) has occurred, but when it is possible to be sure that it *can* be completed within say 15 years. EU membership with the appointment of Commissioners and MEPs etc starts at the beginning, not the end of such a transition period. During this time, laws need not be wholly harmonised and anti-dumping proceedings can be brought against the new members (as happened during the Spanish transition). There is a big difference between this situation and that of the current Europe Agreements: any disputes over market access would be between member states of the Union. The Court of Justice (on which new member states would have representation) would be obliged to settle such disputes in a judicially fair manner. It would also make the enforcement of such harmonisation obligations that the CEEC partners undertake much easier legally and politically. The market access that could be offered during such a transition might even initially be less in a fully-fledged EEA style operation, but the guarantees would carry greater legal certainty that would both serve politically and offer the security that business needs for investment. As far as competition rules are concerned, there could of course be no going back on what has been agreed in the Europe Agreements: it is merely a question of how tightly the obligation to "approximate" laws is to be read.

7.7 Summary and conclusions

Adoption of EU competition rules by the CEECs is desirable for its own sake and as part of the process by which they become part of the EU. Fortunately, the CEEC partners have enthusiastically adopted the EU framework for their own sakes. But the argument of this paper is that close harmonisation of competition law should be seen as part of the accession process rather than as a condition for improved market access during a pre-accession phase. If the CEECs are to become EU member states it is in the EU's economic as well as political interest to allow them to do whatever is best suited to their economic development in the meantime and to allow maximum market access that is not conditional on fine details of legal harmonisation.

Approximation of competition laws and free market access between EU and the CEECs are both highly desirable goals but need to be considered in their own right. Even the total harmonisation of competition law will not remove the scope for other economic asymmetries that anti-dumping laws are intended to compensate for. Institutional and market conditions in the CEECs will inevitably be different from the rest of the EU for some time to come. An early commitment to membership with a long post-accession transition period would seem to be the best way to realise the political commitment that EU leaders have hinted at. Some form of EEA-type regime in industrial products as an intermediate step would be unattractive to the partner countries. It would deny them access for agriculture and to the budget. It would also require the CEECs to cede sovereignty in a wholly asymmetric manner. For example, it would give DGIV a final say on certain competition issue, and the CEECs would also have to apply EU law internally, while having no say in it. It may be that some CEEC governments would accept such an arrangement if accession were certain. However, such a political commitment cannot be made definite. There has been a tendency, above all in the UK, to underestimate the extent to which mutual free trade requires complex legal and political underpinnings.

References

Baldwin, R.(1994), "Towards an Integrated European Economy", CEPR, London.

EBRD (1994), Transition Report.

European Commission, (1995), "White Paper on the Preparation of the Associated Countries of Central and Eastern Europe for Integration into the Internal Market of the Union", Brussels, Com (95) 163..

European Commission (1995a), "Proceedings of Conference on Competition Policy", Visegrad 19-21 June 1995, organised by European Commission and Hungarian Office of Economic Cooperation, unpublished.

Fingleton, J., Fox E., Neven, D. and Seabright, P., (1996), "Competition Policy in Transition Economies", CEPR, London.

Frazer, T. and Holmes P (1995), "Self-Restraint: Cars Complaints and the Commission", European Public Law, 1995, Vol.1, No.1, pp.85-95.

Hawk, B.(1987), America's "Anti-trust revolution Lessons for Europe", European Competition Law Review.

Hoekman, B and Mavroidis, P.(1995), "Linking Trade and competition policy in Central and Eastern Europe", pp. 111-154 in: L.A. Winters (ed.), "Foundations of an Open Economy", CEPR, London.

International Anti-trust Code Working Group (1993), "Draft International Anti-Trust Code", Anti-Trust and Trade Regulation Report, August 19, 1993.

Marceau, G. (1994), "Antitrust and Anti-dumping in Free Trade Areas", OUP.

Marchipont, J-F (1994), "La stratégie industrielle de l'union Européenne pendant et après l'achèvement du marché unique", doctoral dissertation, University of Nancy, II, publication forthcoming.

Messerlin P. (1989),"Anti-dumping regulations or pro-trust laws, the EC chemical cases", World Bank.

Rollo J and Smith A.(1993), "The political economy of E.European trade with the EC: why so sensitive?" Economic Policy, No.16, April 1993, pp 140-166.

Scherer, F.M. (1994), "Competition Policies for an Integrated World Economy," Brookings Institution,.Washington DC.

Thurow, L. (1992), "Head to Head", N.Brealey.

Vigier, P. (1992), "La politique communautaire de l'automobile", Revue du Marché Unique Européen **3** and **4**, 71-113 and 73-126.

Viisi, F. (1996), "The Role of National Competition Laws". Paper presented to Workshop on the Implementation of Antitrust Rules in a Federal Context, EUI Florence, April 1996.

Wang Z.K. and Winters L.A. (1993), "EC Imports from E.Europe: Iron and Steel", EBRD.

8 The Operation of the Internal Market and Approximation to Internal Market Legislation by CEECs

Alexander Spachis[1]
European Commission
DG XV Internal Market and Financial Services
200, Rue de la Loi
1049 Brussels, BELGIUM

Summary

The consolidation and development of the single market are at the heart of the activities of the Community and are major priorities for the Commission. The Single Market, created to promote the competitiveness of European business and therefore the well-being of the citizens of the Union, remains a top priority for the Union. This has of course important implications for the Central and Eastern European countries (CEECs).

In this context, this paper provides background information on the key characteristics of the operation of the single market, explains its importance and describes how the dismantling of barriers was handled. It refers, in particular, to the 1992 single market programme as set out in the 1985 White Paper, constituting the most ambitious and comprehensive supply-side programme ever launched. It then gives some preliminary but clear evidence on the question - "has the single market made any difference ?". It continues by discussing issues of implementation of the single market legislation. It focuses on the enforcement of single market legislation and in particular on administrative co-operation and sanctions. The ensuing discussion on improving the business environment contains references to direct taxation, to information for SMEs and to the Economic and Monetary Union. A brief account of the Single Market Review explains what is the nature and coverage of the first ever exhaustive survey of the impact and effectiveness of the single market measures. Then, the paper goes on to explain that one of the major priorities for the future is the preparation for the integration of Central and Eastern European countries into the single market. It refers, in particular, to the approxi-

[1] I wish to acknowledge the contributions of my colleagues in preparing this material, in particular Mr. A. Dempsey, Mr. N. Bohan, Mrs. L. Cafolla and Ms. J. Hughes for assistance.

mation of single market legislation, to the cornerstone of the accession strategy, to the relevant White Paper of the Commission and to the follow-up. It concludes with some preliminary ideas related to the economic impact of enlargement for discussion.

8.1 The 1992 single market programme

Before giving a preliminary account of the current state of the single market - an account which can only be fleshed out when the Commission has completed the major survey which will be discussed later - the following are the key reasons for undertaking this still unfinished work.

In the mid-1980s, Community business demanded effective action to remove unnecessary and costly non-tariff barriers to intra-Community trade, which it rightly perceived as a threat to the ability of Community firms to withstand world-wide competition. It was not simply a question of increasing the size of the domestic market: rather, the consequence of market fragmentation was that business had been too sheltered from competition from outside its national frontiers, and this had blunted its instinct to develop competitive advantages capable of withstanding international competition. Internal Market integration was perceived as a means of compelling operators to deliver better and/or cheaper products. Greater cross-border competition would serve as a stimulus for a virtuous circle of increased demand, followed by expansion of output, investment and employment.

The programme set out in the 1985 White Paper on the internal market was not, however, a blueprint for the total harmonisation of legislation on goods and services across the Community. It was a limited programme with a limited, but strategic, objective. With the benefit of the experience of the first thirty years of integration, the White Paper set out a workmanlike checklist of some 282 harmonising measures that would be needed to eliminate the legal barriers to a single market by the end of 1992. Relying as far as possible on the principle of mutual recognition developed by the Court of Justice on the basis of the Treaty and proposing harmonisation only where this basic principle could not by itself guarantee free movement, the "1992" programme set out to create, in the now familiar words of Article 7a of the Treaty, *"an area without internal frontiers in which the free movement of goods, persons, services and capital is ensured"*.

The Community institutions have by and large delivered on the package of legislation designed to bring about the single market, although there remains a "hard core" of proposals, some of them very important to European business in the single market, on which the Council has failed to reach agreement. These include the proposal for a European Company Statute, which would greatly facilitate cross-border operations, and proposals on company taxation designed to ensure that companies are not penalised for cross-border activities by double taxation.

It is important to underline, however, that the removal of legal barriers to market entry does not, in itself, create a single market. There is much more to be done, and not just by lawmakers, before a single market in which business treats the entire territory of the Union in the same way as a "national" market can become a reality. In other words, we are not at the end of the road, although one could suggest that we are well on our way.

8.2 Has the single market made a difference?

The big question is not, of course, whether the legislative programme has been adopted but whether it is actually enabling business and consumers to benefit from a true single market. So far, the evidence is incomplete. In the two annual reports it has published on the single market, the Commission has given its assessment, based on the information available. There is preliminary but clear evidence that certain benefits of the single market are feeding through to economic operators. Thus, the elimination of border controls for goods has considerably improved the efficiency of transport services and reduced costs and delivery times for the distribution of goods within the Community. Many companies are winning new public procurement contracts, although delays in transposition and inadequate enforcement of the legislation by the Member States are still causing major difficulties. Most companies trading across frontiers find the current system for value-added tax has brought them considerable savings. Smaller firms have, however, found that the system imposed extra accounting costs at its introduction. Finally, the operation of mutual recognition in the field of the professions is not giving rise to many complaints, although some individual problems can be difficult to resolve.

8.3 Implementation of single market legislation

The Commission has not, in its assessments, tried to conceal the fact there are still problems and that, to some extent, Member States still have to deliver on their commitments. Delays in transposing directives into national law in some fields make it difficult for business to gain the advantages intended by Community legislation, although the overall performance is now good - over 92% of the required legislation is now in place taking the Union as a whole. Delays are particularly evident in a number of areas such as public procurement, intellectual property, advanced technologies and services and general product safety.

Prompt and proper implementation of single market rules is essential for the credibility of the whole exercise in the eyes of citizens and business. Citizens can easily lose faith in the Community if they see that in some Member States their rights under single market rules are not respected. Businesses need to know where they stand in relation to single market rules in every Member State. In other words there should be a "level playing-field" throughout the Union. According to the data referring to early March 1995, the overall level of transposition has now reached 93% (this relates to the EU of twelve, the figures for the new Member States are still being assembled). The ranking of the Member States has changed: Denmark is leading (99,1%), followed by Sweden (96,8%), Luxembourg (96,4%) and the Netherlands (95,5%). The two last places are still occupied by Finland (86%) and Austria (80,5%). Moreover, the level of implementation continues to vary considerably from one sector to another with lower than average levels of implementation in the areas of public procurement (79%), company law (80%) and new technologies (80%). Given the economic importance of these areas, these percentages are also a cause for concern.

The Commission pursues failures to implement legislation on time through formal infringement procedures, while also consulting with the Member States concerned. It is also devoting as much attention as possible, within the limits of the resources available, to examining the quality of the transposition legislation notified by the Member States so as to ensure its conformity with Community law. Again, where this legislation fails to meet Community requirements, the Commission adopts a two-pronged approach based on consultations and infringement procedures.

Paradoxically, there are some areas - such as company law, for example - in which the zeal of Member States in the task of transposition has led them to add detailed requirements not called for by the Community directives. No doubt, in some quarters, the resulting burdens are blamed on the infamous "Brussels bureaucracy"!

One should note here that there are still many areas of legislation for which Member States are solely responsible and which represent a burden for business in that they may well constitute a particular impediment for small and medium-sized enterprises trying to enter their markets from another Member State. If this perception is borne out by the review the Commission is now undertaking, it may well be necessary to set about eliminating unnecessary red tape within each country in the interests of all.

8.4 Enforcement of single market legislation

Proper enforcement of common rules across the entire Single Market is already perceived by many as a major priority. This is likely to be confirmed as a major area for action in the future. It will surely include action related to creating/improving *administrative cooperation*. The importance of such cooperation will be understood by the discussion below:

The quality of implementation and enforcement is not as even as one would wish. Another area of difficulty is the persistence of technical barriers to trade. Often, these are the result of the failure of national authorities to apply the principle of mutual recognition in areas that have not been harmonised at Community level. Problems have been noted particularly with regard to road vehicles, foodstuffs and pharmaceuticals. It can also be difficult for individuals and businesses to obtain redress when they experience difficulties in their internal market operations.

Responsibility for the enforcement of Community law lies with the Member States. But in an internal market without internal frontiers it is clear that effective enforcement of Community law becomes a common concern which calls for greater openness and greater co-operation between the Member States. This is a new challenge for the Community.

Some useful steps have already been taken. In its Resolution of 16 June 1995 on development of administrative co-operation in the implementation and enforcement of Community legislation in the Internal Market, the Council agreed that action was necessary "to increase mutual confidence and transparency between administrations and thereby ensure that Community legislation is enforced effectively, efficiently and uniformly in all Member States".

Since then, three types of action have been conducted by the Commission in close co-operation with the Member States : The first has been to set up and make known named "contact points" so that Member States' administrations can contact each other and the Commission's services in relation to enforcing the Single Market legislation in accordance with the 1994 Council resolution[2] . The second is to pursue the current programme of sectoral discussions with representatives of the Member States to identify needs for administrative co-operation in different areas of legislation. Discussions have been held in committees and groups covering most of the priority areas identified in the Council Resolution, and the intention is for these to be extended to cover the rest as soon as possible. The third action is the further development of Community-level support measures, including exchange programmes for national officials (such as the Karolus and Matthaeus exchange programmes and similar schemes in the area of veterinary control and

[2] Council Resolution of 8th July 1996 on co-operation between administrations for the enforcement of legislation on the Internal Market (96/C224/02)

good laboratory practice), seminars (such as those recently organised for "new approach" testing and certification bodies and motor vehicle type approval bodies) and the compilation of interpretative guides to Community Legislation (such as the recent guide to "new approach" directives). Finally, one should also mention the proposed notification procedure for national measures derogating from the principle of free movement of goods as another potential support measure for correct enforcement[3].

In addition to an enhanced administration cooperation, *sanctions* for infringements of single market legislation present a growing challenge and are being given greater attention at political level.

At the informal meeting of the Internal Market Council in Biarritz, in March 1995, the Commission had the opportunity to discuss with ministers the question of the sanctions which apply to infringements of Community law, which was the subject of a memorandum by the French Presidency of the Council.

The Commission believes, with the Court of Justice, that among the indispensable conditions for effective implementation of Community law must be included the existence of effective, proportionate and dissuasive sanctions for any infringement of Community law.

Significant variations in the treatment of *infringements* between one Member State and another will not only distort competition in the market place but will also undermine the Community's commitment to high standards of protection in the areas of public health and safety, the environment and consumer affairs that are at the centre of EU law. Community law must be seen to be applied strictly but fairly everywhere. In this respect, the Commission is in the process of considering a number of ideas on how to take the political discussions forward. Without wishing to prejudice discussions that must still take place in the Commission, I would like to refer to some of the issues. To begin with, one should distinguish carefully between two issues, namely transparency and harmonisation. Transparency is absolutely necessary. Not only would it be desirable to provide for clear obligations in future Community legislation concerning the putting into place and notification of sanctions by the Member States; it would also be useful to obtain more transparency about sanctions already in place in respect of existing internal market legislation, at least in a few important areas.

As for harmonisation, one should be prudent. Although examples can be found in Community legislation of specific provisions relating to sanctions for infringements, these cases are relatively rare. One should look very carefully at the particular circumstances before extending this approach, although of course it cannot be excluded in cases where serious disparities in national sanctions are identified.

In conclusion, the growing challenge of enforcement will require an innovative approach, which will possibly have to include other actions, in addition to the

---

[3] A recent report on enforcement and administrative co-operation examines developments in each sector, as well as identifying areas in which more progress is needed.

above. No doubt the results of the Single Market Review, expected at the end of 1996, will pinpoint the way forward.

8.5 Improving the business environment

While the phase of major legislative effort with regard to the single market is over, the Community cannot limit itself to ensuring the effective operation of the existing framework. Indeed, some important elements of that framework are still missing. However, there are gaps in Community law which inhibit the development of a truly single market. These include the problem of the free movement of people. The fact that border controls on people remain in place is a matter of regret and certainly damages the individual citizen's perception of the single market. The Commission attaches great importance to this issue and is determined to make progress. In addition, the lack of liberalisation in the energy and telecommunications sectors and the lack of common solutions to the problems of company taxation and company law are also important gaps in the single market framework.

As regards *direct taxation*, the main priority is the elimination of double taxation on cross-border activities. Progress in this area is difficult, resulting in delays in the adoption of proposals and even in the withdrawal, in 1994, of the proposal on the taxation of royalties and interest payments. On this point, we have to find an alternative solution, since the problem which the original proposal had sought to resolve will not go away.

It should be emphasised, however, that apart from those limited areas where harmonisation of direct taxation is needed, the Commission's approach is one of pragmatism and co-operation with Member States in the search for practical solutions to problems.

A number of initiatives have been launched to stimulate debate on the tax environment of SMEs, which are hindered in their efforts to take full advantage of the single market by being more heavily taxed, in some cases, and by having to bear disproportionate costs when they operate across borders. In parallel with its communication of May 1994 on the improvement of the fiscal environment for SMEs, the Commission adopted a recommendation inviting Member States to correct the deterrent effects of progressive rates of income tax payable by sole proprietorships and partnerships on reinvested profits and to eliminate tax obstacles to changes in the legal form of enterprises. A separate communication, published in July 1995, dealt with the legal and fiscal framework regulating the transfer of businesses, since small enterprises are often faced with serious financial consequences when an owner dies.

Another issue considered by the Commission is *information for SMEs*, which sometimes feel uneasy rather than stimulated by the challenges of the competitive environment created by the internal market. This is partially due to a lack of appropriate information on how the internal market works and, therefore, on how to behave in order to handle this new market environment. Individual Member States are the natural interlocutor of their national business community, including SMEs. However, the Commission also has a role and has taken a number of initiatives in these areas. Specifically, it has made special efforts since 1994 to develop a dialogue with citizens and business in order to boost their awareness of how the single market is working in practice and to canvass their own experiences in this field, by organising "Internal Market Weeks" in all Member States. On the basis of a small but illustrative sample of 140 companies interviewed by local Euro-Info Centres in the 12 Member States, it appears that smaller companies have started to market their products in other Member States thanks to the greater trading opportunities offered by the single market programme. However, the enterprises that are already benefiting from the single market are those who anticipated the changing market environment and systematically developed a European business strategy. EU enterprises need to realise that success in the single market will not come automatically.

One of the major problems for enterprises, in particular for SMEs, is knowing where to turn when problems occur. In the Commission's experience, enterprises prefer having a contact point in their home administration rather than having to turn directly to the Commission. The Council has already called upon Member States to establish contact points[4] .. One approach to this is the "single market compliance units" which already exist in some Member States. These units could be backed up by the network of sectoral contact points between the Commission and Member States' administrations that is being built up in the framework of administrative co-operation. As a matter of principle, the Commission tries to associate enterprises with the preparation and evaluation of Community provisions as extensively as possible in order to make sure that their interests are taken into account. Thus, the 1995 working programme of the Commission provided a clear signal for the widest possible consultation of all interested parties. A major step in this direction was the intention announced by the Commission to present more Green and White Papers in comparison with legislative proposals. As an example, in 1995 the intention was to present 67 Green and White papers and 81 legislative proposals. As a further step in this direction, the Commission services are examining ways to improve the procedure to be followed in the preparation of new Community legislation, including consultation of interested parties and the evaluation of the economic impact of the legislation. Finally, as a longer term exercise, the Commission intends, as a first step, to examine the legislation governing the establishment and start-up period of new enterprises.

The absence of *economic and monetary union* is probably the single most important limitation on the efficiency of a single market, particularly for smaller

---

4 Council Resolution of 10th October 1994 on SMEs and 21st November 1994 on strengthening the competitiveness of Community industry.

businesses. Indeed, the most important major step which still has to be taken to consolidate the single market is progress towards economic and monetary union. It is encouraging to see the commitment of many governments, often in the face of a difficult domestic political climate, to maintaining the pace of adaptation needed for economic and monetary union. This shows an awareness of the need to bring to an end the difficulties of operating a single market in the context of exchange rate fluctuations. Currency appreciation is generally an indication of an increase in underlying competitiveness rather than the opposite, but one can understand that fears of protectionist reactions by Member States in the medium term may weaken confidence in the single market.

Eliminating the problems of exchange rate instability will increase trade within the Union both by doing away with the uncertainty that may make firms reluctant to engage in cross-border trade and by eliminating transaction costs or the cost of hedging against currency risk. This will enhance the benefits already expected from the single market through cost savings and the restructuring of production. Business is clear about the need for a single currency, which will also make the single market a more manifest reality in the everyday lives of Union citizens.

8.6 Single Market Review 1996: The impact and effectiveness of internal market measures

The Community institutions were conscious from the outset of the need to monitor the operation of the single market and assess its impact. The Commission is currently working on gathering solid evidence on the effects of the single market, based on the first exhaustive survey of its economic impact and effectiveness conducted since 1994, with results to be published in the fourth quarter of 1996[5]. The detailed account of the Commission's findings will be based on an extensive information-gathering exercise. This comprises 38 studies and an extensive survey of business opinion, as described briefly below:

19 studies of manufacturing and services sectors: each aims to determine whether the Single Market measures under review have led to the disappearance of barriers to free circulation and identify any remaining obstacles to cross-border transactions;

six 'barrier' studies: each aims to assess progress in dismantling the most important non-tariff barriers (technical barriers, public procurement, customs and fiscal formalities, industrial property protection, currency management and capital market liberalization);

[5] Council of Ministers Resolution (1218/92).

the economic impact of removing barriers is examined in a further 13 studies, which deal inter alia with trade and investment flows, price convergence, competition and competitiveness, employment and labour markets, and economic cohesion;

a major *survey* of the awareness, attitudes and reactions to the Single Market programme at company level is coordinated by the Statistical Office of the European Communities (Eurostat), based on replies from 13 000 enterprises in 12 Member States; it asks a representative sample of firms with more than five employees in the services sector and more that 20 employees in the manufacturing sector (24 000 in all) to rate the success of the Single Market Programme and its impact on their strategies and operations.

Other sources of evidence about the effectiveness of Single Market legislative measures are also being considered, including independent studies or surveys carried out in Member States.

The results of this research will be published[6] and will feed extensive debate and consultation of all those interested in the single market. This will allow the Union to assess the extent of problems and to identify others which have not yet been the focus of attention.

The objective of this impact assessment is not to prepare yet another series of reports to provide material for publications and then put it on the shelf. The results are intended to provide a firm basis on which to develop an EU Action Plan for strengthening and developing the single market and reinforcing European business competitiveness.

So, one may well ask, will the Commission use the results as a basis for a new "1992" programme, perhaps to be called, with great imagination, to coincide with EMU, the "2002" programme and comprising yet another 300 or so legislative proposals? The answer is "no!" Contrary to reports in some quarters, the Commission is not interested in red tape. Single market legislation is about replacing 15 sets of national rules with a single one. The big legislative push is now over. The Commission's future action will be based on the approach similar to that adopted under the present Strategic Programme: acting to ensure that the existing legal framework works in practice and legislating only to the degree necessary to fill important gaps and to adapt to changing realities. Where a non-legislative solution provides an adequate response to a single market problem, that is the option to choose; if a possible solution would hamper business more than is necessary, that is a solution to reject.

---

6 The findings as well as the full background research, including the 38 individual studies and the business survey, will be published by the Office for Official Publications of the European Communities in late 1996 and early 1997.

8.7 A priority for the future: preparation for the integration of Central and Eastern European Countries (CEECs) into the single market

This is one of the key challenges facing the European Union as we look ahead towards the single market of the 21st century.

The European Council, at its meeting in Essen in December 1994, invited the Commission to prepare a White Paper on the preparation of the countries of Central and Eastern Europe for integration into the Internal Market. It should be emphasised that the White Paper was conceived as one element in the *pre-accession strategy* for these countries. It forms no part of accession negotiations as such: it is a contribution from the Commission to the preparation of the CEECs for eventual accession negotiations. Progress towards the objectives of *approximation to Internal Market Legislation* by CEECs set out in the White Paper will carry no automatic rewards in terms of market access.

The White Paper contains recommendations about which measures should be tackled first and describes the administrative and organisational structures which should be put in place to make the legal framework work properly. It is intended to guide the CEECs in the complexities of EC internal market legislation and its functioning and to help them align themselves with the Member States of the Union as fast as possible and at the lowest cost.

To this aim, the Commission and the Member States[7] committed themselves to give "all appropriate assistance" to the CEECs. The Commission will help them to establish or modify their national programmes for approximation in the light of the White Paper, to conduct their work, to reinforce their structures, etc. There is also a provision for a new technical assistance office, which will serve as a "one-stop shop" to help with specific problems or general information demands concerning the integration in the internal market.

The White Paper is also a reference document for all who are interested in the functioning of the internal market (academics, students, business chiefs, public, administration, law firms, etc.) in the Member States, giving a global overview of the internal market legislation, its objectives and its functioning.

The Commission makes no secret in its *White Paper,* which is *the cornerstone of the accession strategy* that, although the CEECs have already made a serious effort to approximate their legislation, the task before them is nevertheless a far-reaching and complex one. It also signals that, although the White Paper forms part of the pre-accession strategy adopted at the Essen European Council last December, the completion of the approximation will not automatically open the EU door to them. The acceptance of the "acquis communautaire" as a whole is the

[7] The European Council gave its support to the White Paper at the Cannes Summit on 26 & 27th June 1995.

pre-condition for accession. Consequently, the CEECs' enthusiasm fired by the future prospects of accession could be dampened and their will to bring about the key changes identified in the White Paper weakened. In this respect, the White Paper delivers two messages: first, that although the alignment with the internal market will not automatically lead to the opening of accession negotiations, the Commission will nevertheless take into account the progress made by the CEECs in the light of the White Paper when considering its opinion on a request for the opening of accession negotiations; second, that the approximation work will give concrete advantages to the CEECs long before accession. Alignment with the internal market is expected to reinforce economic reform and industrial restructuring within the associated countries and to stimulate trade. The progressive elimination of barriers will increase competitiveness and encourage the growth of economic activity and investor confidence.

The approach and structure of the White Paper reflects that audience it is addressed to and its objectives. It is addressed to the six countries of Central and Eastern Europe which already have association agreements with the European Union (Poland, Hungary, the Czech Republic, Slovakia, Bulgaria and Romania) and to those with whom agreements will also be concluded soon (Estonia, Latvia, Lithuania and Slovenia). Its usefulness for the CEECs is threefold: it describes the internal market legislation as a whole (as well as legislation in the fields of competition and social and environmental policy which are essential to the functioning of the internal market) and identifies the key measures which should be tackled first; it describes in detail the administrative and technical structures which are needed to ensure that legislation is effectively implemented and enforced; it outlines the way in which technical assistance from the Union can be adapted and enhanced to provide the best possible support to the CEECs' efforts.

Although every piece of Community legislation is important in principle, the Commission considers that it is appropriate in the pre-accession phase to propose a sequence in which the CEECs could take in legislating for each major area. Resources for the approximation exercise are limited in both the Community and the CEECs, whether in terms of legal or technical expertise, parliamentary time or the availability of training. These resources should be focused on areas where they have the greatest impact. The Commission has, therefore, presented the legislation for each area (23 sectors) in a way that distinguishes "key measures" from the total number of measures applicable and then proposes a further breakdown of key measures into two stages. The division into Stage I and Stage II measures shows the indicative priorities which emerge from the logic of the legislation itself and provides a guide to the CEECs for the most effective sequencing of their work schedules for the approximation, implementation and enforcement of legislation.

For each sector, the White Paper gives a general overview of the legislation, describes the conditions necessary to operate the legislation and identifies the key measures to be adopted at Stage I and Stage II.

The main challenge for the associated countries in taking over internal market legislation lies not in the approximation of their legal texts but in adapting their structures (administrative machinery, judicial system and private sector) to the conditions necessary to make the legislation work. The White Paper emphasises the importance of these structures without which the alignment exercise will remain purely theoretical. The presence of the necessary enforcing authorities is crucial in order to create certainty to the members of the Community that legislation is properly implemented. The White Paper describes the relevant structures which are necessary at national (or international) level for each sector. The proper operation of these administrative, judicial or private sector structures, in turn, depends on training and education facilities for the personnel concerned.

In parallel, CEECs will have to launch information campaigns so that public opinion and businesses can understand and come to endorse the functioning of these new structures. In the public procurement area, for example, markets are not being opened in practice, despite the basic legislation being put in place, because firms have not yet accepted that they have a genuine chance of winning contracts or, alternatively, old monopolies have not yet accepted that they may lose contracts. In both cases, they fail to enter bids. Similarly, although consumer legislation has begun to be put in place, it tends to remain a dead letter where consumers do not understand their rights and/or the mechanisms do not exist for exercising them.

The publication of the White Paper is the beginning rather than the end of the story. *The follow-up to the White Paper includes the reinforcement of dialogue with the CEECs, of technical assistance and of co-operation with Member States.*

The Commission organises bilateral meetings with the CEEC countries which request help for the establishment of their national approximation programmes taking account of the recommendations of the White Paper. The CEECs receive the assistance of Commission experts who visit them to discuss the priorities sector by sector and help them in the choice and the adaptation of their national approximation programmes.

The European Union has committed itself to enhancing and adapting its technical assistance response to the challenge of preparing the CEECs for integration into the internal market. For that purpose, the Commission has decided to set up a new technical assistance information exchange office managed by itself and financially supported by a multi-country PHARE programme. Such assistance will come from the Commission, the Member States and private bodies.

Technical assistance from the PHARE programme, enhanced and better co-ordinated, will continue to be delivered. The amounts of financial co-operation as confirmed by the Cannes Summit are 6,693 million ECU over 5 years (1995-1999).

As to the cooperation with Member States, committed themselves at the Cannes Summit to enhancing the co-ordination of their technical assistance to the CEECs in order to avoid overlapping and to improve the effectiveness of their actions on the ground.

8.8 Some preliminary ideas for discussion

The nature and pattern of the EU's economic relations with the CEECs gives a first impression of the likely impact of the enlargement of the internal market on the economic conditions of the existing Member States with respect to the level and composition of trade flows, services trade, capital market flows and labour market integration. Studies have been already been carried out which attempt to furnish such an outlook[8] . It is extremely difficult to predict the evolution of economic relations between the EU and the CEECs in the pre-accession period. Production and consumption patterns in these countries are in such a state of transition that forecasts based on extrapolation of existing trends are completely unreliable. Already, expectations that CEECs would engage primarily in trade of primary and low value-added manufactures have been confounded. Exports of "sensitive" products account for a diminishing share of CEEC exports to the EU (with the exception of textiles), while exports of more sophisticated manufactures and processed goods are increasing (mechanical and electrical engineering products).

Nevertheless, the following broad conclusions seem to be widely accepted: first, that trade flows are to increase progressively but substantially and stabilise at levels 4-6 times higher than current levels; second, that this is likely to involve a shift away from traditional industries in the CEECs and an increase in production of more sophisticated manufactures which are relatively labour-intensive. This will enable the CEECs to exploit perceived competitive advantages resulting from the existence of a labour force which combines low-cost with high skills; third, that while increased investment from the EU and other sources has been noted, it appears that most of this investment is intended to serve the expanding domestic markets of the CEECs rather than involving a relocation of existing EC production to these countries. At this stage it is perhaps premature to draw conclusions about how investment patterns are likely to develop, but it would appear that, as the two trading zones become increasingly interlinked, investment in the CEECs may substitute for investment in the EU, a development which may happen even without accession. Portfolio capital flows from private sources have not received much attention and are probably marginal; and fourth, that the manner in which the CEECs succeed in developing and catching-up on EU income and production levels will vary from one country to another. On the basis of realistic assumptions concerning growth rates in the CEECs vis-à-vis those in the Member States[9] , it is

---

[8] A survey which builds on existing trade flows is the CEPR publication on the economics of enlargement ("Is Bigger Better?"). A more sophisticated equilibrium analysis, which takes account of demand and supply conditions and allows for different levels of competition, is contained in "European Economy", no. 6, 1994 (part C ch. 3).

[9] Assuming growth rates of 4% in the CEECs starting from a per capita GDP equal to 80% of that of Portugal. The latter is assumed to grow at 2% per annum.

possible that some of the richer CEECs will enjoy income levels equal to those of Greece and Portugal within a period of 10 years.

Given the absence of any clear picture about how economic relations between the EU and the CEECs are likely to develop, some preliminary thoughts are provided as a stimulus for discussion in relation to the four fundamental freedoms. With regard to free trade in goods, it might be thought that the availability of cheap labour might confer a competitive advantage on firms located in the CEECs. However, the pattern and level of trade is unlikely to differ greatly between full membership and 'association', given that restrictions on trade are likely to be phased out, whether or not the CEECs become full members. The intensity and composition of trade will continuously increase over the pre-accession period, as the CEECs prosper and exploit competitive advantages in the production of increasingly differentiated products and goods involving higher levels of value-added. At present, the product composition of exports from the Visegrad countries is closer in nature to the EU average than that of existing peripheral Member States. Furthermore, labour costs account for a relatively limited share of overall production costs and any wage cost advantage for the CEECs is likely to be offset by lower levels of productivity in these countries. Thus, it may be misleading to expect dramatic changes in trade flows, although certain sectors in one or other Member State may find themselves in direct price competition with producers from the CEECs.

Looking at *tradable services*, the first remark is that market integration in services often requires establishment of local outlets. In some services (e.g. retail banking), investment in networks may be so expensive as to discourage access (except through take-overs, once indigenous companies develop). Furthermore, their perceived present interests may not encourage CEECs to embark on such investments.

Regarding *capital movement*, the Europe Agreements establish an environment which is conducive to foreign direct investment, by recognising the right of establishment and providing for the gradual liberalisation of investment-related capital movements. Europe Agreements enshrine the principle of national treatment for EC investors, allow full repatriation of profits and allow for some forms of intellectual and industrial property protection. As a result, direct investment flows already occur (although concerns have been expressed in CEECs at the level of foreign ownership of productive assets). These are likely to continue, particularly if accession becomes a certainty. *Portfolio investment* (in CEEC stock and government paper) will be heavily influenced by macroeconomic stability and the depth of financial markets in these countries. In order to limit exchange rate fluctuations, the CEECs may retain capital controls in the pre-accession (and during the transitional?) periods. These controls may restrict the level of integration in financial services.

Finally, with respect to the *free movement of labour*, one should recall that the accession of countries with income levels significantly below those observed in the original Member States has not triggered significant labour movements. It is not expected that the situation would differ in the case of the CEECs.

Enlargement of the Union, and with it the single market, is envisaged for the future. The Central and Eastern European Countries will concentrate on adjusting their legislation from now on. This is no easy task, as the single market is already functioning. However, an early adoption of single market measures could help the acceding countries to quickly exploit the advantages after accession. How this will happen in practice will be strongly influenced by how much the CEECs will ensure not only a complete and coherent legal framework but also the institutions, structures and practices to work with.

9 Integration, Trade Policies, Factor Movements and the European Competitive Order: Problems of CEEC-Accession to the EU

Hans-Jürgen Vosgerau
Universität Konstanz
Universitätstrasse 10
Postfach 5560 D140
D-78434 KONSTANZ

Abstract

The aim of the Europe Agreements is to prepare the CEECs for eventual accession to the EU. At present, they are essentially confined to liberalization of commodity trade, although many barriers remain for sensitive products, and as a consequence, factor price equalization via trade is severely hindered. Immigration into the EU is still under national jurisdiction and practically excluded. The only remaining transmission channels - capital movements and technology transfers - suffer from insufficient financial markets and other unsolved transition problems in most CEECs.

This situation is analyzed in terms of an extended Heckscher-Ohlin model, allowing for transaction costs, which may be different for trade, migration, and capital movements.

9.1 Introduction

Economic relations between the CMEA members and the European Communities have quite a long history, but only since the events starting in 1989, which led to the complete breakdown of the Soviet Bloc central planning system, did they enter into the present stage of continuing rapprochement. Trade between the CEECs and the "West" has since increased considerably at the expense of trade with the Community of Independent States (CIS) i.e. the former Soviet Union. This was accomplished (and partly induced) by the establishment of increasingly closer relations between the EC (since 1993 the EU) and the CEECs with respect to economic but also political cooperation. A series of "Europe Agreements" have prepared the way and codified the first steps for à process of widening and deepening economic association between the EC (EU) and the three "Visegrad Countries" Poland. Czechoslovakia and Hungary. These were subsequently developed and in similar ways extended to other CEECs. The ultimate goal of this development is the eventual accession of these countries ço the EU within five, ten, fifteen or twenty years from now, depending on the performance of the different CEECs, the length of transition periods and the pace of the EU integration process itself.

These few introductory remarks are revealing the vast scope of change in the political, economic, security, institutional, etc. fields which is to be expected in coming years. We shall not try to cover this vast area of problems but concentrate primarily on two aspects: trade policy and the competitive order in Europe. These two issues are, we think, at the core of the process of economic integration. They are closely interconnected and combine economic aspects proper with legal-institutional ones. Competition policy, moreover, is crucial for both the transition and the integration process, as we shall demonstrate. The discussion will be centred on the Visearad countries (which since the separation of the Czech from the Slovak Republic have become four). However, it can be applied with some modifications to many other CEECs, especially Slovenia, the Baltic States and maybe Bulgaria and Romania.

Trade and competition policies in the Europe Agreements are almost completely confined to traditional trade in goods, or more exactly, physical commodities. The ultimate aim of integrating the CEECs into the EU, on the other hand, refers to a much wider field. especially free factor movements. Migration of labour, capital movements and technology transfers are closely related with goods trade.

The topic is of particular interest for future relations between the CEECs and the rest of Europe, not only because the ongoing experiment should allow us to considerably enrich, broaden and deepen our understanding of the complex interrelationships between trade in goods and services, labour migration, capital movements and technology transfer - which even theoretically are not quite clear - but also because of policy alternatives of considerable importance. Eventually, a (competitive) order will have to be established for factor movements, too.

Admittedly, all that can be done at present is to provide a framework for analysis, focusing on sketching the fundamental connections and asking the important questions which will have to be addressed later by more detailed theoretical and empirical analysis.

I shall start with (2) a short documentation of the present state of the Europe Agreements regarding trade and competition regulations and factor movements, develop (3) the fundamental connection between trade and competition policies in removing distortions in the course of increasing integration and proceed by discussing (4) some of the more important problems arising during the necessary structural adjustments. I shall then place these considerations about trade in goods and services into the wider context of factor movements, introducing (5) costs of trade and factor movements, confronting (6) the theory with available evidence and conclude with some general remarks (7).

9.2 The Europe Agreements

One can be very brief here, because the Europe Agreements are well documented and have been extensively commented on and discussed. In essence, they are a special kind of association agreements, special because they are not limited to the opening up of markets for trade as many others do which the EC (EU) has concluded with a multitude of countries. In addition, they contain provisions for political cooperation well beyond purely economic matters. Hence, the special formulation of "Europe Agreement".

The first Europe Agreements with Poland, Hungarv and Czechoslovakia were signed in December 1991. In order to bridge the gap until their ratification by all EC-members, so-called interim agreements were also concluded which went into force in the beginning of 1992. Meanwhile, additional Europe Agreements have been concluded with Bulgaria, Romania, Slovenia and the Baltic States. The original agreement with Czechoslovakia has been adapted to the Czech and Slovak Republics following their separation. Most or the agreements have meanwhile been ratified. On EU Council meetings in Copenhagen and Essen some of the provisions have been moved forward or speeded up.

The contents of the Europe Agreements relevant to the following discussion - - which are similar, but not identical - can be summarized as follows :

- asymmetric improvements of market access for most industrial products, i.e. removal of tariffs and quotas within two five-year transition periods. These will be quicker and more pronounced for CEEC access to EU-markets than vice versa
- continuing protection by the EU against CEEC-imports in the so-called sensitive sectors of steel, coal, textiles and clothing and agriculture
- maintenance of safeguard clauses such as antidumping by the EU
- preparations for an eventual extension of EU competition policy to the CEECs by strong recommendations to establish national competition legislation in these countries in order to support the transition process and eventual adaptation to the EU competitive order. This applies to the private as well as to the public sector, i.e. it concerns not only cartels, take-overs and misuse of market power but also subsidies, public enterprises. etc.

- provisions for the free movement of persons and enterprises are practically non-existent
- the same is true for capital movements, direct investments. etc.

When evaluating these agreements, one has to be cautious not to apply traditional free trade area reasoning too quickly, because in addition to the large endowment differences between the EU and the CEECs - which would of course in themselves strengthen the case for liberalization and mutual gains from trade - the CEECs - have to master a difficult process of transition from a centrally planned to a market economy with its own needs for restructuring. However, even if one argues that adjustment necessary for transition is almost indistinguishable from adjustment to a new trade environment, it remains true that the establishment of the legal, political and social framework with the necessary institutions for the functioning of a market economy takes considerable time, not to speak of the effort and costs, e.g. for the training of personnel, etc.

The importance attached by the EU to the establishment of competition legislation and the support offered for that purpose serves just this purpose. In this respect, considerable progress can be reported: in most CEECs, competition authorities are meanwhile well established and are functioning quite successfully (cf. Holmes [1995], Mavroidis [1993]). Whether national competition policy is able to cope with problems of årowing integration is another matter which will be taken up in the next paragraph.

9.3 Trade and Competition Policies: Their Role in Removing Distortions

The essence of economic integration is the removal of barriers to transactions between the integrating partners. These are traditional tariffs and duties, quantitative restrictions (quotas) and àl l kinds of non-tariff barriers (ntbs), which hinder or prevent not only trade in goods and services but also transborder capital movements, labour migration and technology transfers. In the EU, integration in this sense has been to a large extent completed by the EC-92-program in the beginning of 1993, so that in principle the four freedoms of unrestricted movement between member countries of goods and services, capital and people have been established - at least in principle, since many shortcomings and imperfections still remain.

In line with stated intentions and with theoretical expectations, this removal of barriers has induced a substantial expansion of trade and a restructuring of production. Regions with advantages have attracted those industries which can make best use of the available factor endowment. Economies of scale and scope could be exploited. Technical progress in transport has reduced the cost of bringing inputs to production sites and outputs to markets. In short: the efficiency of production could improve considerably.

At the same time, however, a massive process of concentration via cartels, mergers, etc. set in, which resulted from the (understandable) effort of enterprises to escape from increased competitive pressures within and from without the Community. In order to counteract this threat against the competitive process, the Commission strengthened and enlarged its arsenal of competition policy measures. Articles 85 and 86 of the Treaty of Rome were finally supplemented by the merger control rules of Article 90. In addition, the EU state aid 1 legislation introduced rules for admissible public subsidies by member states while rules for public procurement were also adopted (Vosgerau, 1993).

Within the EC (EU), therefore. by the end of 1992 trade policy had been virtually substituted by competition policy, at least on paper and in principle. Many imperfections and deficiencies, resulting partly from different competition philosophies in member states and partly from massive political interests, still remain. Nevertheless, it is true that considerable efficiency gains are realized by this switch of regime from a "second best" towards a "first best" situation.

The explanation for these efficiency gains is simple - at least in principle. As a rule, trade policy measures have their ultimate reason in some kind of distortion - leaving aside for the moment public choice-type reasons of distribution. The most conspicuous example are anti-dumping and anti-subsidy duties, which are levied (in conformity with present GATT-rules) in order to counteract the trade-distorting effects of a monopoly or state export aids. The problem with this defense measure is that it creates another distortion at the border by driving a wedge between world and home market prices. In fact, as the original distortion which caused the problem in the first place continues to exist, since it cannot be removed by the country afflicted by dumping or state-subsidized exports, we now have two distortions.

Thus, if national sovereignty could be replaced by an inter- or supranational regulatory regime which can directly do away with the original distortion by applying a suitable international competition policy measure, we would move from the second best towards a first best situation with corresponding efficiency gains.

Of course, the distribution of these gains might be such that some agents lose. Some kind of redistributive scheme might be necessary in order to ensure acceptance of an international competition policy. The success and continuing attractiveness of the EU could be attributed to the fact that it has accomplished this in some way. This interpretation is strengthened by the agreements creating the European Economic Space, i.e. the union of EC and EFTA, where a common competition policy along EC lines was accepted bv the EFTA countries in exchange for the abolition of all trade policy measures. Here, the substitution of trade policy by competition policy was quite obvious. (That EFTA has lost much of its importance because of the accession to the EU of most of its members, does not invalidate the argument. Rather, it reinforces it.)

If one sees the Europe Agreements as a step towards more efficiency, the application of this argument to the CEEC case is straightforward. This, at least, is the benevolent interpretation. It implies that, after a not too long transition period, accession of at least the more advanced CEECs to the EU is the ultimate goal. It must be admitted, though, that some formulations in the Europe Agreements and important aspects of real developments contradict this interpretation. We can now turn to a discussion of these contradictions.

9.4 Problems of Structural Adjustment

During the last five years, and especially since the dissolution of the CMEA, trade of CEECs with the EC(EU) has considerably increased at the expense of their trade with the former Soviet Union, as can be seen in tables 9.1 and 9.2.

Table 9.1: EC Trade with Central and Eastern European Countries

	1989	1990	1991	1992	Share(%)
EC imports (mill.$ CIF)					
Poland	4380	6720	7788	9120	1.44
Czech and Slovak Republics	2856	3420	5064	7140	1.13
Hungary	2916	3852	4620	5208	0.82
Romania	2832	167	1824	1824	0.29
Bulgaria	600	63	936	1164	0.18
Baltic States				1080	0.17
NIS	16776	1671	21888	20928	3.31
CEEC	30888	37308	42204	46524	7.36
Extra-EC	496620	595728	616788	63196	100.00
World	1173672	1422816	1459368	1520268	
CEEC/extra-EC(%)	6.22	6.26	6.84	7.36	
CEEC/World(%)	2.63	2.62	2.89	3.06	
EC exports *(mill. $ FOB)*					
Poland	4344	5664	9729	10560	1.90
Czech and Slovak Republics	2628	3324	4740	8112	1.46
Hungary	3312	3684	4332	5256	0.94
Romania	756	1572	1644	2400	0.43
Bulgaria	1644	1152	1200	1440	026
Baltic States				56	0.01
NIS	13896	1158	13896	16644	2.99
CEEC	26592	29304	39444	45468	8.16
Extra-EC	451464	526260	522948	557208	100.00
World	1137060	1361544	1373340	1451856	
CEEC/extra-EC(%)	5.89	5.57	7.54	8.16	
CEEC/World(%)	2.34	2.15	2.87	3.13	

Source: Faini/Portes (1995), p.90

Table 9.2: Foreign Trade Structure by Regions (%)

	1988	1992
CZECHOSLOVAKIA		
Exports		
Total	100.0	100.0
Transition and non-market economies	80.6	25.7
of which former CMEA	76.7	21.5
Developed Countries	15.1	64.1
of which EC	92	49.5
Developing Countries	4.3	10.2
Imports		
Total	100.0	100.0
Transition and non-market economies	79.6	29.7
of which former CMEA	75.7	28.9
Developed Countries	17.2	64.8
of which EC	10.1	43.9
Developing Countries	3.2	5.5
HUNGARY		
Exports		
Total	100.0	100.0
Transition and non-market economies	51.3	23.3
of which former CMEA	46.3	19.4
Developed Countries	44.7	71.2
of which EC	22.6	49.8
Developing Countries	4.0	5.4
Imports		
Total	100.0	100.0
Transition and non-market economies	49.8	25.3
of which former CMEA	44.5	23.6
Developed Countries	48.3	69.7
of which EC	25.6	42.7
Developing Countries	2.0	5.0
POLAND		
Exports		
Total	100.0	100.0
Former CMEA	39.8	14.6
Developed Countries	44.7	68.4
of which EC	29.6	54.9
Rest of the World	17.0	
Imports		
Total	100.0	100.0
Former CMEA	40.9	15.0
Developed Countries	46.0	66.8
of which EC	28.3	49.0
Rest of the World	13.1	18.2

Source: Faini/Portes (1995), p.63

This reflects partly a return to normal trade relations with their western neighbours as they existed before (and even during) the war. Partly, it may be the consequence of liberalisation through the Europe Agreements. That CEECs have deficits in their trade balances and on current accounts (cf. table 9.3) is in conformity with their huge investment needs which make capital imports almost a necessity. Nevertheless, the EU's restrictive import policies in the sensitive sectors is a serious problem, because it is here that the CEECs are particularly competitive because of considerable comparative advantages.

Table 9.3 : **Current Account, Selected CEECs, in Mill. US-$**

	1987	1989	1990	1992	1993
Bulgaria	-720	-769	-1710	-360	-523
Czechoslovakia	371	936	-1227	-31	
Hungary	-676	-588	379	352	-4262
Poland	-379	-1409	3067	-3104	-5788
Romania	2043	2514	-3254	-1506	-1162

Source: IMF, Balance of Payments Staustics Yearbook 1994, Table A.1

It is not difficult to find reasons for EU protectionism: steel and coal, textiles and clothing are shrinking sectors whose difficulties would be aggravated by CEEC imports. But it has to be emphasized that to prevent or at least to decelerate adjustment causes efficiency losses of considerable size. This can be seen quite clearly in the coal industry where subsidies, for instance in Germany, already exceed the value added by the industry.

In principle, the same reasoning applies to agriculture. Both the EU and the CEECs would gain if farm products were produced where they need fewer resources than in Western Europe. The qualification here consists in the existence of the CAP which prevents the industry from shrinking and shifts the losses to consumers and tax-payers. The cost of agricultural protection via the CAP causes increasing EU budget problems. Under present CAP rules, its budget could noç accommodate accession of CEECs to the EU and their inclusion in the CAP.

We must then conclude that potential gains from trade are not being realized, incomes in the CEECs are not rising as much as they could, factor prices are not adjusting as would be possible and, thus, pressure for factor movements is not easing off, as it could be. This is particularly true for labour and wages. I, therefore, now turn to a discussion of the problems of migration but also of capital movements and their connection with goods trade.

9.5 Costs of Trade and Factor Movements

Although economic relations between the CEECs and the EU-members and other European (and third) countries existed before the events of 1989, the subsequent opening up of frontiers can undoubtedly be taken as one of the rare examples for our international economics textbook story of jumping from autarky to trade - not the fairytale of free trade, but some form of regulated trade - not only in material goods but also in services and factors of all kinds. Although the latter are generally neglected in the dominant textbook Heckscher-Ohlin model, Ohlin at least was well aware of the importance of factor movements and their relation to goods trade.

It seems pertinent to start the discussion with the Heckscher-Ohlin model because it is here that one of the most influential notions regarding the relationship between trade and factor movements has its origins: the notion of substitutability between trade and factor movements has been developed and makes sense mainly in a world - a model world and a real world - where trade is occurring between countries with different factor endowments. From the famous factor price equalization (FPE) theorem we know that, under certain ideal conditions, goods trade will completely substitute factor trade, in the sense that, via cross-border transactions of factor contents incorporated in traded goods, factor prices become equal, thereby removing every incentive for factor movements.

The theorem is interesting in itself, especially when one considers its theoretical development, originating with relatively intuitive statements, e.g. in Ohlin (1933), undergoing successive refinements and precisions, mainly by Samuelson (1948), and finally being given a very elegant and general formulation by Dixit and Norman (1980).

Although many of the assumptions necessary for the FPE-theorem to hold are not met in the real world of trade between the EU and CEECs (mainly identical production functions, constant returns to scale and perfect competition), the theorem may help to organize the following discussion. I present it in the Dixit-Norman graph of a factor box in two dimensions and with two products for two countries (figure 1).

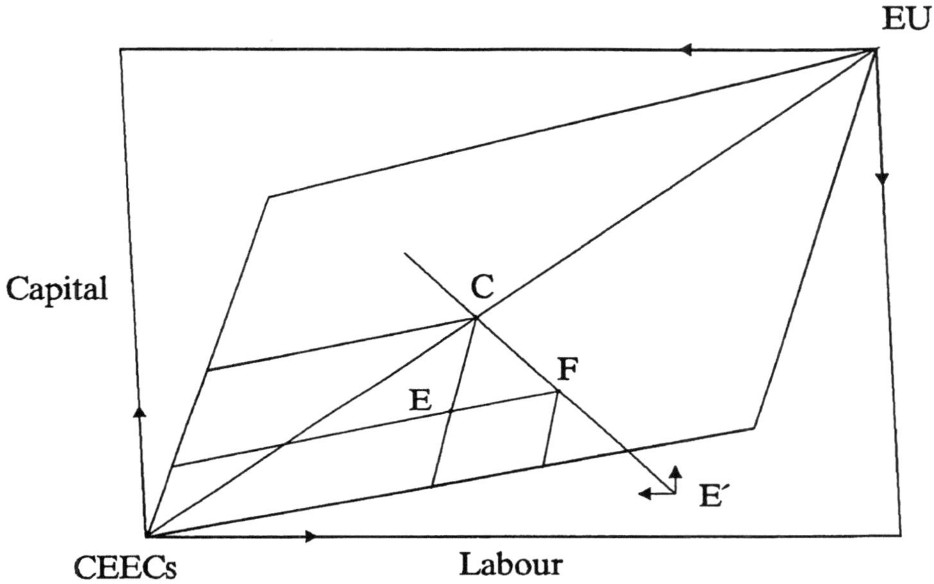

Fig.: 9.1

Here, the area within the parallelogram formed by the two production rays - symmetrical for identical technologies in both countries - contains those endowment points which lead to FPE. If the CEECs are the country with origin at the lower left corner and if labour is measured on the horizontal and capital on the vertical axis, the present situation should be depicted by a point southeast of the diagonal.

If the endowment were at a point such as E, free and unrestricted trade would consist of FE exports of the labour-intensive good from the CEECs to the EU and FC imports of the capital-intensive good into the CEECs. The factor content of trade would be EC, where C is the consumption point and the line CEE' has a slope equal to the factor price (wage - rental) ratio. As E is within the parallelogram, factor prices would be equalised.

If, however, the endowment point lies outside the parallelogram, say at E', trade alone could not equalise factor prices because endowments are too far apart. In this case, wages would be higher and rental rates lower in the EU than in the CEECs and strong incentives for emigration and capital imports would characterise the situation in the CEECs. Emigration would move E' to the left along the arrow, whereas capital imports would move it upwards. These factor movements, which could occur in combination as well, would lead to factor price equalisation as soon as the parallelogram is attained. Note that on the boundaries of the FPE-reaion there will be at least partial specialisation of production.

The analysis so far suffers from the heroic assumptions mentioned above. To remove them would complicate the argument considerably and make graphical representation almost impossible - with the exception of costs of transactions, which have recently been incorporated into the model by Norman and Venables (1995). These costs may take the form of resource-consuming transport costs or of tariffs and other barriers. Usually, they will be different for goods trade and factor movements. In any case, they will prevent goods and/or factor prices from being equalised in consequence of the respective international transactions. In order to surmount the price wedge caused by transaction costs, the endowment differences will have to be greater than would be the case when there are no transaction costs. This means that endowments inducing trade (or factor movements) have to lie away from the diagonal in the factor box - the latter depicting equal endowment ratios in both countries. This is sketched in figure 2.

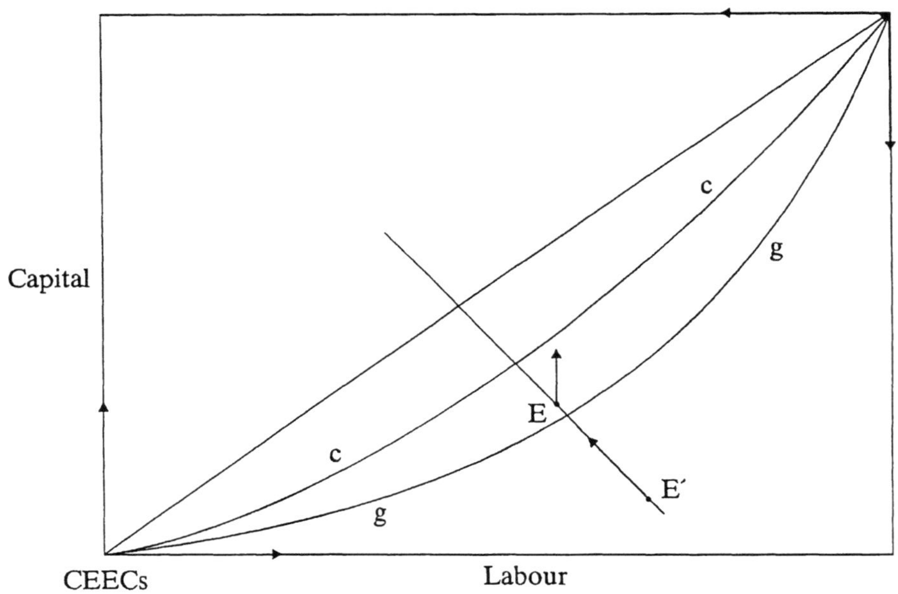

Fig.: 9.2

Regarding, first, transaction costs for trade, we thus have a line, gg, which separates the no trade area between itself and the diagonal from the trade area southeast of gg. Trade can occur only in the latter, for example when E' is the endowment point. If E' is within the parallelogram (not drawn in fig. 2) the factor content of trade is indicated by the arrow pointing northwest from E' towards the goods trade boundary gg. Nothing essential has changed in comparison with the situation represented in figure 1.

But when the endowment point is within the no trade area, say in E, between the diagonal and gg, the situation becomes different. Barriers to trade are now so important that they cannot be overcome by advantages resulting from different endowments. A wedge between goods prices remains and, consequently, factor prices cannot be equalised by trade.

Now, consider line cc, which has been constructed in the same way as the goods trade boundary. It is the capital movements boundary, which incorporates transaction costs of all kinds arising in connection with capital movements, such as information and insurance costs, etc. They are here assumed to be relatively smaller than trade costs with the consequence that cc is closer to the diagonal than gg. This, in turn, means that for an endowment point such as E in fig. 2, capital imports into the CEECs are profitable, indicated by the vertical arrow. On the boundary cc this movement would come to an end. What would happen to trade depends on which particular good causes transaction costs and on whether the capital income is spent in the home or in the host country.[1]

In figure 2 it is implied that there is no labour migration. Graphically, a labour movement boundary ll would be farthest away from the diagonal in the southeast corner of the box indicating prohibitive migration costs. This may describe the situation between the CEECs and the EU rather adequately: in spite of very substantial wage differences, legal migration is close to non-existent.

[1] The analytical details are presented in Norman and Venables (1995) and commented on by Vosgerau (1996).

9.6 Theory and Evidence

Now let us turn back to the real world of today. It is characterized by an average wage differential of around 1 : 10 between the CEECs and the EU (Table 9.4).

Table 9.4 : Wage gaps and population, 1990

	Wage per hour (US-$)	Population (millions)
Eastern Europe		
Poland	0.7	38
Hungary	0.7	11
Czechoslovakia	0.8	16
Bulgaria	0.2	9
Romania	0.6	23
Yugoslavia	1.1	24
USSR (European)	0.9	222
Eastern Europe	0.9	343
Receiving *countries*		
Germany (West)	11	61
France	8	56
Italy	11	57
UK	8	57
EC (total)	9	340
EFTA (total)	13	25
Western Europe (total)	10	365
USA	13	250
Canada	13	27
Australia	14	17

Source: Layard (1992), p.2

This would cause labour immigration into the EU of an order of magnitude of several hundreds of thousands per year, according to estimates presented by Layard and others (1992), if frontiers were open. But immigration is not permitted. The extremely modest numbers of CEEC citizens abroad are documented in tables 9.5 and 9.6.

Table 9.5: Foreign residents who are nationals of central and eastern European countries in selected European OECD countries, last available year

	Belgium 1993	Finland 1993	France 1990	Germany 1993	Italy 1993	Netherland 1993	Sweden 1993	Switzerland 1993
	Number (1000)							
Bulgaria		0.3	0.8	56.7				0.8
Former CSFR	0.4	0.1	2.0	52.0				5.4
Hungary	0.7	0.4	2.9	62.2		1.2	3.4	4.2
Poland	4.9	0.7	46.3	260.5	19.7	6.1	16.1	5.1
Romania		0.3	5.7	162.6		1.8	5.0	2.5
Former USSR	0.9	18.3	4.3	63.6	12.7	3.3		1.6
Total foreigners	920.6	52.8	3596.6	6878.1	987.4	779.8	507.5	1260.3
	Share in total foreign population (%)							
Bulgaria		0.6		0.8				0.1
Former CSFR		0.3	0.1	0.8				0.4
Hungary	0.1	0.7	0.1	0.9		0.2	0.7	0.3
Poland	0.5	1.3	1.3	3.8	2.0	0.8	3.2	0.4
Romania		0.6	0.2	2.4		0.2	1.0	0.2
Former USSR	0.1	34.6	0.1	0.9	1.3	0.4		0.1
Total foreigners	100.0	100.0	100.0	100.0	100.0	100.0	100.0	100.0

Source: Sopemi, p.30

Table 9.6: Immigrants born in central and eastern European countries residing in Australia, Canada and the United States, last available year

	Australia	Canada	United States
	Number (1000)		
	1991	1991	1990
Former CSFR	17.8	42.6	87.0
Hungary	27.2	57.0	110.3
Poland	68.9	184.7	388.3
Romania	11.3		91 ù1
Former USSR	44.3	99.4	389.9
Toçàl of foreign-born	3753.3	4342.9	19767.3
	Share in total of foreign-born (%)		
Former CSFR	0.5	1.0	0.4
Hungary	0.7	1.3	0.6
Poland	1.8	4.3	2.0
Romania	0.3		0.5
Former USSR	1.2	2.3	2.0
Total of foreign-born	100.0	100.0	100.0

Source: Sopemi, p.30

There are several possible interpretations of this behaviour on the part of the EU which is in apparent contradiction with the aim of improving economic efficiency. If one does not think that the underlying Heckscher-Ohlin framework is completely inadequate, several explanations offer themselves. One concerns the missing competence of the EU for migration policy, which is still essentially in the hands of national governments. Another is high adjustment costs in the immigration countries, consisting of social resistance to strangers, with all its emotional aspects. But there are economic aspects, too, such as limitations in public goods and, more importantly, changes in income distribution - negative for wage earners and positive for entrepreneurs - quite apart from employment problems, especially in shrinking sectors.

There may, of course, be also demographic and other longer-term considerations. At any rate, the evidence seems to show that the EUšis not willing to accept the flow of CEEC immigrants which would result from an opening of its borders. Whether one accepts the underlying preferences or not, the choice has consequences that have to be analyzed. One of them concerns capital movements and technology transfers to which we now turn.

In the simplified Heckscher-Ohlin world differences in endowments, factor prices and, hence, incomes between countries can be reduced by trade, migration or capital movements. If one includes technical knowledge as a third factor, productivity differences may also be diminished by technology transfers.

If trade is - because of imperfect liberalization, transaction costs, or for other reasons - insufficient for FPE, and if for whatever reasons migration is not permitted to reduce wage differentials sufficiently, the only remaining remedy are capital and technology transfers. Provided the institutional framework and other conditions are suitable, these may result from voluntary decisions by private agents. But if private capital movements and technology transfers into the CEECs for whatever reasons remain insufficient, convergence between the CEECs and the EU will remain insufficient. The resulting perpetuation of large differences in economic performance, income levels and living standards between Central Eastern and Western Europe will lead to tensions which will force the relatively rich EU members into public transfers. It seems doubtful whether this is a good solution.

Our previous theoretical argument and the available evidence point into the same direction. We have already mentioned the CEECs' typically negative balance on current account in their relation with the EU (table 3). Private foreign direct investment has considerably increased during the last three years. However, this was predominantly concentrated in Poland, Hungary and the Czech Republic, whereas the other CEECs attracted much less FDI (tables 9.7-9.9). Public transfers seem to be rather low. Private credits and portfolio investments are increasing but at a slow pace due to the underdeveloped level of financial markets, etc.

Table 9.7: Stock[(a)] of Foreign Direct Investment in CEEs
by Host Countries 1989-1993 (in mill. US-$)

	1989	1990	1991	1992	1993
Bulgaria			300	320	
ex Czechoslovakia	256	436	1100	1900	
Czech Republic				1669	2100
Slovac Republic				231	366
Hungary	550	1450	3300	4300	6500
Poland	100	352	680	1400	2100
Romania		113	269	538	685 (b)
Total above			5649	8458	
ex Soviet Union	837	1328	5500 (b)		
Belorussia	53	101			
Estonia	45	48	180 (b)		
Latvia	9	27	121 (b)		
Lithuania	14	15	120 (b)		
Russia	617	959	800 (b)		
Ukraine	24	52	670 (b)		

(a) Cumulated flows at the end of the year - (b) October
Source : Schmidt (1994), p.11

Table 9.8: Direct Investment in Selected CEECs -Flows- (in Mill. US-$)

	1987	1988	1989	1990	1991	1992	1993
Bulgaria				4	56	42	55
Czechosiovakia			257	207	600	1103	
Hungary					1462	1479	2350
Poland	12	15	11	89	291	678	1715
Romania					40	77	94
Slovenia						111	112

Source: IMF. Balance of Payments Statistics Yearbook 1994. Table C-17

Table 9.9 : Flows of Foreign Direct Investment into CEECs by OECD Source Countries, 1991 and 1992

		1991		1992	
		mill. $	percent	mill. $	percent
Total Countries	OECD	1654	100.0	2366	100.0
of which :		361	21.8	397	16.8
Austria		210	12.7	167	7.0
France		725	43.8	988	41.6
Germany		185	11.1		
Japan		145	8.7	364	15.4
The Netherlands				397	16.8
United States					

Source: Schmidt (1994), p.12

There are some qualifications and further remarks to be added to this discussion because the transactions mentioned so far are not independent of each other. For instance, exports mean production and, therefore, demand for inputs. With sufficient labour, this implies demand for foreign capital. FDI therefore depends on favourable prospects not only in domestic CEEC markets but also to a large extent in export markets, including those in the EU. Trade and FDI may therefore reinforce each other - not substitute one for the other. This is true at least for private FDI. If they remain insufficient, e.g. because of protection against CEEC imports, pressures for immigration and for public transfers may rise.

9.7 Concluding Remarks

Admittedly, a sketch which compares the two "countries" EU and the CEECs with the Heckscher-Ohlin world, where trade is generated by differences in endowment ratios, can only be a very rough one. But the huge wage/rental differences seem to justify the simplification. In such a world, deficiencies in free trade policy and imperfections in the competitive order prevent goods prices from equalising. This price wedge, in turn, entails factor price differences which would induce factor movements if they were possible and permitted. If labour migration is excluded, the burden can be borne only by trade and capital movements. Figure 2 above has been drawn in such a way that the costs of trade are relatively higher than those of capital movements, increasing the importance of the latter for approaching an efficient solution. Of course, if the trade boundary could be shifted towards the diagonal by liberalising CEEC imports into the EU, the picture would change and capital exports would become less important. If, moreover, artificial migration costs were lowered, an additional gain might be possible.

The theoretical framework has of course to be filled in with quantitative data, which presupposes at least some degree of disaggregation. This goes beyond the scope of the present paper, where the intention was to emphasise the interdependence between goods trade, migration, and capital movements on the one side and to underline, on the other side, the necessity to supplement trade and competition policy for goods trade by an appropriate competitive order for factor movements.

References

Brunner, Petra (1994), Die politischen und wirtschaftlichen Beziehungen der Europäischen Union zu den Visegradstaaten, *IFO-Schnelldiernst* 14, pp. 14 - 22.

Dixit, Avinash and Norman, Victor (1980), *Theory of Irçternatiorcal Trade,* Cambridge University Press.

Eser, Thiemo W. und Hallet, Martin (1993), Der mögliche Beitrag der EG-Regionalpolitik bei einer Ost-Erweiterung der EG: Hilfe oder Hindernis, in: *Osteuropa-Wirtschaft.* 38 Jg., pp. 195 - 217.

Faini, Ricardo and Portes, Richard (eds.), (1995), *European Unioç Trade with Eastern Europe: Adjustmerçt and Opportunities,* Centre for Economic Policy Research. London. p. 63.

Hoekman, Bernhard M. and Mavroidis, Petros C. (1995), Linking Competition and Trade Policies in Central and East European Countries, Ch. 6 in: Winters, L.A. (ed.), *Foundations of an Open Economy,* CEPR.

Estrin, Saul and Cave, M. (eds.) (1993), *Competition and Competition* Policy: A *Comparative Arçalysis of Central and Eastern Europe,* Printer Publishers, London.

Holmes, Peter (1995), Competition Policy and Integration: Levelling or Tilting the Playing Field, in this volume.

International Monetary Fund (1994), *Balance of Payments Statistics Yearbook,* Part 2, IMF, Washington, D.C.

Kennedv, D. and Webb, D. (1993), The Limits of Integration : Eastern Europe and the European Communities, *Common Market Law Review,* 30, 1095 - 117.

Layard, Richard, Blanchard, Olivier, Dornbusch, Rüdiger and Krugman, Paul (1992), *East-West Migration: The : Alternatives.* MiT-Press. Cambridge/ Mass.

Mavroidis, Petros C. (1993), *Handelspolitische Abwehrmechanismen der EWG und der* USA *und ihre Vereinbarkeit mit derc GATT Regeln. Eine rechtsvergleichende Analyse der Verordnung 2641/*84 *(EWG) urcd "Section* 301 " *des "Omnibus trade and competitiveness act " von* 1988 *(USA).* Verlagsgesellschaft Internationales Recht, Stuttgart.

Neumann, Manfred (1994), Öffnung nach Osteuropa, Gefahr oder Chancen für die deutsche Wirtschaft, in: Benkenstein, Martin et al. (Hrsg.), *Osteuropa im Umbruch, Perspektiven für die neuen Bundesländer,* Gabler Verlag, Wiesbaden.

Norman, Victor and Venables, Anthony J. (1995), International Trade, Factor Mobility, and Trade Costs, *The Economic Journal* 105, pp. 1488 - 1504, Blackwell, Oxford.

Ohlin, Bertil (1933), *Interregional and International Trade,* Harvard University Press, Cambridge/Mass. , revised edition 1967.

Samuelson, Paul A. (1948), International Trade and the Equalisation of Factor Prices, *The Ecorçomic Journal.*

Saunders, C. (ed.) (1993), *The Role of Competition in Economic Transition,* St. Martin's Press, New York.

Schmidt, Klaus-Dieter (1994), *Foreign Direct Investment in Central and East European Countries: State of Affairs, Prospects and Policy Implications,* Kiel Working Papers, No. 633, Kiel Institute of World Economics.

Schön, Cordula (1994), *Der rechtliche Rahmen für Assoziierungen der Europäischen Gemeinschaft vor dem aktuellen Hintergrund der Annäherungs- und Mitgliedschaftswünsche der mittel- und osteuropäischen Staaten,* Peter Lang-Verlag, Frankfurt.

Sopemi (1995), *Trends in International Migration. Continuous Reporting* System *on Migration, Annual Report* 1994, Organisation for Economic Co-operation and Development, Paris, France.

Vosgerau, Hans-Jürgen (1993), *Trade Policy and Competition Policy in Europe. Complementarities and Contradictions.* Diskussionsbeiträge des SFB 178 "Internationalisierung der Wirtschaft", Serie II, No. 198.

Vosgerau, Hans- Jürgen (1996), *Trade and Trade Policy, Migration and Capital Movements between the EU and the CEECs: An Analysis of their Inter-relations.* Paper presented at the International Conference "Economic Integration in Transition", Athens, 21-24 August,1996.

Part V Sectoral Issues in the Integration of CEECs into the EU

10 Inward Investment and the Need for Industrial Strategy in Central and Eastern Europe

Christos Pitelis
Judge Institute of Management Studies and
Queens' College, University of Cambridge
Mill Lane, CAMBRIDGE CB2 1lx

Roger Sugden and Rachael Thomas
Research Centre for Industrial Strategy
University of Birmingham

Abstract

The aim of this paper is to establish the almost self-evident, yet often neglected, idea that the objectives of governments and firms need not always coincide. It does so in the context of Foreign Direct Investment (FDI) by Transnational Corporations (TNCs) in Central and Eastern European Countries (CEECs). The paper then goes on to argue for the need for an industrial strategy by CEECs toward FDI.

* The authors would like to thank David Bailey, David Parker and Stan Siebert for helpful comments. An earlier version of this paper was presented at the Workshop on *Foreign Direct Investment from (Less Favoured Countries of) the European Union to (Less Favoured Countries of) the CEECs*, Cambridge, 1995; we are grateful to participants for discussion.

This research was undertaken with support from the European Commission's Phare ACE Programme 1994, Contract Number 94-0719-R.

10.1 Introduction

Following the demise of 'state socialism' in Central and Eastern Europe (CEE) from 1989, a glut of literature emerged dealing with the region's transition to a market based economy and advising on how best to achieve the metamorphosis. Existing commentary stresses the importance of integrating the region into the world economy and emphasises the view that investment by foreign transnationals (TNCs) can play a significant role in assisting Central and Eastern Europe to develop. In line with this, many countries in the region have established agencies for attracting TNCs. Stress has been laid on the initial attraction of all and any investment.

That the region needs to make a transition from the centrally administered economies of state socialism is not disputed. Instead, the discussion focuses on whether current policy towards inward investment will assist CEE governments in achieving their objectives. It would appear that in some overall sense governments desire a 'free market economy'. However, in the face of TNC activities what does it mean to have such a free market system? Moreover, does the introduction of such a system have repercussions for the specific objectives governments have set themselves? Assuming that such a system is preferable to the one it replaces, might governments be able to pursue policies with yet higher benefits? These are the sorts of questions which will effectively be considered. In doing so, the paper explores the motives of both inward investors and host governments in the region and explores the compatibility of these objectives.[1]

The body of the paper is essentially a review of existing literature concerned with the role of foreign investment in Central and Eastern Europe. Section II considers changes in the region since the mid-1940's. The aim is to briefly outline the context in which foreign investment is currently being sought. Sections III and IV discuss, respectively, the motives of TNCs investing in the region and the objectives of governments currently inviting such investors. The aim is to draw a picture encompassing TNCs and governments generally, which is not to deny that there will be exceptions for particular firms and particular countries at specific points in time; this paper attempts to cut through such details. The compatibility between TNCs' motives and government objectives is then the subject of Section V. Some general conclusions are drawn in Section VI.

---

[1] In order to fully address the issue of objectives by governments and/or firms, one would need to delve into and develop a theory of the firm (including the TNC) and the state. This is beyond our scope here, but see Pitelis (1994) for such an attempt. For our purposes here, we take at face value the stated objectives of firms and governments (see below).

10.2 Background

The introduction of centrally administered systems across Central and Eastern European Countries (CEECs) after 1945 brought with it an extensive plan for restructuring, investment being channelled almost exclusively into heavy industry in order to facilitate the shift from agriculture to industry. Despite rudimentary technology, low productivity levels and inefficient organisation, industrial output for the region grew substantially (and in many cases more rapidly than in the West) up to the 1970's, when a widespread decline in living standards and poor productivity became significant features.

This prompted action by CEEC governments to try to narrow the East-West gap by importing technology through 'East-West cooperation' ventures. Financed by foreign credit, the scheme was intended 'to strengthen domestic economic enterprise....creating improved channels for the importation of foreign technology together with related managerial know-how' (McMillan 1986). CEEC governments, however, found it hard to select the appropriate technologies or make them economically profitable. Arguably, many Western companies saw the ventures as little more than a windfall export opportunity, with no gains to be made from long term ties. As a result, the intended means of repayment , exports , never materialised and today most CEECs who used such schemes still have considerable debts with the West.

From the 1970's onwards, much of Central and Eastern Europe saw recession and a sharp decline in production. The ever widening gap between demand and supply for products , exacerbated by the nature of Central and East European industry[2] , led to hyperinflation, market shortages and eventually political crisis in 1989 (Dobosiewicz 1992). With the collapse of state socialism in 1989-90, the view was adopted that the reorganisation and reallocation of resources through a market system where firms compete was the first step towards overcoming the region's considerable problems.

A principal concern is that after decades of high but misdirected capital accumulation there is a need for considerable amounts of investment throughout Central and Eastern Europe[3] , it being necessary to replace the largely obsolescent capital stock and develop the infrastructure in order to increase the level of economic develop-

---

2 Much Central and East European industry is concentrated in heavy manufacturing and engineering. For example, whilst the Czech Republic has output per head of population double that of Austria, its rate of consumption is less than half due to the emphasis, in productive terms, on heavy industry. (Centre for Economic Policy Research, 1992)

3 According to one estimate (The Economist, September 21 1991), the Central and East European economies would need a total of US$420bn investment capital -- per annum -- for the next ten years in order to bring their economies up to equivalence with Western Europe.

ment within the region. Alongside this, the breakdown of intra CMEA trade in 1991[4] led to a loss of markets, poor terms of trade and escalating balance of payments difficulties. With falling real incomes, weak, embryonic local capital markets and existing debt which restrains further borrowing, it has been argued that even modest flows of domestic investment capital in the near future are doubtful.[5] The 1990-94 period has thus seen the CEECs[6] turn to foreign investment as a source of capital investment and as a means of aiding the transition to a market economy.

By 1992, all CEECs allowed 100% foreign ownership of productive assets, provided legal guarantees concerning foreign property and offered special tax concessions to inward investors (Hunya 1992). Investment no longer requires certified approval, except in certain activities such as the manufacture of armaments, the administration of ports and airports, in telecommunications and the media. Increasingly, earnings may be repatriated without limitation, despite shortages of hard currency and a general lack of currency convertibility.

For a region where outright foreign ownership of any firm was prohibited until 1990, Central and Eastern Europe appears to be making a concerted effort to attract foreign investment. For many governments following the practices of the West, attracting foreign investment is perceived as a logical step towards economic development. With this outlook, investment by TNCs tends to be accepted relatively indiscriminately within the region.

---

4 The Council for Mutual Economic Assistance (CMEA) was responsible for facilitating and coordinating the intra-regional trade within Central and Eastern Europe and the former USSR, accounting for the bulk of the region's trade. (Blanchard et al 1991)

5 Central and Eastern Europe has shown high levels of savings and investment in the past (around 20%), implying that it could in principle fund substantial capital investment without reducing its existing levels of consumption. However, since most saving and investment comes directly from the retained earnings of state firms, the view that projected earnings of state firms will not be as large, implies that future saving or investment will have to come from consumers (Blanchard et al 1991). Given the existing low rates of consumption relative to the West, it seems unlikely that consumers would be in a position to raise the quantity of capital required. Merrit (1991) thus argues that there is a need for a substantial transfusion of capital investment into the region given that the level of domestic investment is likely to remain low for the medium term.

6 In particular the so-called Visegrad group -- the Czech Republic, Hungary, Poland and Slovakia.

10.3 Objectives of TNCs Investing in Central and Eastern Europe

Whilst the motives for TNCs investments have been well documented[7], Radice (1993) suggests two principal motives specific to Central and Eastern Europe which have generally influenced TNCs investment in the region; namely market share and low labour costs. Both motives were exhibited by General Electric's investment in the Hungarian light bulb manufacturer Tungsram; 'General Electric (GE) acquired 50% of Tungsram who already had 7% of the West European market. As much as 70% of Tungsram's annual share of this market was shipped to the West from its Hungarian factories where the cost of producing light bulbs was reported to be 30% lower than in Western Europe , due in part to the fact that wages were one tenth those paid in the US. Added to GE's 2% share before the acquisition, this gave GE 9% of the market, making it third amongst its West European competitors' (Business Week, 30 July 1990).

(i) **Market Share** The prospect of gaining market share is suggested as a primary objective for investment in the Central and East European region due to both the maturing state of most Western markets and the potential of reaching 420 million Central and East European consumers. Hamilton and Adjubei (1991) suggest that "the growth potential and prospects for sales are huge ... bucking the trend of Western markets". Given the historical emphasis on heavy industry and the shortages resulting from the collapse of the CMEA, it would appear that some investors see a potential outlet for almost any product or service. Marketing costs are slight compared to the intensity felt in oligopolistic Western markets, and the weakness of indigenous industry in the face of transnational resources might help secure high market shares for foreign investors in many industries. With opportunities existing in various sectors from consumer goods and business services to industrial equipment, Dunning (1994) suggests that the potential for TNCs investment is near infinite.[8]

Alongside this, the relative uncompetitiveness of the region's industry in even the most basic consumer and durable goods suggests that TNCs may not even have to produce 'world class products' in order to gain market share. Lines of production

---

[7] See most recently Dunning (1994) for a comprehensive discussion of the motivation behind investment by transnationals and host governments' justification in pursuing such investment.

[8] Marton (1993) recognises that even in the face of such opportunities 'in several product areas, the relatively small size of the market can only sustain a few enterprises', hence 'in some cases transnationals have invested in local manufacture in order to preempt the market from a competing transnational.'

whose lifecycle has long since expired, or whose production is no longer deemed profitable in Western markets, may be effectively transferred to Central and Eastern Europe. One example of this occurred when car manufacturer Renault switched all production and sales of its ageing R-4 model to the region when this ceased in France (Dobosiewicz 1992). One benefit for TNCs arising from the backwardness of Central and East European manufacturing is that maturing or obsolete lines of production , so called 'cash cows' , may be profitably 'milked' in the new markets of the region. Host governments, which allow technically backward investment to take place, may suffer in the longer term, as relying on imports of outdated technology could limit the region's ability to achieve long term development.

Whilst certain industries in certain CEECs may be attractive to TNCs in their own right, the size of the region as a whole (and its proximity to the rest of the European Union) must also be considered as a motive for investment. It would be misleading to talk of Central and Eastern Europe as a single market given that since the demise of the CMEA in 1991 there is a distinct lack of common mechanisms linking the countries. Yet, Dobosiewicz (1992) notes that many TNCs are investing in one country in order to use it as a springboard for the penetration of neighbouring countries: 'the common view is held that it is easier to export to East European countries from within the region than from outside it'.[9]

It is suggested that TNCs following such a strategy seek to establish market share quickly, without incurring much risk or having to establish physical investment in every country they enter. Hence, the development of distribution networks, warehousing facilities and wholesaling is becoming common practice as a means of exploring or entering neighbouring markets[10] . Moreover, many investments made in the region may involve merely the marketing and distribution of products imported from TNCs' other plants. For example, Jolly (1994) cites the case of SmithKline Beecham, the major TNC pharmaceuticals company, who consider the costs of investing in Poland to be amongst the lowest in the world. Hence, nine new foreign brands were being promoted in Poland alongside Central and East European brands in 1992, although usage is only two thirds that of the UK. SmithKline Beecham's priority was apparently to establish its distribution channels before setting up a manufacturing plant for its Aquafresh brand.[11]

One repercussion of the use of distribution networks and the like is that TNCs have easy access to market share without making any initial physical investment in

---

[9] Dobosiewicz also suggests that this may be true of the region's proximity to the markets of the European Union.

[10] See Pitelis, Sugden and Tsipouri (1994) for a discussion of investment in warehousing and distribution facilities as a means of securing markets in neighbouring countries.

[11] Using the example of Poland, Kozminski (1992) suggests that 'an important condition for the growth of enterprises (be they native, foreign or joint ventures) operating on the Polish market is the early restructuring of the distribution system.'

manufacturing assets, therefore limiting the host country's employment and development benefits.[12]

In aggregate, TNCs seeking to establish market share across the whole region may have limited incentive to establish manufacturing facilities in each country. Indeed observing centripetalism in transnational-led economic development,[13] manufacturing facilities could be distributed across the region unequitably. Certain cities or countries would be favoured over others and used to supply CEECs.[14] This may hinder convergence between CEECs.

Drawing on this it may be suggested that, insofar as there is free trade, a TNC's global strategy could remove the necessity for manufacturing in CEECs 'per se'. With international manufacturing operations, the Central and East European market may be supplied from any manufacturing site outside the region, using distribution networks to maximise market coverage. This raises the issue of the long-term impact of Foreign Direct Investment (FDI) by TNCs, as the very success of FDI in terms of economic growth and development may eventually tend to reduce the attractiveness (eg in terms of labour costs) of the benefitting country vis-a-vis other countries.

(ii) Labour Costs Shifting the focus from market share to take a broader view of TNCs' objectives, a second motive for entering Central and Eastern Europe is the pool of cheap, well educated labour: 'Eastern Europe appears to be ideally suited for setting up the production of labour-intensive goods when to produce such goods in the high wage countries of the West is no longer profitable' (Donges and Wieners 1994).

In line with this, Radice (1994) suggests that Central and Eastern Europe could be a strategic base for European or world markets in labour-intensive operations, 'investment being primarily export-orientated and aimed at supplying Western markets.' Central and Eastern Europe, Radice implies, should follow the development path pursued by the South East Asian region. Given that wage levels in Central and Eastern Europe are as low as 10% of European Union levels, and that the region is historically linked to manufacturing (albeit often using obsolete technology), he suggests that one possible future advantage lies in labour-intensive niche markets such as component manufacture and investment goods.

---

12 Marton (1993) suggests that transnationals 'designed strategies that reduce their exposure whilst permitting them to capture maximum market share.'

13 See Cowling and Sugden (1994) for further discussion of centripetal economic tendencies and the role of TNCs.

14 One influencing factor Merrit (1991) suggests is that 'circles of political instability' have contributed to the favouring of the so-called Visegrad group for transnational investors, as they represent least political or economic risk. The resulting favouritism, Merrit argues, serves to reinforce the existing disparity between regions and the likelihood of political or economic tension.

Thus, it is suggested that whilst a transnational seeks to obtain 'competitive advantage' in Central and East European markets by securing market share, a global strategic advantage may be gained through utilising the region's low labour costs. Generalising more widely, it may also be argued that whilst both market share and cheap labour may provide impetus to the investment decision, it is unlikely that any investment would be undertaken without ascertaining how the strategic position of the firm is affected. Whichever motive presides, the underlying purpose of any investment must be to enhance the competitive advantage of the firm.

It follows that the CEECs should acknowledge that TNC affiliates are a single component in any organisation's global strategy. As such, 'Western ... multinationals are unlikely to treat their East European affiliates as stand-alone ventures, but to treat them as part and parcel of a Pan-European or even international network of activities' (Dunning 1993). Whilst the contribution of any transnational affiliate will tend, if successful, to enhance the global position of the organisation, its effects on the host country are less clear since, 'from the start, the functional and organisational strategies of East European investments will be locked into those currently pursued by the foreign firm' (Dunning 1993). This suggests, for example, that transnational affiliates in individual countries need not always produce sizable returns[15] nor involve high technology production or exports (if these are being secured elsewhere). Hence the overall relationship between inward investment and accrued benefits becomes less clear. For example, it has been argued that Ford's $80m investment in Hungary is not expected to yield the company any significant direct return in Hungary; the attraction lies in the prospect of supplies of cheap parts for its plants in Western Europe making those plants more competitive (Dobosiewicz 1992)[16].

---

15 Wang (1993) suggests that 'foreign firms on the whole were prepared to accept a lower rate of profit in order to pursue their global investment strategy in Eastern Europe aimed at the longer term prospects of enlarged markets'.

16 See the discussion in Naujoks and Schmidt (1994) of TNCs' subcontracting arrangements with production units in Central and Eastern Europe. It is argued that policy-makers in the region bemoan that such arrangements imply a downgrading of subcontractors' production activity, although Naujoks and Schmidt do not share this pessimism.

10.4 Objectives of Governments in Central and Eastern Europe Seeking Foreign Investment

Given the issues facing Central and Eastern Europe , the deteriorating capital stock, the need to rebuild infrastructure and governments' intentions to move from central administration to a market based economy , the governments' objectives in seeking foreign investment are extensive. Against this background, the objectives discussed below are an attempt to generalise and represent some of the more evident motives.

(i) **Technology Transfer and Modernisation** Technology transfer is still one motivating factor for attracting foreign investment, not least because of the slow rate of technological development of the region and thus its impact on industry and the wider economy. Central and East European governments recognise that in opening up the region to foreign competition the relative technological backwardness of the region automatically handicaps the short-term ability of existing domestic industry to 'compete'. Given the apparent historical inability of the state, or even a growing private sector, to mobilise capital effectively and establish a domestic technology base, one view is that foreign investors are needed. What is not so readily considered is the use of foreign investors alongside indigenous organisations to engender development[17] , and it is perhaps salutary to bear in mind Inzelt's (1994) finding that 'foreign companies, in taking over Hungarian firms, tend to cut back R & D expenditure, and to centralise all basic R & D activity in their main, Western locations, leaving their Hungarian research workers to do purely routine work.'[18]

Radice (1993) argues that 'trade competitiveness is seen to depend on the acquisition of the latest technologies, which in turn are owned by TNCs, suggesting that a transnational presence may need to be 'acquired' so that the latest technologies may be secured for domestic development. Alongside this, Cantwell (1994) takes the view that the pace of product innovation and technological development originating all over the world necessitates international linkages due to the high cost of innovation and short product cycles, arguing that 'nationalistic isolation is a recipe for economic backwardness'.

However, in order to make the successful transition to what governments perceive to be a 'competitive' economy, governments need to ensure (not just hope) that modern techniques , from managerial and marketing skills to production methods (with a view to developing export markets) , will accompany the transfer of

---

[17] For simplicity, all existing forms of foreign involvement are lumped together and discussed as 'foreign investment' in this paper. To the extent that, for example joint ventures, include foreign investment in the CEEC, this treatment is legitmate. Differences exist, some are examined below.

[18] See also Bailey (1995) on the Hungarian experience more generally.

technology.[19] Merrit (1991) supports this approach, by drawing on the example of the Asian 'four tigers', who he sees as having successfully utilised technology from the West in order to industrialise and become world market competitors. However, important to note here is the proactive strategy of Asian governments who used foreign technology to empower domestic industry (see, among others, Pitelis (1994) for a discussion).

Both Radice and Cantwell suggest that without involvement from transnational firms, at least with reference to technology and modernisation, Central and Eastern Europe cannot hope to 'compete'. It is thus suggested that whilst foreign **involvement** may be an integral part of economic development, in no way should it be implied that foreign **investment** per se need be critical[20]; countries such as Japan have, in the past, sustained rapid development with little foreign investment but substantial foreign involvement coordinated by the government.[21] In line with this, Cantwell (1994) goes as far as to argue that, given the lack of infrastructure, competitive environment and the weakness of indigenous companies, (pure forms of) FDI may not be the ideal means by which to industrialise. Following the example of Japan, he suggests that a more effective and controlled means of acquiring technology and know-how may be through the use of joint ventures.

Whilst joint ventures may offer a more controlled means of acquiring technology, Dobosiewicz (1992) emphasises the need for mechanisms to ensure that governments have some degree of control over the quality of technology which is 'acquired'. He thus infers that whilst the technology transferred may be more modern than that hitherto used, and hence may reduce the development lag between countries, 'it is not a long-run solution as the lag still exists'[22]. The lag is only reduced or surmounted if the technology imported is planned or controlled to meet some wider government strategy and is of a quality which domestic entrepreneurs are able to utilise to build 'sustainable competitive advantage'. Dunning (1994)

---

[19] For example, Marton (1993) suggests that, 'several transnationals in Hungary produce standardised, relatively low-technology products ... mostly for Western export markets. In these cases, the initial investment requirement is low, and the fast and high returns make Hungary an attractive location.' Their is little suggestion of a broader range of skills being transferred.

[20] Kozminski (1992) also suggests that in the case of Poland, 'equity ties are a must ... Poland cannot be just a passive 'customer' for foreign investors', but alongside this 'no Polish company can attain a global competitive position 'single-handed''.

[21] See Ellman (1992), Evans (1979), Wade (1990) for discussions of how foreign investment aided the development of Brazil and the South East Asian region.

[22] Marton (1993) suggests that 'transnationals have reduced the initial investment necessary for local production by importing used equipment from their home country or from other foreign affiliates'.

notes the strategy followed by Japan as a singular example,[23] where the technology imported and licensed throughout the 1950-60s was targeted and specific, not a 'cast-off' from the West. By utilising and further developing imported or licensed technology, Japan's domestic industry was able to compete on the world market. It is clear that Japan was not made successful by inward investment alone.[24]

Two lessons arise for Central and Eastern Europe from the Japanese experience of modernising industry. Firstly, the industrialisation which took place was not directly the result of foreign involvement 'per se'. Instead, it was due in part to the type of involvement which took place. Secondly, inward investment was used by domestic entrepreneurs to the advantage of indigenous industry.

Whilst Central and Eastern Europe may learn from the Japanese example, caution must be exercised when comparing experiences of modernisation from other regions or countries. For example, the quantity and quality of entrepreneurs who adapted imported technology and know-how in order to become 'competitive' in domestic and international markets cannot be taken as given in Central and Eastern Europe.[25] Radice (1994) takes the view that Central and Eastern Europe 'lacks not only capital but capitalist entrepreneurs',[26] and suggests that the success of Central and Eastern Europe in utilising foreign investments to industrialise may depend on the development of an entrepreneurial culture. Given the overhang of 50 years of central administration, it might seem unlikely that the number of entrepreneurs needed is merely 'waiting in the wings'.

Hence, it is suggested that whilst arbitrary, uncoordinated investment may not achieve the governments' objective of technology transfer or modernisation, domestic industry may not be capable of realising this objective without the use of transnational involvement to some extent.

(ii) Competition and the Introduction of Market Forces Another function suggested for foreign investment by Central and East European governments is to serve as a means of introducing new standards and greater competition into their domestic economies.

Central and East European industry has been traditionally very concentrated due to the monopolies and informal cartels created by state-owned industry. Low productivity, overmanning and inferior quality were all tolerated through the system

---

[23] For further discussion of the development strategy taken by Japan, see Dunning (1993), Cantwell (1994)

[24] See also Bailey, Harte and Sugden (1994) for details on the Japanese case, and Teranishi (1994) for a discussion of lessons from Japan for change in Central and Eastern Europe.

[25] Wade (1990) emphasises the role played by domestic entrepreneurs and industries in creating sustained development and industrialisation in the South East Asian region.

[26] In light of government objectives to introduce market systems into the economy, Radice assumes that this necessitates the development of a 'capitalist' system.

of central administration. By acting as a 'role model' for indigenous companies, Dobosiewicz (1992) notes that TNCs' 'superior efficiency, productivity and profitability creates a potent 'demonstration effect''; forcing domestic firms to emulate transnational standards in order to remain in business implies that they evolve over time to compete with trannationals for domestic market share.

Foreign investment is thus perceived as a means through which favourable market forces may be introduced, assuming that the 'superior efficiency, productivity and profitability' is achievable for indigenous industry. Should indigenous industries be 'overwhelmed by superior technology, quality or marketing' (Radice 1994) and fail to reach such standards, a consequence of introducing rival producers into the region might be the displacement of domestic firms from the market. Radice suggests that domestic producers might survive in the long term by imitation and that input suppliers might develop to meet the investors' requirements. However, this need not be a foregone conclusion, raising the possibility for a potential role for government.

In contrast to this, Merrit (1991) suggests that the ethos of 'only the strong survive' is 'in aggregate no bad thing' for the restructuring of the region's economies, arguing that 'better and more efficient producers drive out the bad'. However, it may also be worth noting that he takes little account of where the restructuring in the market will take place and of the aggregate effect of this on the region's development. The introduction of transnational firms into the domestic economy has repercussions for both large- and small-scale indigenous firms, though 'restructuring' may have more serious repercussions for the latter. The existing private sector consists of a large number of small firms, arguably few of which are likely to survive in competition with TNCs. Alongside the private sector, 80% of most Central and East European economies comprise large state owned firms. In the face of foreign investment, whether they remain in state ownership or are transferred to the private sector, it seems that few will be forced to leave the market by virtue of their size and resources. Hence, the impact on large industry is likely to be less pronounced. The introduction of transnational investment into the Central and East European economies need not reduce the region's existing emphasis on large firms as the basis for their economic development. This could be a problem. For example, Ellman (1992) suggests that 'the development of a large number of medium and small enterprises will have to be an important part of the structural change process', given that 'the traditional absence of both foreign competition and the possibility of entry of domestic competitors creates a monopolist's dream.' Monopolisation of industry can make the transition to **competitive** market relations very difficult and thus the 'market forces' injected into the economy by foreign investment may serve to reinforce the existing oligopolistic structure of the domestic economy rather than loosen it up.

(iii) Privatisation At the forefront of the process of transition to a free market economy have been privatisation programmes aimed at reducing the level of involvement of the state as an owner from approximately 80-90% to 20-30% (Alter and Wehrle 1993). It is suggested that 'without converting a substantial part of state property of productive assets into private ownership, the market economy cannot emerge' (Donges and Wieners 1994).

Dobosiewicz (1992) identifies what he perceives to be a vital role for foreign investment in the process[27] and in doing so suggests that a feedback relationship exists between privatisation and foreign investment. First, Dobosiewicz suggests that foreign investment creates greater momentum in the privatisation process by supplying the capital necessary to purchase enterprises. Second, he suggests that privatisation itself creates more 'normal' market conditions , attracting further foreign investors who may be reluctant to enter an industry dominated by the state.

Taking first the role of foreign investment in supplying capital to the market, Hunya (1992) argues that 'privatisation projects in Central and Eastern Europe must rely to a large extent on foreign capital because internal savings comprise only a small part of the value of assets to be privatised and governments do not want to wait until domestic capital accumulates.' In order to assess the need for foreign investment, it is useful to distinguish among different types of privatisation. Whilst the sale of land and small to medium sized enterprises has been considerable, with the majority of transfers taking place at the domestic level, domestic capital has been less forthcoming in the privatisation of large firms. Given the basic lack of funds and managerial experience, it appears that domestic entrepreneurs have also been reluctant to accept the risks inherent in large scale privatisation[28] .

If an objective of any Central and East European government was to retain domestic ownership, the small scale privatisation might be regarded as a mixed blessing as domestic ownership prevails. Given this, one solution to the problem of privatising large scale firms might be to break up elements of the latter, to facilitate domestic sale. However, the emphasis placed on large firms as the principal means by which the region may develop has meant that the breaking up of large firms has been largely rejected by the CEECs.[29] As such, the role for foreign investors in large scale privatisation has been elevated.[30]

---

27 Dobosiewicz's assertion is well founded given that 'most transnationals that entered the country for local manufacture acquired assets and production facilities through the privatisation of state-owned enterprises', Marton (1993).

28 In the Czech Republic,where coupons were distributed throughout the adult population with the aim of achieving equitable democratic distribution of enterprises, 72% of coupon owners were reluctant to act independently. Most relied on institutional investors and mutual funds during the auctions, both of which have heavy foreign involvement. Hence, the intended domestic nature of the privatisation scheme was lost due to the general apprehension of the population. (Hunya 1992)

29 Only in Romania have large state firms been broken up into smaller units to encourage domestic sale.

30 Radice (1994) argues that 'the massive asset transfers [of foreign investors] overshadow the organic growth of the small business', hinting at the significant role which

Direct sale to foreign investors has caused much debate and concern amongst the population, chiefly 'that in the absence of domestic sources of finance, foreigners will acquire a large part of industry at fire-sale prices' (Hamilton and Adjubei 1991). This echoes fears of foreign domination of the economy expressed by other regions in the past. However, this does not appear to be influencing the governments' policies. For example, in 1990 the Hungarian Department of Industry issued guidelines on 'How to buy a company in 100 days'. These were targeted directly at foreign interest, and selected 20 large enterprises whose sale to foreign investors was seen to be a high priority. The government stated that it was 'open to offers' for all and any of the 10,000 concerns on the state's privatisation list (Merrit 1991).

For large privatisations, Central and East European governments have thus been quick to switch their attention to outside investors, but in doing so they have tended to downplay the need for (at least some) domestic ownership.

It appears that in assessing the impact of sale to foreign investors, governments tend to over-emphasise the immediate gain from a large influx of capital. Existing privatisation schemes appear to lack coherent purpose or strategy, other than that of achieving widespread speedy transfers of ownership, with relatively little consideration being given to the potential long-term consequences of the wholesale transfer of large enterprises to foreign concerns.

The second role that Dobosiewicz (1992) suggests for privatisation is that of a spur to further foreign investment. By speeding up the transformation to a market economy, it is argued, privatisation creates a free market system of competing firms which acts to encourage further foreign investment in Central and Eastern Europe. However, the assumption that the existence of free market forces **must** attract foreign investment is questionable. Indeed, foreign firms may favour a degree of protection from competition and even request this as a prerequisite for investing in a country, so as to operate in an attractive industrial environment.[31]

Evidence (Hunya 1992, McMillan 1993) suggests that the largest purchases by foreign investors have been in sectors where the state monopoly has been the highest, ie automobile manufacture, cigarette production and electronics. Rather than moving to a system whereby competition results in market share, privatisation of large firms may enable TNCs to buy an automatic oligopolistic market share. Radice (1994) suggests that 'even if governments are anxious to develop competitive market structures, it is clear that the attraction of a significant if not dominant market share is important to foreign companies'. The ability to buy a large market share, even gain a monopoly position, may be a discerning factor for recent transnational investment activity.

---

small indigenous industry may have to play, a point often neglected by Central and East European governments.

[31] Interestingly, CEECs may use such requests as a means for introducing a degree of protectionism (as in Japan and the 'Four Tigers').

An example of this is the Volkswagen (VW) acquisition of Czech car manufacturer Skoda in 1992. Skoda was deemed strategically important by VW, representing over 70% of car sales in the Czech Republic. VW acquired 31% of Skoda in 1991, with an option to acquire a further 40% by 1995. Plans are being made to expand its dealer distribution networks within the region in order to increase Skoda's sales in Czech and other Central and East European markets (Dobosiewicz 1992).

It follows that a presumption that FDI will necessarily increase competition between firms warrants further investigation.

10.5 Compatibility of Objectives

The example of privatisation illustrates the need to explore the degree of compatibility between government and transnational objectives. Having explored these in the previous two sections, the question is raised: will TNCs pursuing their own objectives necessarily yield the outcomes which governments desire?

The specific objectives of governments that have been discussed , technology transfer and modernisation, competition and the introduction of market forces, and privatisation , may be reduced to essentially one thing: the desire to introduce a free market system (so as) to create a more efficient, competitive economy. One way to achieve this is by introducing competition between firms. Transnationals' role in this process has been likened to 'a battering ram beating down the many obstacles to the introduction of the free market economy' (Merrit 1991). It was also suggested that transnationals pursuing the objectives of market share and low labour costs may do so with and eye to achieving market power in both Central and East European and global markets. Many opportunities arising within Central and Eastern Europe which promise to lead to the realisation of this underlying aim have been grasped by TNCs, illustrated by their involvement in the privatisation process and in their use of distribution channels.

Consider first privatisation. Whilst identified as a means of introducing new capital flows into the region, more importantly privatisation has been advocated as a means of introducing free market forces in the economy. The programmes, if evaluated solely at this level, might be presumed a 'success', since sizable inflows of capital have accompanied the sale of large state-owned firms in areas such as car manufacture and, as public ownership rights have been transferred to the private sector, a free market system might be said to have emerged. However, given that the introduction of greater competition between firms was deemed an important component of a free market system, TNCs' management of the privatisation process brings into question this underlying presumption. In some cases, privatisation aimed at spurring competition may have resulted in reduced rather than heightened levels of competition. Insofar as TNCs have taken over once publicly-owned, large and monopolistic enterprises, this does not imply a necessary increase in competition, other things being equal. Nor does it necessarily imply an outcome that can be meaningfully labelled 'competitive'. Moreover, insofar as these privatisations may result in smaller indigenous producers being forced off the market, as contemplated in Section IV, levels of competition may be further reduced. Any restructuring which takes place as a result of the sale of large firms to TNCs might usually be identified as a necessary signal of the free market driving out its temporary inefficiencies. Yet, if the aim of a free market system is to allocate resources efficiently through competition between firms, reducing the number of firms that are competing raises question marks about the nature of the market system being established.

Furthermore, to the extent that privatisation in Central and Eastern Europe may represent the transfer of dominant market power from **public** and **domestic** to **private** and **foreign** hands, it may be inferred that the objective of increased competition need not be attained. If follows that, unless governments can and do design appropriate **industrial** strategies with **their objectives** clearly laid out and with **consequent** roles for transnational investment clearly identified, it may be the case that 'any industrialisation taking place is purely incidental to the [TNCs'] main objective', Evans (1979). The CEECs cannot afford this.

Governments 'buying into' elements of a market system , introducing competition, welcoming inward investment , expect it to yield the alleged benefits heralded by other supposed free market economies. Theoretically, it is argued that in a free market system where actors pursue their own motives, the 'invisible hand' of the market leads to an efficient allocation of resources.[32] Neoclassical economics has honed the argument, suggesting that an economy will be Pareto-efficient if it comprises actors who pursue their own interests in a system of complete perfect competition. Hence, it is perhaps unsurprising that Central and East European governments find the notion of the invisible hand so appealing. Yet, the forgoing discussion illustrates that TNCs may proactively remove themselves from the rigours of perfect competition. In doing so, however, the assumption that a market system will yield a Pareto-efficient outcome is undermined.

---

32 Adam Smith's analogy of an 'invisible hand' has been at the forefront of the concept of 'private enterprise', whereby the entrepreneur, 'intends only his own gain, and he is in this ... led by an invisible hand to promote an end which was no part of his intention. Nor is it always the worse for the society that it was no part of it. By pursuing his own interest he frequently promotes that of society more effectually than when he really intends to promote it' (Smith, 1950). Marris and Mueller (1980) observe: 'few would disagree that Adam Smith's invisible hand theorem is the heart of the economist's *Weltanschaung*. Ask whether trade barriers should be lowered, the spread of multinational corporations restrained, oil prices deregulated, cartels dissolved, or more fundamentally whether a market-based capitalist system is economically superior to a state-run socialist system, and economists almost certainly will begin to answer the question by trying to apply the theorem'.

To the extent that, in this instance, the attainment of desirable outcomes is not predetermined by the application of a free market system, it becomes necessary to examine the implications for the pursuit and attainment of government objectives more widely. To this end, it is perhaps revealing to use the discussion of technology transfer and modernisation from Section IV as a further example of an objective for governments seeking foreign investment. Again, the potential disparity between the objectives of governments and those of TNCs suggests that the market system will not automatically lead to a desirable outcome from the point of view of governments.

The Central and East European market is, unarguably, in need of modernisation , from physical plant and infrastructure to management techniques and best practice methods , and to this end governments are pursuing transnational 'packages' as a means of moving to a more modern, efficient economy. As a means to achieve this, Section III discussed the possibility that Central and Eastern Europe might utilise its low cost workforce to attract transnational investments, which it is hoped will spur the transfer of technology and the modernisation of industry.

Consider, however, transnational investments motivated by cheap labour. Central and Eastern Europe offers a cost advantage by means of its low cost workforce. By manipulating this 'competitive edge' , using the region as a base for simple, labour-intensive operations , TNCs are able to obtain a competitive advantage over their rivals. Hence, Central and Eastern Europe might, in response to this, attract transnational investment on the basis of offering a cheap site for labour intensive exports. The two sets of objectives may initially appear compatible: Central and Eastern Europe offering cheap labour which TNCs want and TNCs supplying the technology and know-how which Central and Eastern Europe needs. However, to the extent that Central and Eastern Europe may be attracting low-technology, labour-intensive operations by virtue of its low-cost labour force, it is not clear how this will contribute to the governments' objective of modernisation if the technology used in such investments is , by definition , simple. Alongside this, the potential use of distribution channels and warehousing by TNCs as a means of reaching markets without investing in manufacturing indicates that in some cases essentially little technology may be imported as part of the transnational package. Last but not least, the long term viability of a reliance on low labour costs is precarious, as new cheap leabour sites emerge.

To summarise, it has been argued that government objectives of modernisation and technology transfer are not necessarily attainable through the uncoordinated activities of TNCs. It, therefore, cannot be presumed that CEEC development needs can simply be attained through TNCs pursuing their own agenda.

Looking behind the South East Asian 'miracle', proactive government industrial strategies for the use of transnational investment emerge as pivotal to the success of that region. Objectives were stated and an industrial strategy provided government with a direct means of controlling how transnational activity influenced its economy, with a view to cultivating indigenous industrial strength. On this basis, the supposition that Central and Eastern Europe might use foreign investment in order to achieve economic development is welcome. However, an obsession with transnational investment 'per se' could undermine the development of indigenous industry as the development of the economy is 'contracted out' to TNCs.

All these point to the need for identifying policies by governments and TNCs which ideally favour everyone's objectives, i.e. maximise the compatibility of objectives and (thus) competitiveness. Given that an important factor for achieving this could be government policy towards industry in the form, for example, of an industrial strategy, it is as crucial to analyse the conditions which enable governments to do so (namely minimise the problem of 'government failure'). These are complex issues which are beyond the modest scope of this paper. All we wanted to establish here is the rather obvious, yet often neglected, possibility that government and TNC objectives need not always coincide and that exploring further the conditions which facilitate such 'coincidence' to everyone's benefit is a useful objective.[33]

10.6 Conclusion

The principal focus of this paper is to identify and explain both the motives of transnationals in investing in Central and Eastern Europe and the objectives of governments in attracting such investment. These issues preoccupy Sections III and IV, which centre on a review of existing literature. The aim is to depict the general situation, cutting through the details associated with specific firms and particular countries. Section V deepens the analysis by exploring the compatibility of the motives and the objectives.

All government objectives discussed in Section IV appear to have the common aim of making Central and East European industry 'competitive' by Western standards through the modernisati5on of industry, the creation of market systems and the transfer of state owned enterprises into private hands. It seems that it is hoped by governments that indigenous industry will develop to become efficient, more marketable and ultimately an 'international player.' What becomes apparent from the discussion in Section V, however, is the potential weakening of indigenous industry and the regional governments' loss of decision-making power, weakening the region's ability to determine its own future development. This suggests that using FDI to develop particular activities or industries which need Western technology or know-how can best be achieved as part of a coherent industrial strategy. The extent to which it is possible to achieve this in Central and Eastern Europe, particularly given its history of economic mismanagement by government,

---

33 This we pursue in further related work. (See, for example, Cowling and Sugden (1994), Pitelis (1994).

is highly questionable. This points crucially to the need to analyse the conditions which may enable governments to undertake the role entrusted to them by their citizens. Moreover, it points to the need to examine the conditions which ensure the compatibility of objectives between TNCs and governments, ideally leading to a 'positive sum game'. These issues are beyond the scope of this paper, the modest aim of which was to establish the obvious; that CEECs' and TNCs' objectives need not always coincide.

References

Alter, R and Wehrle, F (1993) 'Foreign Direct Investment', *Intereconomics*, May/June.

Bailey, David (1995) 'Transnationals and the Transition: The Role of Foreign Direct Investment in Hungary's Economic Transformation', *Occasional Papers in Industrial Strategy*, No 32, *Research Centre for Industrial Strategy*, University of Birmingham.

Bailey, David, Harte, George and Sugden, Roger (1994) *Transnationals and Governments. Recent Policies in Japan, France, Germany, the United States and Britain*, London: Routledge.

Blanchard, Oliver, Dornbush, Rudiger, Krugman, Paul, Layard, Richard and Summers, Lawrence (1991) '*Reform in Eastern Europe*', Massachusetts: MIT Press

Cantwell, John (1994) 'The Internationalisation of Business and the Economic Development of Poland and Eastern Europe', University of Reading Department of Economics, *Discussion Papers in International Investment and Business Studies*, No 180.

Centre for Economic Policy Research (1992) *Monitoring European Integration , The Impact of Eastern Europe*, London: Centre for Economic Policy Research.

Cowling, Keith and Sugden, Roger (1994) *Beyond Capitalism: Towards a New World Economic Order*, London: Pinter .

Dobosiewicz, Zbigniew (1992) *Foreign Investment in Eastern Europe*, London: Routledge.

Donges, Juergen B and Wieners, Jürgen (1994) 'Foreign Investment in the Transformation Process of Eastern Europe', *The International Trade Journal*, Vol VIII, No.2, Summer.

Dunning, John H (1993) 'The Prospects for Foreign Direct Investment in Central and Eastern Europe', University of Reading Department of Economics, *Discussion Papers in International Investment and Business Studies*, No.155.

Dunning, John H (1994) 'Globalisation, Economic Restructuring and Development', University of Reading Department of Economics, *Discussion Papers in International Investment and Business Studies*, No.187.

Ellman, M (1992) 'General Aspects of Transition' in: Ellman, M, Gardar, E T and Kolodko, G (eds) '*Economic Transition in Eastern Europe*', Oxford: Blackman.

Evans, P (1979) *Dependent Development: the Alliance of Multinational, State and Local Capital in Brazil*, Princeton: Princeton University Press.

Hamilton, Geoffrey and Adjubei, Yuri (1991) 'Analysing the First Wave of Foreign Direct Investment to the Countries of Eastern Europe 1987-1990' in: Schenk, Monkiewicz, Wass-v-Cege (eds), *New Dimensions in East-West Business Relations*, New York: Verlag.

Hunya, G (1992) 'Foreign Direct Investment and Privatisation in Central and Eastern Europe', *Communist Economies and Economic Transformation*, Vol.4, No.4.

Inzelt, Annamaria (1994) 'Privatisation and Innovation in Hungary: First Experiences', *Economic Systems*, Vol 18, No 2.

Jolly, Adam (1994) 'Business Development in Eastern Europe', in: *Eastern Europe and the Commonwealth of Independent States*, London: Europa Publications.

Kozminski, Andrzej (1992) 'The Main Issues of Industrial Policy for Poland', *Communist Economies and Economic Transformation*, Vol.4, No.2.

Marris, Robin and Mueller, Dennis C (1980) 'The Corporation, Competition and the Invisible Hand', *Journal of Economic Literature*, Vol.XVIII, March.

Marton, Katherin (1993) 'Foreign Direct Investment in Hungary', *Transnational Corporations*, Vol.2, No.1, February.

McMillan, C H (1986) 'Trends in Direct Investment and the Transfer of Technology', in: Csikos-Nagy, Band and Young, D G (eds) *East-West Economic Relations in a Changing Global Environment*, London: IEA/Macmillan.

McMillan, C H (1993) 'The Role of Foreign Direct Investment in the Transition from Planned to Market Economies', *Transnational Corporations*, Vol.2, No.3, December.

Merrit, M (1991) *Eastern Europe and the USSR*, London: Kogan Page.

Naujoks, Petra and Schmidt, Klaus-Dieter (1994), 'Outward Processing in Central and East European Transition Countries: Issues and Results from German Statistics', Kiel Institute of World Economics, *Kiel Working Paper*, No 631.

Pitelis, Christos (1994) 'Industrial Strategy for Britain in Europe and the World', *Journal of Economic Studies*, 21 (5)

Pitelis, Christos, Tsipouri, Lena and Sugden, Roger (1994) 'Outward Investment, International Competitiveness and Industrial Development: The Case of Greece', *Occasional Papers in Industrial Strategy*, No 23, *Research Centre for Industriel Strategy*, University of Birmingham.

Radice, Hugo (1993) 'Global Integration, National Disintegration? Foreign Capital in the Reconstitution of Capitalism in Central and Eastern Europe', *School of Business and Economic Studies Discussion Paper*, University of Leeds.

Radice, Hugo (1994) 'Organising Markets in Central and Eastern Europe: Competition, Governance and the Role of Foreign Capital', *School of Business and Economic Studies Discussion Paper*, University of Leeds.

Smith, Adam (1950) *An Inquiry Into the Nature and Causes of the Wealth of Nations*, London: Methuen.

Teranishi, Juro (1994) 'Economic Recovery, Growth and Policies: 'Gradualism' in the Japanese Context', *Economic Policy*, Vol 19, Supplement.

Wade, R (1990) *Governing the Market: Economic Theory and the Role of Government in East Asian Industrialization*, Princeton: Princeton University Press.

Wang, Zhen Quan (1993) 'Foreign Investment in Hungary: A Survey of Experience and Prospects', *Communist Economies and Economic Transformation*, Vol.5, No.2.

11 Agricultural Issues in the Integration of the CEECs in the EU

George J. Mergos
Dept. of Economics
University of Athens
8, Pesmazoglou - Stadiou Str.
Athens, GR-105 59

Abstract

The major challenge for Europe at the turn of the century is the integration of the CEECs and, perhaps unexpectedly, agricultural issues play a major role. The discussion has focused up to now on the impact of enlargement on the CAP. This paper reviews available evidence and critically assesses the agricultural issues in the process of establishing a wider, integrated Europe. The twin objective of transition and integration requires changes of a massive scale, something that is not fully realized in the CEECs. In a pre-accession strategy, the main issue is alignment with the internal market as the most important step towards membership. CEEC agricultural policies should reinforce the emergence of markets and institutions and, here, a new role for the state is required. Finally, the paper claims that integration will be facilitated by reinforcing intra-CEEC cooperation with the creation of a free trade area by expanding the existing CEFTA, instead of the present bilateralism of the Association Agreements.

11.1 Introduction

The integration of Central and Eastern European Countries (CEEC)[1] with the European Union is the greatest challenge facing Europe at the turn of the century. The major issues are whether integration of EU and CEEC agriculture is possible;

---

[1] Originally, the term CEEC included Poland, Hungary, the Czech Republic, Slovakia, Romania and Bulgaria. Now, it refers also to those Eastern European countries that are in the process of negotiating Europe Agreements, such as Slovenia, Estonia, Latvia and Lithuania.

if yes, what impact that might have on EU agriculture and the Common Agricultural Policy (CAP); and, finally, what options are available for the process of integration.

Although the issue of agriculture in the context of EU enlargement has been intensely discussed, it is far from settled. The discussion up to now has focused more on the impact of enlargement on the CAP and much less on its feasibility or on the specific agricultural issues associated with enlargement. It is vigorously argued that the expansion of EU to include new members will be facilitated if the EU undertakes necessary reforms, mainly by further reforming the CAP and reducing the structural funds[2]. According to this view, the CAP at least in its present form is incompatible with the integration of new members into a wider Europe, either as members of the EU or as priviledged trading partners. On the other hand, proponents of maintaining the CAP, at least in principle, claim that this is an opportunistic position that takes advantage of the circumstances to destroy the CAP and that a sweeping reform of the CAP is not necessary for CEEC accession and integration into a wider EU. Although accession of the CEECs is considered as helping both the new members and the EU, the process of achieving integration is far from settled.

Several studies have so far focused on agriculture. Thus, an early study which explored the future of the CAP also discussed the issue of enlargement (Larsen, 1994). The study of Nallet and van Stolk (1994), commissioned by DG IV of the Commission, and four more studies published in the beginning of 1995, commissioned by the DG I, focused on the issue of convergence between EU's and CEECs' agricultural policies, in view of the CEECs future accession to the EU (Backwell et al, 1995, Mahe et al, 1995 Tangerman et al. 1995 and Tarditi et al, 1995). These studies examined what can be done during the pre-accession period to further facilitate convergence and integration of the agricultural sectors in the EU and CEEC. More recently, a series of reports have been published by the Commission for each country (EC, 1995a). Still open, however, are issues on: (a) how and how soon internal market rules with respect to agriculture can be adopted by new members; (b) what is the role of agriculture in the economy of the CEECs and what are the required short term measures to stop decline and stabilize income and production in CEEC agriculture; (c) what trade strategies they should follow and what are the available options for increasing intra-CEEC and CEEC-CIS agricultural trade relationships; and (d) what are the policy options that are more consistent with CEECs macro-economic stabilization plans and EU obligations to the GATT.

Sectoral policy options, however, including those of the agricultural sector, should properly be considered within an overall frame of economic integration,

---

[2] An interview of Commission President J. Santer to *The Financial Times* was commented on in the editorial of *The Wall Street Journal* on 19 May 1995 which stressed that bringing in new members depends chiefly on further reforming of the CAP.

taking into account the particular situation of economic transition. The external economic integration and internal economic transition of the CEECs are intimately tied together and, in fact, jointly determine the process and feasibility of integration (see Bosworth and Ofer, 1995). Hence, focusing on CAP reform as the main obstacle for integration may be inappropriate, since a reform of the CAP may not be sufficient or even necessary for the integration of the CEECs into a wider Europe, in the absence of other fundamental changes in their economy and society.

Economic integration can take several forms, from "shallow integration" with an expansion of trade in goods and services and factor transfers to a deeper integration involving the establishment of common economic and institutional frameworks with the creation of similar legal, regulatory and social institutions (Bosworth and Ofer, 1995). After a long period of central planning with emphasis on autarky and central control, the CEECs will face immense difficulties in adjusting and approximating their administrative, economic and social structures to those of the EU, with implications that cut through all economic sectors. It is questionable whether these countries can skip many of the evolutionary stages through which other countries have passed. The creation of markets is a difficult process and one cannot expect that the rate of establishing markets in the CEECs would be faster than that of advanced market economies (PMI, 1994, p.75). Markets do not just spring up from the ground but are complex institutions requiring strong social organization and state involvement (Stiglitz, 1993).

To a large extent, the legacy of the past determines not only the process of transition but also the process of integration. Central planning mentality still haunts policy thinking, the economic organization is still structured along vertical branches of economic activity, administrative control still suppresses a large range of activities required for the operation of markets. Further, the emphasis during the central planning period on self-sufficiency has eliminated the region's long established competitive advantage in food and agricultural products. The failure of the system is highlighted by the poor quality of domestic products in comparison to those available in the global market as a result of lack of competition. Last, the establishment of a legal system protecting property rights and enforcing contracts to replace the previously existing administrative controls and hierarchical structures seems a daunting task.

It is also recognized that the piece-meal trade arrangements of the Association Agreements[3] and the lack of a coherent strategy for integration are serious handicaps. Not only some countries have not yet been included but the bilateralism tends to marginalize CEECs economically and politically. The best way, it is argued, Western Europe can help transition and integration is by building a

---

3 Europe Agreements establish bilateral associations between each of the CEEC and the EU with major aims policy dialogue, closer economic integration, and further cultural and financial cooperation. See for an earlier survey and assessment of the impact of Agreements in agriculture Tracy (1994).

sensible path that can be followed by the CEECs as a group, instead of the present "hub-and-spoke" bilateralism (Baldwin, 1994). However, it should be noted that most CEECs favour this bilateralism.

The purpose of this paper is to review available evidence and critically assess the agricultural dimension in the process of establishing a wider, integrated Europe. The principal question is whether integration of EU and CEEC agriculture is a feasible endeavour. The paper aims to contribute to the debate by considering what types of policies are compatible with the objective of integration and by discussing alternative options for action. The structure of the paper is as follows. First, it presents a brief survey of the situation in CEEC agriculture and provides an assessment of the situation of the agricultural sector, of the role of agriculture in their economies and of the status of the reform. Then it examines the issue of adopting the rules of the internal market, as well as a number of other policy issues in the EU and the CEECs. Finally, it concludes with an examination of alternative options for the process of integration of CEEC and EU agriculture.

11.2 Beyond Privatization of CEEC Agriculture

Economic performance in the CEECs does not match the early optimism for growth rates of 7% (CEPR, 1990). Yet, despite modest and uneven progress in privatization and economic performance across the region during the early reform years, political objectives have been elevated from transition to accession which calls, in fact, for an economic integration of historic magnitude.

Researchers and politicians alike consider agriculture as one of the key sectors for the convergence of the CEECs to the EU. This is because expansion of the EU to the East to include the six (or ten) CEECs would increase agricultural land of the EU by one third, double agricultural employment and raise agricultural output by 30% to 60%, depending on the product (more if all ten countries are included). The GDP of the EU after accession of the six CEECs, on the other hand, would be increased by only 3,5%. Also, the current decline of agriculture in the CEECs is not considered permanent but rather is viewed as being mostly related to factors of transitory nature. It is expected that agriculture will recover once the process of transition approaches completion. The region is well endowed with agricultural resources. Although the six CEECs have only 2.2% of the world population, they have 3.1% of the world's land resources and a large production potential.

Since 1990, the region has experienced a substantial decline in agricultural production. The decline is considered by policy makers and the public as a disaster and is to a large extent attributed to the transition. Despite the decline, agricultural production in the CEECs remains high compared to that of the EU. For instance, production of grains in the six countries (1993) was 67 million tons compared with 160 million tons in the EU and there is still a large production potential that is not realized. Given resource endowments and average EU yields, the six countries can increase their production substantially (see Tyers, 1994). Nevertheless, this production potential may take decades to materialize, given the state of agriculture in the CEECs. This production potential is much larger in the case of crops, as livestock farming in the region is relatively backward compared to EU.

Besides differences in size, moreover, the sector plays a much more important role in the CEECs than in the EU. Agriculture occupies a position in the economy of the CEECs which is in fact much more central than is the case in the EU. The share of agriculture in GDP ranges from 4.5% to 21%, while the EU average is only 2.8%. Agriculture's share in employment ranges from 6.5% in the Czech Republic to 32.3% in Romania, while it averages only 5.8% in the EU. Taking into account agriculture's linkages to the rest of the economy through upstream and downstream sectors, the importance of agriculture in income generation in the CEECs becomes all too obvious. Furthermore, it should be noted that in some of the CEECs agricultural employment operates as a safety net during transition, in particular in Romania, Bulgaria and Poland.

In addition, unlike in the EU, agriculture and food policies have significant distributional implications. Food consumption in the CEECs has declined substantially since 1990, mostly as a result of the collapse in incomes. However, caloric consumption in the CEECs is still higher than the EU average, mainly due to substantially different food consumption patterns. Hence, despite the recent decline in total food consumption, no substantial increase in food consumption per capita is expected in the future, at least for traditional food items. An increase might be expected for fruit, vegetables and perhaps meat, but a decrease should be expected for grains and other staples. Protecting the urban and rural poor is an important concern when food prices are rising. Although price reforms imply raising prices to provide incentives to producers, eliminating subsidies has important distributional implications and price reform adversely affects the welfare of the poor urban groups. This state of affairs cannot be overlooked. A prosperous agricultural sector is important for the CEECs in their effort towards a strong market economy (Brooks et al., 1991). Nevertheless, domestic policies vary considerably across the region and in many cases do not lead to convergence with EU policies. Since 1990, the rural economy of the CEECs is experiencing fundamental change. Urban unemployment has put significant pressure on the rural economy for new jobs and agriculture's role, besides its strong contribution to GDP and employment, has become instrumental in revitalizing the rural economy and regions affected by industrial restructuring. Privatization of agriculture, including upstream and downstream activities, is slow. Land reform has contributed in some way to the creation of a large number of subsistence farms. Land fragmentation, lack of capital or land for many individuals wishing to engage in farming, lack of support services and poorly accessible upstream and downstream activities place a heavy burden on newly-established private farms and preclude any development possibility, locking them in subsistence.

In most CEECs, the process of transition is still slow and privatization is only partial. The agricultural sector of the CEECs - in particular the newly-established private sector - is frequently exploited by upstream and downstream industries that still possess characteristics of state or regional monopolies. Marketing and distribution systems generally operate with much lower efficiency than expected. Farmers and agricultural service operators are short of capital and investment is lagging. Rural credit is, perhaps, the most critical constraint for increasing the private sector's share in agricultural production. Obsolete technology in the agro-industrial food chain, inefficient industrial organisation and inexperienced management and markets with pronounced monopolistic characteristics create severe constraints to the expansion of agricultural production. Because of such factors, the economic environment for agriculture under prevailing conditions is very difficult and a rapid expansion of production is highly unlikely.

The monopolistic position of State Owned Enterprises (SOEs) inhibits efforts to provide private sector services. The observed reluctance in some countries to reduce the role of SOEs involved in the provision of services, inputs and in food processing and distribution has delayed the creation of an efficient, private agriculture and of a decentralized and diversified rural economy. There is a need for continuous support in strengthening economic growth and market reform in agriculture, mainly with policy reform and institution building.

Agricultural policy in the CEECs is still dominated by the legacy of the past with an excessive emphasis on self-sufficiency, mainly in grain production, as a means of achieving national food security. Agricultural policy formulation is uneven and partial. Policy measures are often conflicting and administratively motivated, leaving very limited choices for the emerging private sector. In some countries (mainly the Visegrad four) a CAP-like policy is starting to emerge with the prospect of EU membership. A protectionist attitude is emerging across the region, as a result of the belief that international markets are distorted by subsidised exports from the EU and the US. Macro-economic instability is perhaps the main obstacle in the process to reform agriculture and in the emergence of a healthy private sector. This macro-economic instability is manifested in large budget deficits, high inflation, inability to collect taxes and the rapid devaluation of the currencies which has a strong negative impact on all productive sectors. The legacy of the past and on-going power struggles in the economic and social spheres still persist and make the transition a long and painful process.

Although the countries share an eonomic structure inherited from the similar socio-economic systems they have been under for about fifty years, they do exhibit some important differences that create significant diversity within the region with respect to agriculture. Thus, there are three countries (Hungary, Romania, Bulgaria) with a substantial agricultural production potential. Hungary and Bulgaria were substantial exporters of agricultural commodities during the period of the previous regime. Recent developments in both countries point to the direction of re-establishing production structures. Romania, on the other hand, despite a large production potential, thanks to its land resources, has been severely affected by the adverse agricultural policies of the previous regime and it may take much longer before becoming able to reinstate an efficient production structure. In addition, there are significant differences among countries in their transformation policies (see for example Swinnen, 1995) which strongly influence the process of transition and integration.

Another dimension of diversity in the CEECs is the different role of agriculture in the economy. Some countries, like the Czech Republic and Hungary, are more advanced and have a similar structure to that of EU countries. As a result, agriculture's importance in their economies is rather small. In others, however, like Poland, Bulgaria and Romania, agriculture's role is much stronger, either as a safety net for unemployment or as a contributor to economic development. In Poland, where private farming dominated even in the past, agriculture's role as a safety net against poverty and unemployment is being increasingly recognized. Similarly, in Romania, where the transformation of the economy is lagging, agriculture can provide employment and income in regions that are being adversely affected by industrial restructuring.

11.3 The Agricultural Dimension of Integration

Having reviewed the progress of transition in agriculture so far, we turn now to the issues of integration. The achievement of the dual objective of economic transition and integration requires actions in various interrelated areas. Not only is the scale of change massive but also current policy thinking in the CEECs lacks the problem-solving approach that prevails in any market environment. To add to the complexity, the fragile political environment is not conducive to the required changes, despite agreement on the broad agenda of reform. Price liberalization, privatization, establishment of property rights, macro-economic stabilization and foreign trade reform are all well understood and part of the ongoing transition process. However, economic integration puts further constraints on the process requiring, at the same time with transition, adaptation to new economic, legal, regulatory, and social institutions. The massive change that is required to this end is not fully understood in the CEECs, caught as they are in their pre-accession euphoria. Some of these issues related to agriculture are discussed next.

11.3.1 Alignment with the internal market

The main task for all CEECs in the context of preparation for accession is alignment with the internal market of the Union in a process of approximation and harmonization. It is important to recognize, however, that the main challenge is not the approximation of legal texts, but the change and adaptation of the administrative, economic and social institutions needed to make the legislation operational. The legacy of the past renders this process complicated involving fundamental changes in the responsibilities not only of the national administrative and judicial systems but also of the emerging private sector as well. In addition, improvements in the operation of these administrative, judicial and private sector structures depend not only on changes in candidate countries but also on assistance provided by the EU on these matters as well as on training and transfer of experience (EC, 1994).

Although accession to the Union will involve acceptance of the *acquis communautaire* as a whole, priority during preparation for accession is placed on alignment with internal market requirements. Harmonization of legislation and adoption of the *acquis communautaire* is a pre-condition for accession. The CEEC can accede to the Union when they are able to take on the obligations of membership, including the aims of political, economic and monetary union, the development of a market economy with a capacity to withstand competition from the economies of the European Union and the development of institutions and guarantees in the functioning of democratic institutions, rule of law, respect for human rights and respect and protection for minorities. A Commission White Paper sets out the obligations of the Associated Countries with respect to the internal market of the Union, identifying the key measures in each sector of the internal market and suggesting a sequence with which the approximation of legislation should proceed (EC, 1995b).

Alignment with the Union's internal market is considered the first and most important step towards membership of the Union and it is expected to reinforce economic reform and industrial restructuring, stimulate trade and prepare the countries for integration into the EU. It involves the creation of conditions for promotion of economic freedom, removal of trade barriers, introduction of transparent competition rules, satisfaction of minimum social standards, adequate protection of the environment and putting into place legislative and regulatory systems, as well as standards and certification methods compatible with those of the European Union. It, also, involves achieving progress in macro-economic stabilization and structural reform, as well as commitment to and support for privatization, as essential steps in the preparation for integration into the internal market. To that end, several actions need to be taken by the CEECs including: (a) strengthening privatization and private sector development; (b) achieving progress in macro-economic stabilization and structural reform; (c) taking decisive steps towards elimination of state aids; (d) demonstrating commitment to and support for privatization and restructuring; and (e) supporting the development of an efficient financial system as a prerequisite of market development.

Education, training and experience transfer from the EU in this area is one of the main tasks of the approximation exercise. EU assistance has been from the beginning an important tool for the CEECs in the transition of their economies from plan to market. After the Essen meeting, EU assistance is given the twin mandate: (a) to assist the CEECs in accelerating economic development and growth in order to narrow the gap with the member states of the EU; and (b) to support the CEECs in their preparation for accession to the EU by providing assistance for the transformation of their economies and for the approximation of the legal systems.

In the context of agriculture, although the discussion up to now has centred on budgetary issues, the capacity of the countries to adopt the internal market rules has been overstated. An important question is whether these countries are expected to be able to adopt internal market regulations within a reasonable time frame, at least within the time frame discussed for the accession. The internal market is not considered as an end in itself, but rather as the principal instrument for achieving economic integration with a whole series of objectives, such as balanced and sustainable growth, high levels of employment and social protection, better standards of living and quality of life and economic and social cohesion. Economic integration achieved in a frontier-free internal market goes beyond other forms of cooperation such as free trade areas, customs unions and common markets which retain their physical frontiers. Hence, the creation of a frontier-free internal market is expected to maximize economic benefits by allowing a larger scale of production, improving economic performance through increased competition and stimulating investment (Spachis, 1995).

The requirement that the CEECs accept the internal market legislation has one precedent: that of the EFTA countries. Are the CEECs ready to adopt internal market rules and regulations in the pre-accession period? The operation of the internal market requires mutual confidence and equivalent regulation. Further, so as not to undermine the operation of the internal market, prospective members will have to achieve a high degree of alignment ahead of accession since any substantial failure to apply internal market rules puts the whole system under risk. However, a realistic process of alignment might be a logical sequential process of adopting internal market rules in the pre-accession period (EC, 1995b). This process is related to the characteristics of each country and the pace of its economic reform. Given that the CEECs are at different stages of macro-economic, and, sometimes, political stability, their capacity to adopt internal market regulations varies widely, with the Czech Republic being far ahead in this respect and Romania being the most distant from this objective.

This may have important implications for the time horizon of accession. The CEECs appear to compete for membership in order to ensure the political security and the economic benefits of EU membership and each is worried that its entry might be delayed if there is a need to wait until the other is admitted. This applies to Hungary and the Czech Republic versus Poland and Slovakia on the one hand and between the Visegrad four and the Balkan countries (Romania and Bulgaria) on the other. However, it seems that the Eastern enlargement is several years away, given that entry negotiations will not start before the end of the Inter-Governmental Conference of 1996. Hence, a realistic time frame for the enlargement is perhaps the year 2005 or even a later date. What seems proper during this pre-accession period is for the CEECs to develop market connections among themselves that lead to convergence with the EU internal market rules. Such connections may take the form of cooperation in stages, starting with a coordination of policies and leading to a free trade area and further increasing the ties of the group with the EU, instead of each individual country racing to join first and seeking bilateral ties with the EU.

11.3.2 Agricultural policies in the CEECs

A second important agricultural issue in the context of integration is what strategy should the CEECs adopt in formulating their agricultural and trade policies in the pre-accession period. In all CEECs agricultural output has fallen after 1990. The causes include a fall in internal demand, although production has also been affected for various reasons. The livestock sector was particularly hit by the fall in production. Governments have responded by providing support for producer prices in the form of minimum prices for certain major products, while others provide export subsidies. Although the European market cannot be the only outlet, the associated countries look to it as a natural destination of their products and one that can ensure satisfactory prices. However, exports of agricultural products from the associated countries have decreased recently while their imports of agricultural products from EU countries have increased creating a negative trade balance. Against this background it is crucial that the agricultural policies of the associated countries evolve in a way which is compatible with the reform of the Common Agricultural Policy as well with the GATT commitments entered into by these countries and by the European Union.

The agricultural policies of the CEECs have evolved through several stages since the beginning of the reform. Initially they started with a complete price liberalization that lasted for about two years and was followed by the gradual introduction of import restrictions and export promotion measures. The arguments for the adoption of protective policies included national food security, distorted international markets and the protection of domestic farm incomes. This has resulted in a variety of border measures that distort trade and have in most cases to be modified and significantly reduced under the GATT. It would be helpful if such coordination between the CEECs on these border measures and on domestic policy matters is achieved before negotiations for accession are initiated.

Policies in the CEECs should aim to reinforce the creation of a market economy with concerted efforts in the areas of macro-economic, institutional and sectoral policies. The most important factor contributing to the establishment of a market economy in agriculture is macro-economic stabilization. Although significant achievements have already been made in this respect, there is room for improvement, particularly towards a reduction of the high unemployment rate. Other priorities in the establishment of the market for agricultural inputs and outputs are the introduction of private initiatives in collective action and in supplying inputs to newly created private farms. Profitable markets do exist but new firms lack the capital and the knowledge to take advantage of such opportunities.

Although some CEECs have already started to increase agricultural prices by means of protective measures, high prices may not be helpful for the development of an efficient agriculture because they inhibit the flow of resources to other sectors and insulate the domestic economy from the competitive conditions of the international market. Given the uncertainty on the CAP's direction, as far as price support is concerned, the best policy option for the CEECs is to follow a low support policy (close to world market levels) by giving a low priority to price policy and avoiding interference with the market. This would mean a new role for state and government policy with an emphasis on measures that aim to correct market failures and to create a well functioning market environment that could be achieved by accelerating the privatisation process and by encouraging competition at all production and distribution levels (Stiglitz, 1993).

Impact on the CAP and the budget Given that, for internal EU reasons, the CAP is itself in the process of change, it represents a "moving target" for the CEECs. Although there has been a major recent reform (1992), several other changes are currently being considered, not to mention that further changes are likely to happen over the next decade, resulting from the EU's commitments to the GATT, even without accession of the CEECs. It should be mentioned that the new round of GATT negotiations is to start in 1999 and will focus on environmental issues. In these negotiations, however, the EU will be most probably a *demandeur* (Ockenden and Franklin, 1995). Although it may be possible for the present range and level of support to survive unchanged until the turn of the century, its maintenance will become progressively more difficult thereafter. In the absence of some unforeseeable event, quotas, set-aside and compensatory payments will probably, at the turn of the century, still exist and EU prices will still be maintained significantly above world market levels, although by a smaller margin than the one of mid-1990's. Despite all the arguments in favour of market prices, reduction of quotas and direct payments, there are no sufficient reasons from both the budget and the GATT agreement to justify further deep changes in the CAP. Hence, even without a CEECs enlargement there will most probably not be any nominal price cuts by the year 2000, but some supply control measures may be undertaken to meet the export volume constraint set by the GATT agreement by the year 2005 (Ockenden and Franklin, 1995).

The cost of the CEECs' accession to the CAP and the EU budget has been the subject of a long and hot debate. Estimates of the budget implications of the CEECs' accession vary widely, depending upon the assumptions used to develop alternative scenarios. Some of the estimates are realistic and plausible (such as cost estimates produced by Mahe et al. (1995), i.e. from 6 bn ECU to 13 bn ECU). Other estimates, however, are quite unrealistic and their derivation is simplistic and speculative. For instance, Tarditi et al. (1995) use an EU average per capita transfer of ECU 328 to arrive at an estimate of 32 bn ECU as the budget cost of the CEECs' accession, assuming full rights of new members under present CAP rules. Such an estimate is not plausible, given current productivity levels in CEECs as well as a highly probable low absorption capacity, as the experience of the Mediterranean enlargement has shown. Hence, given the low absorption capacity of the CEECs and the slow process of development of their agricultural production structures, a more realistic estimate of the annual cost of accession to the CAP would be, even with full rights enjoyed by the new members, of the order of 6 to 8 bn EC, which, of course, is still quite substantial.

What assistance should the EU offer Between December 1991 and March 1993, "Europe Agreements" were signed between the EU and the six CEECs establishing Associations as a first step to EU accession and integration into a wider Europe. Soon, similar Association Agreements are to enter into force for Slovenia and the three Baltic states. The objective of accession is included in all Europe Agreement texts as a goal for the CEECs and the preambles stress the importance of strengthening the links between the EU and the CEECs following their emergence as new democracies.

Accession, however, goes far beyond the provisions of the Europe Agreements and even beyond harmonization with internal market legislation. Many politicians from the CEECs have expressed their dissatisfaction that the integration of Eastern Europe is not considered as a mainly political issue (PMI, 1995, p. 19 and 64). But this only reveals that decision makers in the CEECs do not fully realize the magnitude of the task they are embarking on or the complexity that the process of deep integration involves. The task they face is certainly much more difficult than that faced by the Mediterranean countries at the time of their accession (Baldwin, 1994).

Assistance from the EU would be extremely helpful for the CEECs in achieving their objectives of transition and integration. However, public opinion in the EU considers that much of this assistance is being wasted, while in the CEECs an erosion of the public image of the west is evident in recent years. Hence, a rethinking of the EU assistance strategy seems in order if it is to facilitate transition and integration.

EU assistance to agriculture should concentrate on four key areas: (i) assist the development and improvement of institutions and infrastructures, with emphasis on marketing, price information, market infrastructure, restructuring and privatisation, food and product quality standards, marketing agencies, export promotion extension services, rural credit, land registration; (ii) help counteract the adverse employment effects of agricultural restructuring with training programmes for displaced workers, establishment of decentralised educational and training centres and preparation of vocational teachers; (iii) encourage the transformation process by providing investment credit for new or reformed enterprises (agri-business and food processing, downstream and upstream); (iv) step up efforts and help the CEECs to establish the institutional and legal preconditions necessary to implement the CAP, once the CEECs have joined. The latter involves harmonisation of legislation and creation of appropriate legal and institutional framework for the smooth operation of the internal market.

Last, trade is an area where EU assistance can have a strong impact on both transition and integration. Food security reasons for the protection of agriculture are not considered credible any more (Winters, 1990). Agriculture is the sector where the CEECs need special support for easier access to EU markets, but it is unrealistic to expect further EU agricultural trade concessions during pre-accession. Although CEEC exports to third counties are affected by EU export subsidies, for instance in the case of the Newly Independent States (NIS), the claim that there are subsidised EU exports to the CEECs is unfounded (Tangerman, 1995).

Recently, an increase in trade between former CMEA countries is observed, despite constraints imposed by serious foreign exchange shortages. Hence, the EU can support intra-regional trade and establish credit lines and/or offer export credit guarantees for the CEEC agricultural exports to the NIS. An important constraint to export expansion is also the lack of adequate export and marketing infrastructure. Assistance from international financial institutions can play here a catalytic role in mobilizing resources from other donors (Zecchini, 1995).

While the overall economic cost of assistance in these areas to the EU would be small, the impact on CEEC agriculture would be large. In general, assistance in the trade area has several advantages. Namely, it creates fewer distortions and at the same time helps the CEECs generate income out of their own resources making them economically more self-reliant, which in turn reduces protectionist attitudes in the EU.

11.4 Options for Integration of CEEC and EU Agriculture

Transition and integration have become the twin objectives of the CEECs. However, there is no precedent on the process of achieving them, let alone on how to evaluate alternative courses of action. Although one could list the changes required in the system and the characteristics of a market economy, it would be difficult to provide a concrete sequence of actions to achieve the objective of integration. The dilemma is known in the literature as the "gradualism versus shock approach" but in reality no path follows either the one or the other approach and most countries have largely followed approaches involving mostly trial and error.

The principal question posed at the beginning of this paper was whether an integration of EU and CEEC agricultures is possible, and, if yes, what is the magnitude of the problem and what options are available for achieving a smooth integration. Obviously, as it becomes evident from the preceding analysis, the process of integration and the time horizon are important parameters of the issue. The principal variables are production, consumption and net trade in agricultural and food products. The question is, therefore, in what time horizon and following which process is integration of EU and CEEC agriculture feasible, while commitments to the GATT can be met by either parties and the budget cost of extending the CAP to these countries can be contained within reasonable limits.

Food is a highly political issue associated with strong state involvement, so that free trade in food is extremely rare (Winters, 1990). The EU will be unwilling to dispose of the CAP, at least in principle. However, despite resistance from farming circles, some reform of the CAP towards lower price support and an increase in direct payments should be expected in the future, perhaps around 2000. This is not necessarily a consequence of the EU enlargement but it will certainly facilitate it.

Prices in the CEECs are below both CAP price levels and world market levels. Although a protectionist attitude is emerging in certain CEECs resulting in higher farm prices, the region's production potential may take some time to materialize, as discussed earlier. Hence, only moderate supply response should be expected in the CEECs, at least in the medium term. If this is the case, the EU markets are not threatened even if there are cost advantages in the CEECs and some economic benefit from trade liberalization will probably occur with respect to GATT.

As mentioned earlier, estimates of the cost of CEEC accession to the CAP vary widely depending on the particular assumptions used in the calculations, but most probably costs have been overstated. Besides, it should be underlined that direct payments may not be given to farmers who have not suffered price cuts, i.e. the farmers in CEECs. Nevertheless, focusing just on budget costs is not helpful, because not only are costs difficult to estimate but it is also misleading to look only at costs without estimating benefits as well, especially when these benefits could well balance the costs. Any increase in trade between regions in the expanded EU would give rise to a larger market, with significant economic gains to European consumers. Also, in the absence of an external shock (e.g., integration), the transition within the CEECs will be long. In any case, integration will confer wider benefits to the entire European economy that cannot be easily monetized.

With respect to agriculture, three main options have been considered for transition and integration (OECD, 1995). The first option is a full and immediate adoption of the CAP upon membership, which is not regarded as a viable option overall. A variant of this, which calls for enlargement of the EU without the CAP, although a feasible option, might not be politically acceptable. A second option is the operation of a different CAP for the CEECs than the one for the EU-15. Despite lower price levels in the CEECs, some production response would still be expected, thanks to the stable environment created for investment. The CEECs would also make lower budgetary contributions, as they would not have access to the full benefits of membership. However, the drawback with this option is that a complex system of border controls between the CEECs and the EU-15 will have to be established in order to maintain price differences. This would be difficult, if not impossible, to achieve, given the requirements of the internal market. The outcome would be the suppression of agriculture only in new members. Hence, the option of creating a differentiated CAP in the CEECs should be rejected. It makes no sense in the absence of a wider CEEC common market and, moreover, from an operational point of view, it poses large problems in agreeing a common price level, in managing the prices, given the exchange rate instability, and in financing the common policy. A third option is the gradual enlargement of the EU, where different CEECs could be admitted to the EU as and when they were deemed ready, without waiting for other CEECs to catch up (variable geometry approach). In purely agricultural terms, admission of the Czech Republic would create the fewest problems and could be undertaken far earlier than the admission of, say, Bulgaria or Romania. In a wider view, an early accession of Poland would have considerable merit, given the size of its economy. Such a gradual approach offers many advantages and, despite being politically unattractive, is an approach which will sooner or later be considered, at least with respect to the Baltic States, Slovenia and the rest of former Yugoslavia.

However, from a different perspective, as indicated previously, the CEECs can start bringing themselves closer to each other by coordinating their policies, including agricultural and trade policies, as they strive for convergence with the EU. Baldwin (1994) has proposed an "Association of the Association Agreements" and then an Organization of European Integration (with the CEECs participating in the EU's Single Market without agriculture, without transfers and without voting), that would create the intermediate step in the process of European integration. Following a slightly different line of thinking, a free trade area may be one option, a customs union may be a second option and a common market the third option.

The creation of a free trade area between the six countries has definite merit, given that it already exists for the Visegrad four (CEFTA) and can be expanded to all countries that aim at accession. The operation of a free trade area offers several advantages: it will assist macro-economic and price convergence; it will encourage greater dialogue leading to agricultural policy convergence; it will increase competition and market size; and, finally, it will prepare the CEECs for joining the internal market of the EU. Although there are problems in creating a free trade area (bringing down border barriers always causes pain for some parts of the economy), the benefits far outweigh costs.

A recent evaluation of CEFTA (Inotai and Sass, 1994) gives a positive balance, pointing out its favourable impact on intra-regional trade, especially in terms of preventing trade diversion. However, it also points out to some cautionary signs, such as the slow pace and limited extent of liberalization, potential conflicts among members and the predominance of security issues over economic issues in the relations among CEFTA countries.

A customs union involves, in addition to a free trade area, a common external tariff, while a common market would duplicate almost all of the actions of the EU common market that they eventually have to adopt. Despite some benefits to be derived from the creation of a customs union or a common market by the CEECs, the associated costs will be much greater than the benefits. Hence, establishment of a free trade area would be an advantageous solution for the countries in their preparation for accession.

11.5 Conclusions

Agricultural issues have been at the centre of the debate on the EU's eastward enlargement. Many consider the impact on the EU budget as the main issue. However, alignment with the internal market is the major task and here the capacity of the countries to adopt internal market rules has been overstated. Agricultural and trade policies in th e CEECs have to be coordinated and bring the domestic markets closer to the international market. Agriculture's role as a contributor to economic growth and to consumer welfare, as well as as employment provider in regions affected by industrial restructuring, requires strengthening of the market and supporting the emerging private sector. The CAP will probably remain more or less in its present form up to the year 2000 but will come under pressure for change thereafter, in the direction of lower price support, coupled perhaps with higher direct income transfers. The main priority for agricultural policy in the CEECs is to create a well-functioning market environment by strengthening the privatization process and encouraging competition.

Considering alternative options for the integration of EU and CEEC agriculture, the main priority is to step up the integration of the CEECs as a group. There are several benefits from such an approach that outweigh the costs. For instance, this will strengthen collaboration and will stop the present race of these countries to achieve EU membership bilaterally. Further, it will create competition, expand the market, encourage greater dialogue and prepare the countries for joining the EU internal market. Economically, the best instrument for this objective is the creation of a Free Trade Area of all the countries of the region that aim at accession. Their success in joining the Free Trade Area would determine their prospects for joining the group of those who would achieve accession first. Going further down regional integration by establishing a customs union or a common market would be a waste of resources and may lead to diverging directions with respect to the EU.

References

Baldwin, R.E.(1994) Towards an Integrated Europe, CEPR, London

Bosworth, B.P. and Ofer, G. (1995) Reforming Planned Economies in an Integrated World Economy, Brookings Institution, Washington D.C.

Brooks, K. et al. (1991) "Agriculture and the Transition to the Market" The Journal of Economic Perspectives, Vol. 5, No. 4, pp. 149-160.

Buckwell, A. et al. (1995) Feasibility of an Agricultural Strategy to Prepare the CEEC for EU Accession, report to DG I of the European Commission, Brussels.

Centre of Economic Policy Research (CEPR) (1990) Monitoring European Integration: The Impact of Eastern Europe, CEPR, London.

European Commission (1995a) Agricultural Situation and Prospects in the CEECs-Summary Report and Individual Country Reports, EC-DG VI, Brussels.

European Commission (1995b) White Paper - Preparation of the Associated States of CEEC for Integration into the Internal Market of the Union.Brussels.

European Commission (1994) Agriculture: Progress and Strategy Paper, PHARE, Brussels.

European Commission (1994) Follow up to Commission Communication on "Europe Agreement and Beyond: A Strategy to Prepare the CEEC for Accession",Brussels.

Inotai, A. and Sass, M. (1994) "Economic Integration of the Visegrad Countries: Facts and Scenarios" Eastern European Economics, Vol. 32, No. 6, pp. 6-28.

Larsen, A. et al. (1994) "EC Agricultural Policy for the 21st Century" European Economy, 1990/4.

Mahe, L. et al. (1995) L'Agriculture et l'Enlargissement de l' UE aux PECO, report to DG I of the European Commission , Brussels.

Nallet, H. and van Stolk, A. (1994) Relations between the European Union and the CEEC in matters concerning Agriculture and Food Production, report to DG VI of the European Commission, Brussels.

Ockenden, J. and Franklin, M. (1995) European Agriculture: Making the CAP fit the future, The Royal Institute of International Affairs, London.

OECD (1995) "Pre-accession Agricultural and Trade Policies for the group of PECO-6", mimeographed.

Philip Morris Institute (PMI) (1994) Is the West Doing Enough for Eastern Europe?, PMI, Brussels.

Spachis, A. (1995) "The Operation of the Internal Market and Approximation to Legislation by CEECs', presented in the international conference Economic Interdependence and Cooperation in Europe, 28-29 Sep. 1995, Athens.

Stiglitz, J.E. (1993) "Remarks on the Design of Financial Systems for the Newly Emerging Democracies of Eastern Europe" in Clague C. and G. Rausser (eds) The Emergence of Market Economies in Eastern Europe, basil Blackwell, Cambridge.

Swinnen, J.F.M. (1995) Policy and Institutional Change in Central European Agriculture, Avebury Publishers, London.

Tangerman, S. and Josling, T. (1995) Pre-accession Agricultural Policies for the CEEC and the EU, report to the European Commission DG I, Brussels.

Tarditi, S. et al. (1995) Agricultural Strategies for the Enlargement of the EU to CEEC, report to the European Commission, DG I, Brussels.

Tracy, M. (editor) (1994) East-West European Agricultural Trade, APS, Brussels.

Tyers, R. (1994) "Economic Reform in Europe and the Former Soviet Union: Implications for International Food Markets" Research Report No. 99, IFPRI, Washington D.C.

Winters, L.A. "Digging for Victory: Agricultural Policy and National Security" The World Economy, Vol. 13, No. 2, pp. 170-190.

Zecchini, S. (1995) "The Role of IFIs in the Transition Process", Journal of Comparative Economics, Vol. 20, pp. 116-138.

Contributors

GELB Alan
Chief Economist, The World Bank

HILLMAN Arye
Professor, Department of Economics, Bar-Ilan University, Israel

HOLMES Peter
Reader, School of European Studies, University of Sussex

KORLIRAS Panayotis
Professor, Department of Economics, Athens University of Economics and Business

MLADENOV Mileti
Deputy Governor of Bulgarian National Bank, Sofia

MERGOS George
Associate Professsor of Economics, Department of Economics, University of Athens

PETERSEN Hans-Georg
Professor, Faculty of Economics and Social Sciences, University of Potsdam

PITELIS Christos
Fellow, The Judge Institute of Management Studies, University of Cambridge

PITIC Goran
Assistant Professor, Department of Economics, University of Belgrade

SAVIC Nebojsa
Professor, Head of Economic Research, Economics Institute, Belgrade

SPACHIS Alexander
European Commission

URSPRUNG Heinrich W.
Professor, Department of Economics, University of Konstanz

VOSGERAU Hans-Jurgen
Professor, Department of Economics, University of Konstanz

MIX
Papier aus verantwortungsvollen Quellen
Paper from responsible sources
FSC® C105338

If you have any concerns about our products,
you can contact us on
ProductSafety@springernature.com

In case Publisher is established outside the EU,
the EU authorized representative is:
Springer Nature Customer Service Center GmbH
Europaplatz 3, 69115 Heidelberg, Germany

Printed by Libri Plureos GmbH
in Hamburg, Germany